1506074538

AF805122

University of Bristol Library
Tyndall Avenue, Bristol BS8 1TJ

INSTITUTIONS AND ECONOMIC ORGANIZATION IN THE ADVANCED ECONOMIES

CENTRAL ISSUES IN CONTEMPORARY ECONOMIC THEORY AND POLICY

General Editor: **Mario Baldassarri**, *Professor of Economics, University of Rome 'La Sapienza', Italy*

Published titles include

Mario Baldassarri and Massimo Di Matteo (*editors*)
INTERNATIONAL PROBLEMS OF ECONOMIC INTERDEPENDENCE

Mario Baldassarri, Cesare Imbriani and Dominick Salvatore (*editors*)
THE INTERNATIONAL SYSTEM BETWEEN NEW INTEGRATION AND NEO-PROTECTIONISM

Mario Baldassarri, Alfredo Macchiati and Diego Piacentino (*editors*)
THE PRIVATIZATION OF PUBLIC UTILITIES: THE CASE OF ITALY

Mario Baldassarri, Luigi Paganetto and Edmund S. Phelps (*editors*)
EQUITY, EFFICIENCY AND GROWTH: THE FUTURE OF THE WELFARE STATE

Mario Baldassarri, Luigi Paganetto and Edmund S. Phelps (*editors*)
THE 1990s SLUMP: CAUSES AND CURES

Mario Baldassarri, Luigi Paganetto and Edmund S. Phelps (*editors*)
WORLD SAVING, PROSPERITY AND GROWTH

Mario Baldassarri, Luigi Paganetto and Edmund S. Phelps (*editors*)
INTERNATIONAL DIFFERENCES IN GROWTH RATES: MARKET GLOBALIZATION AND ECONOMIC AREAS

Mario Baldassarri and Paolo Roberti (*editors*)
FISCAL PROBLEMS IN THE SINGLE-MARKET EUROPE

Mario Baldassarri and Franco Modigliani (*editors*)
THE ITALIAN ECONOMY: WHAT NEXT?

Mario Baldassarri (*editor*)
MAFFEO PANTALEONI: AT THE ORIGIN OF THE ITALIAN SCHOOL OF ECONOMICS AND FINANCE

Mario Baldassarri, Luigi Paganetto and Edmund S. Phelps (*editors*)
INSTITUTIONS AND ECONOMIC ORGANIZATION IN THE ADVANCED ECONOMIES: THE GOVERNANCE PERSPECTIVE

Institutions and Economic Organization in the Advanced Economies

The Governance Perspective

Edited by

Mario Baldassarri
Professor of Economics
University of Rome 'La Sapienza'
Italy

Luigi Paganetto
Professor of Economics
Dean of the Faculty of Economics and Business Administration
University of Rome 'Tor Vergata'
Italy

and

Edmund S. Phelps
McVickar Professor of Political Economics
Columbia University
New York

in association with
Rivista di Politica Economica, SIPI, Rome
and
CEIS, University of Rome 'Tor Vergata'

First published in Great Britain 1998 by
MACMILLAN PRESS LTD
Houndmills, Basingstoke, Hampshire RG21 6XS and London
Companies and representatives throughout the world

A catalogue record for this book is available from the British Library.

ISBN 0–333–71575–6

First published in the United States of America 1998 by
ST. MARTIN'S PRESS, INC.,
Scholarly and Reference Division,
175 Fifth Avenue, New York, N.Y. 10010

HB 99.5 INS

ISBN 0–312–21276–3

Library of Congress Cataloging-in-Publication Data
Institutions and economic organization in the advanced economies : the governance perspective / edited by Mario Baldassarri, Luigi Paganetto and Edmund S. Phelps.
p. cm. — (Central issues in contemporary economic theory and policy)
Includes bibliographical reference and index.
ISBN 0–312–21276–3 (cloth)
1. Institutional economics. 2. Economic policy. I. Baldassarri, Mario, 1946– . II. Paganetto, Luigi. III. Phelps, Edmund S.
IV. Series.
HB99.5.I55 1998
338.9—dc21 97–41071
CIP

© Servizio Italiano Pubblicazioni Internazionali Srl 1998

All rights reserved. No reproduction, copy or transmission of this publication may be made without written permission.

No paragraph of this publication may be reproduced, copied or transmitted save with written permission or in accordance with the provisions of the Copyright, Designs and Patents Act 1988, or under the terms of any licence permitting limited copying issued by the Copyright Licensing Agency, 90 Tottenham Court Road, London W1P 9HE.

Any person who does any unauthorised act in relation to this publication may be liable to criminal prosecution and civil claims for damages.

The authors have asserted their rights to be identified as the authors of this work in accordance with the Copyright, Designs and Patents Act 1988.

This book is printed on paper suitable for recycling and made from fully managed and sustained forest sources.

10 9 8 7 6 5 4 3 2 1
07 06 05 04 03 02 01 00 99 98

Printed and bound in Great Britain by
Antony Rowe Ltd, Chippenham, Wiltshire

UNIVERSITY OF BRISTOL
15 NOV 2019
WITHDRAWN

UNIVERSITY
OF BRISTOL
LIBRARY

Contents

List of Contributors

Michele Bagella	Director, Department of Economics and Institutions, University of Rome 'Tor Vergata'
Leonardo Becchetti	Doctor of Research and Master of Science (LSE), Department of Economics and Institutions, University of Rome 'Tor Vergata'
Andrea Berardi	Researcher, Banca Comerciale Italiana, Milan, and London Business School
Giovanni Caravale	Professor of Economics, University of Rome 'La Sapienza'
Alberto Dalmazzo	Researcher, Department of Economics, University of Siena
Carlo Dell'Aringa	Professor of Economics, Catholic University, Milan
Avinash Dixit	Professor of Economics, Princeton University
Fabio Gobbo	Professor of Economics, University of Bologna and member of Italy's Authority for Competition and the Market
Bruno Jossa	Professor of Political Economics, University of Naples
Giancarlo Marini	Professor of Economics, University of Rome 'Tor Vergata'
Mancur Olson	Professor of Economics, University of Maryland
Luigi Paganetto	Dean, Faculty of Economics and President of CEIS, University of Rome 'Tor Vergata'
Edmund S. Phelps	McVickar Professor of Political Economics, Columbia University, New York

Pasquale Lucio Scandizzo	Professor of Economics, University of Rome 'Tor Vergata'
Andrei Shleifer	Professor of Economics, Harvard University
Giovanni Somogyi	Professor of Industrial Economics, University of Rome 'La Sapienza'
Salvatore Zecchini	Deputy Secretary General, OECD, Paris, and Director of CCET

Governance and New Institutional Economics: Some Introductory Remarks

Luigi Paganetto*
Università «Tor Vergata», Roma

New Institutional Economics, writes Arrow, opens a new methodological perspective on to political economy by posing the question of why economic institutions are created.

Institutions, according to North's definition, are man-made constraints which condition political, economic and social integration. They translate into both informal contraints, such as codes of conduct and traditions, and formal rules, such as rights of ownership, laws and constitutions. Institutions, as well as the «standard» constraints on which economic theory grounds its analyses, define the set of choices available to economic operators. According to the game theory, players who intend to maximize their profit tend to cooperate when the information they have is complete, there is a small number of players and the game may be repeated. In other circumstances cooperation becomes more difficult. If one assumes, as one must do in order to introduce a greater degree of realism in the behaviours hypothesized in economic theory, that the rationality of *homo economicus* is limited and that the information available to the partecipants in the dealings is conditioned by the incompleteness of the contracts, then the dealings will entail certain costs which must be taken into account to assess their convenience.

---

* The author is Dean of the Faculty of Economics at Tor Vergata University, Rome and President of CEIS-Tor Vergata.

The costs connected with the transactions would make cooperation between the operators unviable and any dealings difficult pursue if there were no economic institutions, which, in the perspective of new institutional economics, represent the response to the transaction costs.

Transaction costs are represented by both the *ex ante* costs for the completion of the contract and the *ex post* costs incurred in relation with its management, although it must be remembered that transaction costs connected to interpersonal relations must be included in the production costs, in the sense that the economic operators tend to minimize, in their calculations, the sum of the transaction and production costs.

The institutions make it possible to increase the amount of information available to the dealers and are a tool for obtaining penalties/bonuses for those who depart from a cooperative attitude.

A certain degree of «opportunism» in the behaviour of the operators is another reason for the need of institutions aimed at avoiding any «contractual hazards», the presence of which would bar otherwise possible investments. Opportunism generally rises from the possibility of behaving in a contrary or different manner to the one laid down in the contractual relations, and it is precisely to prevent or limit this opportunism that general rules and obligations are set forth, which stiffen contracts with the consequent and relative costs.

This affects economic policies at both micro-economical, where regulatory policies are the key aspect, and macro-economical level, in the so-called «announcement» policies, by means of which commitments are officially undertaken to control inflation and the national debt, and procedures are defined for the approval of the budget. In the perspective of «governance», the authorities responsible for regulating competition in real and financial markets are not considered in the light of their capacity to realize efficiency of allocation, but as the articulations of institutional mechanisms and procedures capable of realizing defined social welfare objectives.

Contracts concerning matters characterized by information asymmetries or moral hazards are generally long-term contracts and are entered into in order to regulate recurrent transactions, in respect of which continuous negotiations would represent a less efficient solution, as demonstrated by Tirole. This is especially true in the circumstance where the contractual relationship entails non-recoverable investments related to the transaction; for example, if one of the parties is required to improve the characteristics of the product he receives before putting it on the market. In a similar manner, in the case of in-house contracts, long-term contracts are deemed the best solution because the company is an institution destined to last in time. Therefore, it is interested in creating the right environment enabling it to adapt to the changing circumstances over time and maintain its reputation. This objective provides a satisfactory explanation as to why cooperative mechanisms prevail in long-term transactions. We are all aware of the fact that the analysis of transaction costs is a decisive step, with regard to the relationship which is established between the marketplace and the hierarchy.

According to Williamson, markets are the tool used to organize transactions when there is the possibility and need of independent adaptations, while hierarchy comes into being for those transactions where cooperative activies prevail. In this perspective, markets and hierarchies are a complementary couple, and are more related than economic plans and the market, because, as Coase points out, in a competitive system there is an optimum amount of planning. This fact comes to the fore in the more complex contractual relations, through which the parties concerned artificially, albeit freely, restrict their choices. When transaction costs are high and the penalising mechanisms connected to contracts inadequate, the alternative to long-term contracts is the integration between the parties, realized through some form of authority, which generally takes the shape of the hierarchy. This is the best organizational solution to solve the problems of labour division arising between parties characterized by imitated rationality.

Coase has pointed out that in a world without transaction costs the efficient allocation of resources would be independent of the distribution of the rights of ownership. On the contrary, Hart and More state that when there are transaction costs the owner is the necessary agent for reducing the transaction costs. The relationship between principal and agent is the answer to the differences of interest in the industrial organization, beginning with that between owners and managers, when the available information is incomplete and asymmetrical.

This relationship is grounded on the distribution of risks and the management of incentives, given the different propensity to risk amongst owners, managers and workers. The separation of ownership and control poses important problems with regard to «governance». The agent entrepreneur, in fact, must not abuse of his power of control, for example, by aiming only at the satisfaction of his own interests.

At the same time, however, it is necessary to admit a minimum of interference in his actions to avoid reducing his accountability, with regard to the use and development of companies' assets. In this perspective, the fiduciary relations between investors and entrepreneurs are of great importance, as are the monitoring of banks and institutional investors who have employed financial resources in the enterprises and the threat of any takeovers.

In conclusion, the neo-institutionalist paradigm is a way of modifying the functions of the economic operators, and is represented in both the conditioning suffered from the «institutional environment» and their concrete manifestations, wherein «governance» of contractual relations assumes a decisive role.

What becomes clear to us is the evolution of a process of alternative organizational structures, a comparative appraisal of which may be made by taking account of the amount of adjustment costs incurred in passing from one model to the other. On the other hand, by broadening one's visual field, the institutional environment may be seen as a set of political, social and legal rules serving as the foundation for production, trade and distribution.

The rules governing elections and forms of government, such as federalism, which may be included in the neo-institutionalist theory of hierarchical forms, even the economic Constitution itself, are essential aspects of the issue of «governance».

Collective actions, performed by organized groups both large and small, acting in collusion or applying pressure to improved the well-being of their members, pose the problem of how collective actions are formed and the impact of these actions on the efficiency of the economic and social system. As Olson points out, the actions of the large organizations, such as the trade unions for example, may produce an increase of benefits for their members, but these benefits must be divided amongst a large number of members, therefore, the actions often produce inferior results compared to the expended cost. The claims made by a large organization may produce significant effects in terms of loss of efficiency of the national revenue, with important consequences for the numbers themselves. His conclusion is that small groups do not worry about the effects of their actions on the national economy, whereas the larger groups, which do worry, for purely selfish reasons, have a propulsive effect on economic growth.

Another important aspect of the relationship between institutions and the economy is the greater capacity of democratic systems with strong bodies representative of certain interests to act on the plane of distribution efficiency. Democratic governments when faced with efficient representative institutions are encouraged to support the institutions and not to excessively increase tax rates; for example, because otherwise they would run the risk of losing the support of the electorate. The role of this insitutional arrangement is very important. To convince oneself of this it is sufficient to consider the effects of the presence or absence of representative bodies at federal level and the manner in which the market regulatory authorities interpret their role.

When individual preferences are not homogeneous and are distributed in a non-uniform manner, the federal system allows the decentralization of decision-making, thus enabling the improved satisfaction of the preferences expressed by the peripheral units, increasing the number of satisfied individuals, with regard to their set of preferences.

Lastly, «governance», defined as the set of institutions, rules and behaviours determining the organization of the economy, is a perspective within which the capacity of the institutional bodies to influence the internal growth processes plays a decisive role. Organized minorities may sometimes take control of economic policy-making and push for redistribution to their own benefit.

The political system's desire to directly control and manage the economy is based on motivations on the opposite side of those determining privatization. The latter are related to the idea that, with regard to the key aspects of demand and supply, where information plays a decisive role, the marketplace is superior to any «governance» structure, especially if public in nature. The idea behind this is that the State has a comparative advantage because it is the maker of rules and that it must, therefore, restrict itself to regulating the interactions between private operators, since it is incapable of achieving any special benefits in the production and distribution of goods and services.

If one looks at the State from the point of view of «governance» one may observe certain structural weak points concerning its capacity to access the information held by the private sector, which is what ultimately contributes to the achievement of the combinations of market and hierarchy determining the economic organization. Citizens' lack of access to the information held by the public officials allows the State to become non-accountable for its actions. Consequently, it is difficult, if not impossible, to assess the motivations and objectives of the public administrators, who are called to implement procedures and transactions of great importance for the «governance» of the economic system. A significant measure would be the introduction of incentive systems and the continuous monitoring of their activities. A system whereby the administrative functions of the operators agree with their personal interests, also by means of incentive bonuses for ensuring the correspondence between their personal interests and their duties, would be of great help for enabling the «governance» expressed by the private system to generate internal growth mechanisms, in respect of which the State would intervene solely in order to establish a set of rules for interpreting the evolutionary trends.

Why Poor Economic Policies Must Promote Corruption: Lessons from the East for All Countries

Mancur Olson [1]
University of Maryland

At a time when Italy's political system has been overturned by charges of official corruption, it might seem that the study of economic policy and economic growth cannot demand the most urgent attention. I shall argue, on the contrary, that the best way to understand corruption is to start by looking at economic institutions and economic policy, that is, at the main determinants of economic performance. Remarkably, the same ideas that mainly explain the major anomalies in economic performance also mainly explain the most conspicuous variations in the extent of official corruption.

The counterintuitive connection between corruption and economic performance will become evident when we compare what happened to the formerly Axis countries after they were defeated in World War II with what has happened to the once-communist countries after the collapse of comunism. What happened to the Axis countries after they were defeated was dramatically different from what has happened to the formerly communist countries after the collapse of the communist dictatorships.

West Germany, Japan, and Italy enjoyed economic miracles afrter World War II, but in many of the formerly communist societies

---

[1] The author thanks the US Agency for International Development for supporting his research through the Center on Institutional Reform and the Informal Sector (IRIS).
Copyright by the Author, all Rights reserved; portions of this article have appeared in other publications by the author.

N.B.: the numbers in square brackets refer to the Bibliography at the end of the paper.

economic performance is even worse than it was under communism. Postwar West Germany and Japan have shown little or no tendencies toward geographical fragmentation or devolution, and Germany has even, after the collapse of the German Democratic Republic in 1989, seen a reunification. Though Italy's Northern League has proposed secession, this is trivial compared to what has happened in several of the formerly communist countries: Yugoslavia, Czechoslovakia, and the Soviet Union have broken into parts, and Russia has experienced not only some secessionism by Chechens, Tatars, and others, but also a devolution of power from Moscow to Republics and other regional or local units of government.

These dramatic differences between what happened after the defeat of fascism and after the collapse of communism are all the more remarkable in view of the expectations at the time and the desires of the victorious countries in World Wat II. The expectations about the economic growth of the countries defeated in World War II were quite pessimistic. Though there was a concern in the US that it might need to feed the defeated populations indefinitely, the winning countries were initially not much concerned about the poor prospects of the defeated countries. At the end of the Second World War and for some time afterwards, the victorious countries were fearful that Germany and Japan, at least, would again emerge as aggressive dictatorships, so they did not want them to have either strong industrial economies or to become substantial and unified countries.

Though Italy – which shall be separately touched upon in a brief postscipt – is a more complex or intermediate case, it is clear that West Germany and Japan also have enjoyed a tranquil social order and their citizens have not been especially victimized by crime and official corruption[2]. By contrast, many citizens and firms in some formerly communist countries complain bitterly about mafias and corrupt officials, corruption in the former Soviet Union has reached astonishing levels.

---

[2] Though Japan has lately suffered from corruption by some of its best-known politicians. Japanese society has far lower crime rates than most other countries, and its bureaucracy is relatively honest. Except in certain areas such as construction of public works, most Japanese individuals and firms can go about their work without being troubled by corruption.

The dramatic contrast between the outcomes in the formerly fascist and the formerly communist societies has not previously been explained. The reason, I, believe, is that an idea or theory that is indispensable for a full understanding of the matter has not been available. We must have a deeper understanding of the ways in which post-communist societies function – better insight, as it were, into their social physiology – to obtain a correct diagnosis of the disease that sometimes keeps them from having economic miracles, from eliminating official corruption, and from preventing political fragmentation.

The first task is to develop the ideas or theory that we need to diagnose the disease. We shall then show that the theory illuminates a crucial feature of the experience of the formerly fascist countries and of other market democracies. We then extend the ideas to examine the ageing process of the type of political and economic system created by Stalin. An understanding of this process provides a new diagnosis of the pathologies of the transition from communism. I conclude with the policy prescriptions that follow from the diagnosis and suggest that they also have some implications for Italy and the West in general.

1. - A Theory of Power

What is needed here is a theory that focuses on coercive power and the gains from wielding it, on the incentives to acquire coercive power and the incentives facing those who have it. Any adequate intellectual framework must, of course, also encompass the market and the voluntary transactions in it, but (as we shall see) this is not the place to begin. Practical results depend not only on the incentives and self-interest of those with power, but also on their characters and morals and many other things. But the problem that confronts us will become impossibly complex if we do not take things one at a time. Thus I shall focus now only on the incentives, the inducements to self-interested action, that face those with power.

To make it obvious that I am focusing only on coercive power and analyzing only self-interested behavior, I shall use a criminal metaphor to start the analysis. Clearly, we cannot understand robbery as either a voluntary trade or a moral act, and thus it will help us focus only on the self-interested use of coercive power. With a precise focus, we will be able to see what is beneath the surface and to construct the needed theory. Since, in any successful society, criminal behavior is the exception rather than the rule, the criminal metaphor will also remind us of the extent to which we are abstracting from the complexity of human nature.

Consider the incentives facing the individual criminal in a populous society. Other things being equal, a criminal is better off in a rich than in a poor society: there is more to steal. Theft also makes societies less prosperous than they would otherwise be, the time devoted to theft produces nothing, but it reduces the rewards from productive work and investment and induces a diversion of resources from production into guards, locks, police, courts, and the like. Therefore, the crime committed by each criminal reduces the wealth of society and thus also the amount that is available to steal. Does the individual criminal curtail his crime because crime reduces the amont that is there to steal?

Everyone already knows that he does not, but it is important to see why. The typical individual thief in a society of, say, a million people, might bear something like one-millionth of the loss to society that occurs because his crime makes society's output less than it would otherwise be, but he alone is likely to bear the whole loss of whatever opportunities for theft he passes up. Thus the gain to criminals from a wealthy society and the fact that crime reduces society's wealth does not keep crime from paying, it is society's punishment of criminals and the efforts of individuals and firms to protect themselves that, sometimes, keeps crime from paying. Though each criminal does have a stake in the prosperity of society, that stake is so minuscule that the criminal ignores it.

As we shall see, it makes a great deal of difference whether individuals with coercive capacities have a tiny or "narrow" stake in the society, on the one hand, or an "encompassing" interest, on the other.

Now let us shift from the individual criminal to the head of a mafia "family" or other criminal gang that can monopolize crime in some neighborhood. Suppose that in some well-defined turf, a criminal gang can not only steal more or less as it pleases, but also prevent anyone else from committing crime there. Obviously, the mafia family has an incentive to keep other thieves out of its domain. Will it gain from stealing whatever it finds on its own ground?

Definitely not. If business in this domain is made unprofitable by theft, or migration away from the neighborhood is prompted by crime, then the neighborhood will not generate as much income and there will not be as much to steal. Indeed, the mafia family with a true and continuing monopoly on crime in a neighborhood will not commit any robberies at all. If it monopolizes crime in the neighborhood, it will gain from promoting business profitability and safe residential life there. Thus the secure mafia family will maximize its take by selling "protection", both against the crime it would (if not paid) commit itself as well as that which would (if it did not keep other criminals out) be committed by others. Other things being equal, the better the community is as an environment for business and for living, the more the protection racket will bring in.

Accordingly, if one family has total power to commit and monopolize crime, there is (apart from the protection racket) little or no crime. The considerable literature on monopolized crime makes it clear that secure monopolization of crime does lead to protection rackets rather than ordinary crime, and that outbreaks of theft and violence in such environments are normally a sign that the controlling gang is losing its monopoly[3].

The individual robber in a populous society obtains such a narrow or minute share of any loss or gain to society that he ignores the damage his robbery does to the society. By constrast, the mafia family that monopolizes crime in a community has, because of this monopoly, a moderately encompassing interest or stake in the income of that community, so it takes the interest of the community into account in using its coercive power[4]. A gang with a secure monopoly over crime in a neighborhood will be able to obtain a significant fraction of the total income of the community from its protection "tax", and thus it bears a significant fraction of any social loss from robbery and burglary in its domain.

---

[3] See, for example, GAMBETTA D. [6].

[4] For the concepts of encompassing and narrow interests, see OLSON M. [12].

What would happen if the head of the mafia family succeeds in taking complete control of some region or country?

2. - The First Blessing of the Invisible Hand

Part of the answer to this question came to me by chance when I was reading years ago about a Chinese warlord[5]. In the 1920's, China was in large part under the control of various warlords. They were men who led some armed band with which they conquered territory and who then appointed themselves lords of that territory. They taxed the population heavily and pocketed much of the proceeds. The warlord Feng Yu-hsiang was noted for the exceptional extent to which he used his army for suppressing bandits and for his defeat of the relatively substantial army of the roving bandit, White Wolf. Apparently most people in Feng's domain found him to be preferable to the roving bandits. At first, this puzzled me: why should warlords who were stationary bandits continuously stealing from a given group of victims be preferred, by those victims, to roving bandits who soon departed? The warlords had no traditional legitimacy and had not been chosen by the population or by anyone else.

In fact, if a roving bandit settles down and takes his theft in the form of regular taxation, and at the same time maintains a monopoly on theft in his domain, then those from whom he exacts tax-theft will have an incentive to produce that they do not have if they will be picked clean by roving robbers. A stationary bandit will take only a part of income in taxes, because he will be able to exact more tax from his subjects if he leaves them with an incentive to generate more income. Thus the victims of the stationary bandit, like the bandit himself, will be better off than with roving banditry.

If the stationary bandit successfully monopolizes theft in his domain, then his victims do not needs to worry about theft by anyone other than the stationary bandit. Since all of the settled bandit's victims are for him a source of tax payments, he also has an incentive to protect them.

---

[5] See SHERIDAN E. [17].

With the monopolization of theft, the victims of the theft can also expect to retain whatever capital they accumulate out of after-tax income and therefore they also have an incentive to save and to invest, thereby increasing their own future income and tax receipts for the stationary bandit.

In a world of roving banditry there is little or no incentive for anyone to produce or accumulate anything that may be stolen and thus little for bandits to steal. Bandit rationality accordingly induces the bandit leader to seize a given domain, to make himself the ruler of that domain, and to provide a peaceful order and other public goods for its inhabitants, thereby obtaining more in tax-theft than he could have obtained from migratory plunder.

Thus we have "the first blessing of the invisible hand", the rational, self-interested leader of a band of roving bandits is led, as though by an invisible hand, to settle down, to wear a crown, and to replace anarchy with government. The gigantic increase in output that normally arises from the provision of a peaceful order and other public goods gives the stationary bandit a far larger take than he could obtain if he did not provide government.

Since the stationary bandit takes a part of total production in the form of tax-theft, it will also pay him to provide other goods, besides a peaceful order, that the market will not provide. It is now widely understood that the market will not provde large populations with goods – such as flood control, quarantine against contagious disease, or defense – whose benefits inevitably go to a broad population: the individual who strives to obtain such goods for himself will find that he reaps only a minute part of the benefits. Thus individuals and firms in the market will not have an incentive to obtain or provide a peaceful order or any other "collective" or "public" goods[6].

But the rational stationary bandit will have such an incentive. He would reap a significant gain through increased tax receipts from any public goods that increased the productivity of the economy or the size of the population he controls.

---

[6] Since this reasoning is set out fully in OLSON M. [13]. I will say no more about it here.

3. - The Logic of Narrow Versus Encompassing Interests

With the model inspired by our criminal metaphor, we can see the precise and general logic behind the foregoing stories. As we recall, our individual criminal in a society of a million has only a narrow or minuscule interest in the prosperity of the society, which it is not worth his while to take into account, and his interests are best served simply by taking all of the cash in any till he robs.

The mafia family that has the power to monopolize crime in a given neighborhood, but not to keep the government tax collector out, will steer away from socially costly crimes like robbery and strive for a protection racket instead. In this protection racket it will not rationally demand everything in the till, it will not take 100% of all the assets a business or household possesses. This would lead to the failure or outmigration of the very businesses and households that the mafia family, given the encompassing interest in the neighborhood implied by its criminal monopoly there, hopes will thrive, thereby enabling absolutely larger protection tax payments. So the rational protection racket has a less than 100% protection tax[7].

The rational stationary bandit leader with secure autocratic power will not raise the percentage of his tax-theft beyond the point where the distortions due to this tax-theft reduce the society's total income so much that his share of this loss is as great as his gain from obtaining a larger percentage of the total. To see this, suppose there is a simple flat tax and that the tax rate that would maximize the

---

[7] If there is both a mafia family and a maximizing autocrat extracting resources, the combined protection-racket tax plus autocrat's tax will be higher than if only one of them had been taxing. When the mafia leader, for example, is deciding on the protection-racket charge and is aware that activity in the neighborhood is curtailed by the protection charge, he notes that some of the loss takes the form of lower governmental tax collections, and the mafia family has no incentive to take this loss into account in deciding on the rate of protection payment it demands. If a mafia family were, like our bandit gang that settles down, strong enough so that its protection-racket charge was the only tax, then the aggregate tax rate imposed on citizens would be lower and the income of the neighborhood would be higher. In other words, competition among autocratic rulers for power over the same domain is bad for the subjects and monopoly by a single ruler is better for them. By contrast, competition in a democracy between two parties to obtain a majority that gives the winning party a term during which it has a monopoly of government means a significantly lower tax rate than under a single autocrat, and a much lower tax rate than results from a stationary bandit plus a mafia family.

tax-take for a given autocrat was exactly 50%. Then the last dollar collected in taxes would reduce the national income by two dollars, and the autocrat would bear half of this loss, so he would be at a point of indifference, i.e., at the peak of his tax revenue function. More generally, the stationary bandit finds that he cannot gain from increasing the share, S, of the national income that he takes beyond the point where the national income goes down by $1/S$. The stationary bandit's encompassing interest in the society means that he is led, again as though by an invisible hand, to limit the rate of his theft.

This encompassing interest also makes him provide public goods. Specifically, he gains from using his resources to provide public goods up to the point where the national income increases by $1/S$ times as much as the marginal cost of the public goods. If his optimal tax rate is 50%, he will gain from spending an extra dollar on public goods so long as that dollar adds two dollars or more to the income of his domain. A secure stationary bandit uses his power, in part, constructively.

Let us now consider a democracy under the control of a unified majority, and impartially assume that this majority has the same self-interest as the autocrat and redistributes income from the minority to itself. Since the members of the majority not only have the same control of the tax and transfer system as the autocrat, but also earn income in the market, they necessarily have a more encompassing interest than the autocrat. It follows that will treat the minority better than the autocrat treats his subjects. This, in combination with some inherent reasons why there are superior individual rights to property and contract-enforcement in the long run in lasting democracies, greatly strengthens the traditional case for democracy. But since these advantages of democracy are not necessary to the present argument and have been explained elsewhere[8], no more will be said of them here.

4. - The Anti-Social Incentives of Special-Interest Groups

Consider now situations where the firms or workers in an

---

[8] See OLSON M. [14], and formal proofs and additional results are provided in MC GUIRE M. - OLSON M. [8].

industry or the individuals employed in some occupation or profession are organized to act collectively, as a lobby or a cartel. The firms or workers in any single industry or occupation are unlikely to be a majority of the electorate and unlikely to earn any substantial percentage of the national income of a country. Because they are not a majority, they cannot obtain complete control of the taxation and spending power of a government. They must instead take advantage of the "rational ignorance" of the electorate about the details of public policy and about their particular industry or occupation. They will then often through lobbying obtain special-interest measures, such as protection against imports, regulations that limit entry and competition, tax loopholes, or subsidies. They may also be able to cartelize or collude to obtain monopoly prices or wages in their market.

To what extent will the organizations for collective action that represent particular industries or occupations have an incentive to refrain from any redistribution to themselves that will do great damage to economic efficiency?

The profits and even the value added in a typical industry and the wages in a typical craft or occupation are a small faction of GDP. Suppose, for ease of calculation, that a given organized interest obtains exactly one percent of the GDP. Then it will pay this organized interest to press for both governmental and cartelistic redistributions to itself up to the point where the social losses are 100 times as great as the amount it obtains: only then will its marginal share of these social losses be as great as its gain at the margin from further redistribution. Thus the typical special-interest group has a very narrow rather than an encompassing interest. It therefore faces incentives that are by no means so wholesome as those facing majorities. Unfortunately, they are much more detrimental to society than those facing the secure stationary bandit, often also worse than those that face the gang with a protection racket, and not much better for society than those facing the individual criminal.

Those in particular industries and occupations are sometimes not organized for collective action. Collective action must overcome the free-rider problem. It can emerge only when the gains from organization benefit just a small number of actors (like the few big firms in a concentrated industry) or when there are "selective incentives" (rewards or punishments that, unlike the collective good the organization provides its constituents, can be applied to or withheld from individuals depending on whether or not they contribute to the costs of the collective action)[9].

Even when small numbers or potential selective incentives make organization for collective action possible, it normally takes a long time before it occurs. Thus only long-stable societies have dense and powerful networks of organizations for collective action.

5. - Testing the Argument on the West

I have argued that it takes a long time for a society to accumulate many organizations for collective action, and that industry-specific, occupation-specific, and other narrow organizations for collective action are most harmful to economic efficiency and dynamism. We can therefore test whether the theory fits the facts by looking at the experience of the market democracies of the West. If my theory is right, we should expect that societies that set up a good legal order, after a catastrophe has destroyed organizations for collective action, will, for a time, grow extraordinarily rapidly. Similarly, long-stable societies ought to grow much less rapidly than societies that are in other respects comparable.

The society that has had the longest period of stability and immunity from invasion and institutional destruction is Great Britain. As the theory predicts, Great Britain also has had the "British disease" the poorest economic performance of the major developed democracies. The economic miracles of Germany, Japan, and Italy after World War II are also consistent with the argument. With appropriate elaboration, the aforementioned theory also explains the general pattern of regional growth in the United States since World War II, as well as other evidence. Most of the test and evaluations by others are mainly corroborative[10].

---

[9] The arguments in this and the immediately preceding paragraphs are developed in OLSON M. [12] and [13].

[10] See, for example, CHOI K. [2]; GALLOWAY L. - VEDDER R. [5]; CHAN S. [1]; WEEDL E. [20]; ERSSON S. - LANE J.E. [4]; SANDLER T. [16]; RAUCH J. [15]; OLSON M. [12]; MULLER D. [10]; VARIOUS AUTHORS [18] and [19].

6. - The Hidden Sources of Honest Government and Law-Abiding Behavior

We do not yet have an explanation of why there has been an epidemic of complaints about official corruption and mafia crime after the defeat of communism whereas there was no such epidemic after the defeat of fascism. Though they occasionally have suffered from notorious scandals, the citizens of West Germany and Japan – and of most of the other Western market democracies – have not complained nearly as much about official corruption and mafia gangs as many people in some formerly communist countries have.

As has long been known, one source of law-abiding behavior is a strong government that efficiently punishes illegal acts. West Germany and Japan, and most of the other major market democracies, appear to have had stronger government than Italy had, and this helps explain why Italy, in its southern region, has had major problems with mafia families when most of the other major market democracies have not. (Ethnic and racial divisions and the degree of elaboration of the legal rights of defendants may also make a difference and help to account for the extraordinary levels of street crime in the large cities of the United States).

But the strength of the government is by no means a sufficient explanation of the extent of crime and corruption, in part because we also need an independent explanation of official corruption. If government officials are corrupt, lawbreakers can buy immunity from prosecution and there cannot be a strong government combatting crime.

There is another source of law-abiding behavior and honest government in most societies that seems to have escaped notice. This source of law-abiding behavior and official integrity was missing under communism. To undestand it, we must consider countries with market economies and good economic policies and institutions.

The self-interest of the individuals and firms in a market economy with good economic policies and clearly delineated property rights is a major force for crime prevention, lawful behavior, and law enforcement. Consider the prevention of theft or the maintenance of property rights (theft is of course taking something from someone who has a property right to it). The self-interest of the owners of goods leads them to guard against theft. In a society with private property, the self-interest of individuals and firms leads them to install locks, hide valuables, hire guards, and keep watch.

The self-interest of individuals and firms in the private sector also often helps the police, the courts, and the government generally in apprehending and punishing theft. When a family or a firm is the victim of a theft, they normally help the police apprehend the thief. Sometimes firms and individuals will even offer rewards for information that leads to the apprehension of criminals who prey upon them.

I must not exaggerate and neglect the self-interest of the thieves. The thief has an incentive to try to avoid apprehension and prosecution by the police and the courts, and sometimes to bribe the police or the judges to let him off without punishment. So the self-interest of criminals works everywhere to undermine the law.

Yet in a market economy with good institutions and economic policies there is always, on the other side, the victims and potential victims of crime who not only use locks, guards, watchfulness, and a vast variety of behaviors to guard against theft, but who also pressure the police to recover stolen property and normally gladly assist the courts by testifying in trials against the offenders.

This obvious point about theft and property is only the tip of a large iceberg. Consider contract enforcement. Suppose that somebody has borrowed money but decides not to pay it back. The borrower, of course, does have an incentive to work against the enforcement of the agreement, i.e., the law that grows out of the contract that the two parties have signed. But the lender has exactly the opposite incentive. The lender will try to induce the borrower to pay the loan back by threatening his reputation and access to future credit and if necessary by getting the courts to seize borrower's assets. In the case of theft, the victims and potential victims push the authorities to enforce the law and therefore offset the efforts of the violators.

Because lenders, in deciding to whom to lend, are picking the borrowers that they think are most likely to pay the loan back, a higher proportion of cases the loans will be paid back than if lenders did not exercise this judgment. That of course makes the paying back of loans more common and generates a habitual obedience to the private law that grows out of a mutually agreed contract.

Thus much law enforcement and law-abiding behavior comes about because the self-interest of the firms and individuals leads them to do what they can to avoid being victims and to assist the government's system of law enforcement. In societies with market economies and good economic policies and institutions, private firms and individuals do much more to discourage violation of the law and to help enforce it than to undermine the law.

What about differences in the power and wealth of the people and firms in the private sector? Usually, in a successful market economy, the same inequalities in wealth and power that are, in other respects, a problem, help maintain law and order. When theft and the enforcement of contracts are at issue, the more substantial and wealthier interests will normally be on the side of upholding the law. If the average burglar is not as prosperous, as well placed, or as politically influential as his victim, that means that the net force of the private sector is on the side of the law. If lenders are on average more influential than borrowers, this makes loan-contract enforcement work better. This not only works in favor of contract enforcement, but it also helps those who can gain from borrowing money by creating an environment where money can be borrowed on reasonable terms. The net private force in support of many laws is, I think, is a matter of extraordinary importance.

Now let us look at countries that do not have good economic policies and institutions. Suppose that the government fixes prices and sets a price lower than the market-clearing price. If there is a price that is lower than the market-clearing price, the quantity demanded will be higher than the quantity that the suppliers, at that lower-than-market-clearing price, want to supply. So it will then be the case that there can be a mutually advantageous trade, one with two parties, a buyer and a seller, gaining – at a price that is higher than the controlled price and lower than the market-clearing price. Here is a situation in which both parties gain by violating the law – essentially all of the parts of the private sector act to undermine the law. The same thing holds true if the government sets a price above market-clearing levels.

Suppose now that the government determines how much of some good will be produced, and that the quantity chosen by the planners is lower than the quantity that the market would have generated. There will then be some buyers who do not get as much as they would like and also some potential sellers who would profit from supplying these buyers at a price they are willing to pay. Both parties can gain from evading the law and, if necessary, corrupting the officials who are supposed to enforce it.

Now assume that it is ordained by the government that some good must be produced in excess of the amount that the market would dictate, or that some good must be produced which the market would not produce at all. There are then enormous costs that producers can escape if they do not produce this good or do not produce the prescribed amount of it, and (since the production is by stipulation uneconomic) the good is not worth nearly so much to buyers so they do not put up much of a fight for it.

The general point is that any legislation or regulation that is "market contrary" must leave all or almost all parties with the incentive to evade the law and is likely to promote criminality and corruption in government.

Thus one reason why many societies have a lot of corruption in government is that they prescribe outcomes that all or almost all private parties have an incentive to avoid, and almost no one has an incentive to report violations to the authorities. When caught in violation of the rule, moreover, those on both sides of the market have the same incentive to persuade or bribe the policeman or government official not to enforce the law. Not only is the net incentive of the private sector to evade the law, essentially all of the private sector incentives are on the side of undermining the rules. With lots of market-contrary regulation, sooner or later the private sector – because everyone or almost everyone in it has an incentive to undermine or suborn its market-contrary actions – makes the government corrupt and ineffective.

The governments of the third world attempt to impose incomparably more market-contrary policies than do the governments of the prosperous market economies. As the foregoing argument predicts, they also have vastly more corruption in their governments. The huge informal economies in the third world are evidence not only of the extent of market-contrary policies, but also of the extent to which these policies have led over time to the corruption and ineffectiveness of third-world governments.

As everyone knows, the communist regimes allowed very little in the way of private property. This meant that self-interest of the people in the communist countries was not brought to bear to prevent theft and to aid the government in apprehending and prosecuting theft. Market-contrary activity was, of course, also the norm in the communist countries. As many people who lived under communism testify, in the Soviet-type countries sometimes a factory manager could not even get his work done – could not fulfill his quota – without engaging in quasi-legal or illegal deals to obtain inputs. The whole system of Soviet-style planning was so market-contrary that even the high officials – and perhaps especially high officials – had to violate the rules and the plan in order to comply with the orders and targets they were given. In other words, the market-contrary activity even often stood in the way of achieving some of the objectives of the regime.

We now have a part of the explanation of the chorus of complaints about crime and official corruption in the East, but only a part. As we shall see, we greatly understate the extent to which Soviet-type arrangements undermined law-abiding behavior and the integrity of government officials by saying that the Soviet-type societies restricted private property and markets to a unprecedented degree. The type of system that Stalin initiated had a more fundamental feature that prompted even more illicit activity and official corruption than could be accounted for by the foregoing argument.

It turns out that this additional corruption-inducing feature of the Soviet-type systems was, paradoxically, a side-effect of the very same thing that made the Soviet countries as powerful and imposing as, for a time, they were. The same thing that made the Soviet Union a super-power also in the long run corrupted it and accounted for its decline and ultimate collapse.

To understand what enabled Stalin to make his domain a superpower – and also led to its corruption, decline, and collapse – we must return to the criminal metaphor with which we began, and especially to the theory of the autocrat as stationary bandit.

7. - The Theory of Power Extended to Cover Stalinist Regimes

The theory of autocracy earlier in the paper puts the spotlight on two reasons why the Soviet empire for a time offered both an economic and military challenge to the United States and its allies. Stalin's Soviet Union was an autocracy and therefore:

1) it was governed by an encompassing interest: the more productive the Soviet domain was, other things equal, the more resources were available to achieve the autocrat's objectives, so Stalin had a powerful incentive to make his empire more productive;

2) Stalin, as an autocrat, extracted the largest possible surplus from the society to increase his political power, military might, and international influence.

Important as these two factors are, they do not explain why autocracies in the Stalinist pattern – i.e., what has come to be called the communist or Soviet pattern – were organized the way they were. Before Stalin consolidated his control over the Soviet political system at the end of the 1920s, no autocrat (not even Lenin) had organized his domain the way Stalin organized the Soviet Union. Why did Stalin impose on the Soviet Union (and later on the satellite countries) an economic system with almost universal state-ownership and a vast proportion of the prices and wages set by the regime?

The conventional assumption – that the choice for a centrally planned economy was because of Marxist-Leninist ideology – is inadequate. Saying that the actions of autocrats are explained by their ideologies adds only a word rather than an explanation unless we can, in turn, explain what inspired that ideology and why an autocrat chose that ideology.

After he obtained unchallenged power, Stalin adopted policies that he had previously opposed: total state absorption of the economy with brutal collectivization of agriculture. Stalin was not a consistent adherent of any ideological position. Marx's writings also did not require the economic organization that Stalin imposed; Marx had focused on capitalism and said almost nothing about the organization of socialist or communist societies. In time, because of Stalin's practice and propaganda, Marxism-Leninist ideology came to be identified with the type of economic and political system he had imposed, but this later rationalization cannot explain the choices Stalin made when he initially obtained dictatorial power.

Especially in view of the inadequacy of existing explanations of the special economic system in the communist autocracies, we need to extend the model of autocracy so that it can explain the special economic system in the communist autocracies and the special problems its collapse has bequeathed the societies in transition.

8. - The Limits on Autocratic Extraction

What limits the amount of resources that an autocrat can extract from his society? To answer this question, we must distinguish autocrats who have a secure hold on power and take a long run view from those that do not. I argued earlier that a roving bandit leader, if he could secure and hold a given domain, had an incentive to become a public-good-providing king. When insecurity about how long he will be in power or anything else makes an autocrat take a short-term view, we must stand this logic on its head. An autocrat by definition has sovereign power and thus the power unilaterally to take any asset that he wants. If an autocratic ruler has a short-term view, he has an incentive, no matter how gigantic his empire or how exalted his lineage might be, to seize any asset whose total value exceeds the discounted present value of its tax-yield over his short-term horizon. In other words, just as the roving bandit leader who can securely hold a domain has an incentive to make himself a king, so any autocrat with a short time horizon has an incentive to become, in effect, a roving bandit.

But, except in a special case we will cover in a moment, a rational autocrat with a long time horizon will not confiscate the assets of his subjects because this will reduce investment and future income and therefore also his own long-run tax receipts. As was shown earlier, the rational autocrat chooses the revenue-maximizing tax rate. Is there anything he can do to obtain still more? It appears that the expropriation of capital goods, because it reduces future investment and income, cannot increase the tax receipts of an autocrat over the long run. But there is one way that it cȧn, and Stalin was the first one to discover this way.

9. - Confiscations that Increase Savings and Investment

Stalin confiscated all of the farmland and natural resources of the Soviet Union, and all of the commercial and industrial property that had been privately held in the period of the New Economic Policy, and the rate of sayings and investment increased substantially. In general, the Soviet Union after Stalin's innovations, and the other societies on which the Stalinist system was imposed, had far higher rates of savings and investment than most other societies. Stalin's innovation was to take almost the total natural and tangible capital stock of the country through a 100% wealth tax, i.e., an expropriation, and then to use these resources to produce a mix of output that was much more intensive in capital goods, and other goods Stalin wanted, than would otherwise have been produced. By determining himself how much of the nation's resources would be used to produce consumer goods, and keeping this proportion much smaller than it was in most other societies, Stalin gave the Soviet Union an extraordinarily high rate of capital accumulation at the same time that he augmented his annual tax receipts by an amount approximately equal to all non-labor income. In the long history of stationary banditry, no other autocrat seems to have managed this while at the same time greatly increasing savings, investment, and the level of output[11].

---

[11] In the very short run, just after the collectivization of agriculture and other productive assets, there was apparently a period of "indigestion" and confusion when output may have significantly declined. But for most of the rest of Stalin's reign, the output that Stalin cared about was far higher than it had been before he imposed Stalinization on the USSR.

10. - How Taxes Can Increase the Incentive to Work

Stalin and his advisors also discovered a second innovative idea about how to increase the amount of resources he could obtain for his own purposes. Though most of Stalin's resources were obtained by taking all of the profits of state-owned enterprises rather from explicit taxes on individuals, we must recognize that this was an implicit if inconspicuous form of taxation, and thus analyze it as a form of taxation.

We must also understand that, when an autocrat has different tax schedules for individuals of different productivities, he can collect much more tax revenue. In the typical modern democracy, high-income people confront higher tax rates or brackets than do low-income people, but everyone faces the same tax law or schedule. When everyone faces the same tax schedule, it is impossible to tax people more on their first hours of work than on their last or marginal hours of work and also to have very high tax rates. Obviously, if each of us was taxed heavily on the first four hours a day of work, less on the next two, and not at all on hours after that, then we would have an incentive to work a lot more. We would have a stronger incentive to work because, if we were taxed heavily enough on the first few hours of work, we would be poorer and the "income effect" of taxation would make us work more. If we were not taxed on our last hours of work, we would also have a greater post-tax reward for additional work, so there would be what Western economics calls a larger "substitution effect", which would also make us work more than we would under ordinary Western types of taxation. Economic efficiency and the national income would also increase. So in some sense the Western democracies would be more efficient and productive if somehow it were possibile for their citizens to be taxed more on their first hours of work, but not taxed on their last or marginal hours of work.

But that is not a real possibility in a society with the same rule-of-law for everyone: then everyone must face the same tax law – that is, the same set of income tax brackets. Suppose that the United States decided to tax the first $ 5,000 a person makes a year at 99%, the next $ 5,000 at 98%, etc., and to tax what each person makes in excess of, say, a million dollars at 0%. This method – reversing the progression and regressively taxing lower incomes at much higher rates than higher incomes – would create a situation where the least productive people would not have even enough income to survive. The productivity and efficiency-enhancing policy of taxing people more on their first hours of work – or, more generally, on their infra-marginal income – but not taxing their marginal income, is not only morally repugnant but also practically impossibile when the same laws apply to everyone, when any society has the rule of law.

11. - From Each According to His Ability, to the Man in Charge

here is, however, a way that a cunning autocrat can tax infra-marginal income at far higher rates than marginal income, and thereby obtain great increases in both tax collections and national output. Somehow, Stalin or someone from whom he borrowed the idea hit upon this method. Stalin was power-hungry and ruthless enough to put it into practice. The method is to set the salaries and wages of each occupation and ability level in the society with the purpose of collecting the maximum income for the autocrat's purposes from every individual in the economy.

First, Stalin had the subordinates he put in charge of the economy set wages and salaries very low, so people could not afford much leisure. Second, he established a system of bonuses and of special rewards for people who were Stakhanovites or model workers. He also used progressive piece rates, that is, piece rates that increased the per-unit payment with the amount that the person produced. Stalin's combination of bonuses, progressive piece rates, prizes for Stakhanovites, and special perquisites for other especially productive workers was a system that provided people with a large proportion of the marginal output that they produced, but at the same time implicitly taxed them very highly indeed on their infra-marginal work.

In effect, Stalin's system of wage and salary setting had the effect of implicitly confronting individuals in different jobs or with different ability levels with a different tax schedule. This made it possible to impose higher average tax rates on the more able individuals who

UNIVERSITY
OF BRISTOL
LIBRARY

could produce a larger surplus over subsistence[12], while at the same time taxing the first hours of work severely and the last hours only lightly. To paraphrase an old saying, it was "from each according to his ability, to the man in charge".

The Stalinist regime obviously knew that it took more ability to be a factory manager than an unskilled factory worker, and it must have known roughly what ability and education level was appropriate for each major type of job. To motivate the more able people to take on the jobs needing more ability, Stalin made the total pay – including bonuses and other forms of marginal pay – for the jobs demanding higher ability higher than the total pay for the less demanding jobs.

Note that the familiar Western progressive income tax would not have served Stalin's purposes at all. Thus it is no coincidence that the Soviet Union, even as it attacked the market democracies for their inequalities of income, did not in any serious way use the progressive income tax. For a long time, the maximum rate of income tax in the Soviet Union, for example, was only 13%.

As I mentioned above, and as Ronald McKinnon's important work on this subject explained earlier[13], the main source of tax revenue for the Soviet-type societies was the profits of industrial enterprises (and turnover taxes that were, in effect, mainly taxes on the profits of these enterprises). Stalin not only claimed for the regime all of the profits of state enterprises, but also had his planners set inframarginal wage rates and prices at levels that would make industrial profits – and thus implicit taxes – very high.

The proportion of income in the Soviet Union in Stalin's time that was devoted to personal consumption of the population was lower than in any noncommunist country, and that is exactly what the theory of "totalitarian taxation" put forth here predicts. Stalin was able to obtain a larger proportion of the national output for his own purposes than any other government in history had been able to extract.

---

[12] I am grateful to James Buchanan for pointing out to me, at a very early stage of my work on the hypothesis that Stalinism was fundamentally a tax-collection system, that a communist tax-maximizing system would not only try to raise the ratio of infra-marginal to marginal taxes, but also try to take more taxation from those who were more productive.

[13] See McKinnon [9], an IRIS publication also available in Russina translation published by The Foundation for Economic Literacy in Moscow.

The origins of Stalin's innovative system of tax collection showed up most starkly in agriculture. The collective farm was designed to be "collective" in the sense of "collection", not as in "collectivist". After providing extensive labor services to the collective farm, the farmers were allowed to use any leisure time for work on the tiny private plots that were allocated to them. As the theory here predicts, the income from these plots was not, in general, taxed.

From Stalin's point of view, the food collection system worked. During World War I the Tsarist state (even though at times it also used coercive measures to collect food) was not able to provide enough food to people in the cities to maintain its control: the February revolution began as a protest over the shortage of bread. By contrast, during World War II, the Soviet regime had at its disposal a well-developed procurement system... Despite a disastrous fall in food production per head of the collective farm population, the share of total meat and grain output taken by the government rose[14].

Though Stalin was often considered the Pope of Marxist religion, he was not, in fact, a sincere ideologue. Though ideology no doubt played a role explaining some of his support, the hypothesis here is that Stalin was not blinded by – or even faithful to – what had previously been called Marxism. If Stalin had been a committed ideologue he would not have done many of the things he did, like kill off all of the people who had participated with him as initial leaders of the Bolshevik revolution, or purge those Bolsheviks who dared to defend their Marxist principles, or make the Nazi-Soviet pact. Stalin also did nothing whatever to bring about the withering of the state that Marx had predicted and advocated.

Yet he did a great deal to increase the size and power of the Soviet military and the industrial and scientific base that it required. Though the main features of the Stalinist system were not required by Marx's writings, nor by Lenin's example in the period of the somewhat market-oriented New Economic Policy, they are consistent with the hypothesis that Stalin wanted, above all else, the power that increased tax collections could give him.

---

[14] See GATRELL P. - HARRISON M. [7].

12. - A Test: the Ratio of Power to Income

If the theory offered here is true, the military or geo-political power and the expenditures on projects that add to the status and prestige of political leaders should have been greater, in relation to the standard of living of the population, than in other societies, even other autocratic societies. A casual glance at the historical record is enough to show that this was the case.

Tsarist Russia, though much the largest country on earth, was not able to give a good account of itself in the Crimean War. Nor was it able to defeat even the then-backward island society of Japan in 1904-1905. Similarly, Chiang Kai-Shek's China, though it had the world's largest population, was military impotent.

Compare also Tsarist Russia in World War I with Stalin's USSR. In World War I the gigantic Empire of the Tsars was defeated essentially only by Germany[15], even though the German army had its hands full fighting on a second front against the French and British from the beginning of the War and normally used only a small fraction of its forces against Russia. By contrast, in World War II Stalin's Soviet Union was victorious against Nazi Germany, even though the Germans committed the great bulk of their fighting troops to the Soviet front: there was no "second front" until the Normandy invasion in June of 1944. Though German ground and air munitions production was 2.6 times as large in World War II as in World War I, Soviet munitions production was 24.5 times as high in World War II as the Russina Empire's munitions production in World War I[16].

---

[15] The army of the Austro-Hungarian Empire was also used against Tsarist Russia, but this army was often said to be poorer than that of any other combatant country in World War I, and it did not play an impressive role in the defeat of Russia.

[16] See GATRELL P. - HARRISON M. [7], Table 9 and pp. 425-52. Gatrell and Harrison point out that «In World War I... only Germany's failure to disentangle itself from the Western front prevented the speedy victory over Russia which Germany intended. Even so, a small fraction of Germany's military power was able eventually to bring about Russia's defeat and disintegration. In the second war... the scale of Soviet mobilization, when combined with overwhelming economic superiority of the Allies, was sufficient to destroy Germany completely as a military power... the USSR made a contribution... that was disproportionate to the size and level of development of the Soviet economy» (pp. 438).

Whatever interpretation may be offered for the fortunes of the different Russina autocracies in World Wars I and II, there can be no doubt that after World War II the Soviet Union was universally accorded a superpower status that the Tsarist autocracy never achieved and that the Tsars never managed a prestige coup comparable to the Soviet initiation of flight in space. When the Stalinist system was applied in China, Vietnam, and North Korea it again made the communist autocracies incomparably more powerful militarily and politically than other third world regimes.

13. - The Inefficiency and Decline of the Stalinist System

Having given the Stalinist devil its due, we must not forget the well-known point that the Soviet system, even at its best, was inefficient. The Soviet system mobilized a fantastic amount of resources, but it also wasted a lot. Stalin's confiscations eliminated many of the markets needed for an efficient economy. To obtain all of what would, in a market economy, have been interest, rent, and profit, Stalin had to rule out private asset and rental markets for land and other natural resources and for capital goods. He also eliminated privately-owned firms, and society lost the gains from the innovations that private entrepreneurs would have undertaken. By setting wage and salary levels and differentials administratively in order to obtain colossal implicit tax collections out of labor income, Stalin also distorted labor markets, though by much less than expected because his taxation fell mainly on inframarginal earnings. As a result of all of the eliminations and distortions of markets required by Stalin's confiscations and implicit taxes, the "total factor productivity" (the output in relation to the inputs) of the Soviet-type societies was lower – and was growing less rapidly – than in market economies of comparable levels of development.

In the early years, the Soviet societies achieved rapid economic growth, in spite of their slow growth of total factor productivity, because they had extraordinarily high rates of investment. These exceptional rates of saving and investment were, as I argued earlier, due in turn to the uniquely high proportion of national output that they could capture for investments that made them formidable and expanding competitors in the race for international influence and power. For about the first two decades after World War II, the societies that grew out of Stalin's innovations and conquests were able to make up for their inefficiency through their wondrous savings and investment rates.

We already know that, as time went on, the Soviet-type societies began to stagnate. Though they continued with their high saving and investment, they were after a time unable to obtain even moderate rates of growth of productivity[17], even though they still had a long way to go to catch-up to Western levels[18].

This is because the Soviet Union and the other countries on which the Stalinist model had been imposed suffered from a sclerosis analogous to the one that was described above when analyzing the market democracies and the "British disease" of slow growth. But, for reasons that will soon be evident, the red sclerosis was far more severe than the form that afflicts the market democracies of the West. As time went on, the Soviet Union and (to a lesser extent) the societies that became communist only after World War II became severely sclerotic. Eventually this sclerosis reached fatal proportions and communism collapsed.

How could a system that served Stalin so well – that made him arguably the most powerful individual in the world – become so sclerotic that it could not, in the long run, even survive? This was not a question that Stalin himself had to worry about. To paraphrase Keynes: in the long run, Stalin was dead.

But it is an overwhelming problem for the societies in transition from communism. As we shall see, the drop in income levels that most of these societies have endured and their continuing difficulties are mainly due to the sclerotic structures that continue to plague the societies in transition. So the "red sclerosis" must be understood if the societies in transition are to find the therapy that will cure the disease from which they suffer.

---

[17] See Easterly W. - Fischer S. [3].
[18] See Murrel P. - Olson M. [11], vol. 15, pp. 239-65.

14. - How Can there Be Sclerosis without Freedom of Organization?

Obviously, the communist countries did not have freedom of organization. It would be absurd to suppose that lobbying organizations of the kind that buy advertisements in the American media or labor unions such as those that have played such a large role in the United Kingdom could be responsible for their sclerosis. The red sclerosis was very different from that in societies with freedom of organization, and not only because it reached the point of being fatal. It was also incomparably more discreet and subtle.

The key to the gradual decay of Stalin's system under his successors was its dependence on the decisions of subordinates in the bureaucracy. Though the role of markets in Soviet-type societies was much larger than is often supposed[19], the Stalinist system of implicit tax collection obviously had to limit markets more than any other societies have done. To maintain and increase investment after confiscating the capital stock, the Soviet-type regimes had to control consumption and saving decisions. After seizing all the tangible capital and natural resources in the society, there could be no private firms. If infra-marginal wages are to be set far below the free market levels, they cannot simply be left to the market. Thus a system of the type Stalin founded obviously must handle an awesome number of matters through its command and control system, and for this it had to rely on a vast army of nomenklatura and lesser administrators.

How could the leadership of a Soviet-type economy, given that it had to make through a bureaucracy millions of decisions that in other societies are governed mainly by markets, obtain an even faintly rational allocation of resources? That such a system would be insensitive to consumer demands and would also have major inefficiencies is so well-known that it should no longer need to be discussed. But how could it work well enough to create and sustain a superpower? I have explained how the encompassing interest of the Soviet dictator gave

---

[19] Because it is impossible for any bureaucracy to make decisions about all of the countless goods and services produced in a vast economy, innumerable decisions were in fact left for negotiations and contracts among state enterprises and to diverse legal, informal, and black markets.

him a strong incentive to make his domain as productive as he could in the interest of increasing his total tax collections. We still need to explain how the autocrat was able to obtain the information, plans, and implementation of decisions from his bureaucracy that were needed to obtain even a semi-coherent allocation of resources. Thus we face the extraordinary intellectual challenge of explaining how such a system could work at all.

Economists, operations researchers, and systems analysts have, of course, long understood theoretically what would be needed for a fully efficient planned economy. The leader of a communist society would need to have enterprise managers and other subordinates estimate the input-output possibilities or "production functions" of each and every enterprise and spell out the leader's goals or "objective function" in great detail. In principle, economic planners could then calculate the optimal allocation of resources for the leader. The leader would have his subordinates impose this allocation. Since conditions and technologies are constantly changing, optimality requires that the whole process continually be redone.

As has long been known, a bureaucracy cannot obtain or process all of the information needed to calculate an optimal allocation or put it into practice. Of course, the communist countries did not need optimality to compete against their most imperfect competitors – they needed only a tolerable level of efficiency.

15. - Obtaining the Information Needed for a Coherent Plan

For a Soviet-type economy to obtain tolerable efficiency, indeed, for it to function at all, the bureaucracy must centralize and utilize a staggering amount of information. The experience of actual conditions becomes evident only at the front line of the production processes and it is only there that the performance of most workers can be monitored. The information has to be passed up layer of bureaucracy to the top. The orders worked out in the light of this information also have to passed through all of these layers of officials on the way down. In any large bureaucracy, there is inevitably a large loss and distortion of information, even with the best efforts of all concerned.

For fundamental reasons, the best efforts of all concerned are not usually available. A manager's chances of promotion or bonuses are lowered if a superior learns of mistakes. Subordinates, therefore, have an incentive to hide all those shortcomings of their performance that can be successfully concealed from a superior. There is also an incentive to overstate the difficulties faced and to understate potential production. The more one reflects about these problems the clearer it becomes that there must be a countervailing factor, or the centrally planned economies would not have been able to function at all.

16. - Competition Among Bureaucrats

Competition among bureaucrats is such a countervailing factor. The strong incentive for production facing the leader of a Soviet-type society can at times be translated into tolerable performance because of the constraints on bureaucratic misrepresentation and negligence that arise because each bureaucrat or manager can be constrained and monitored by others. Suppose that a manager understates the output that can be produced with the inputs that are being allocated to him or that he produces much less than he could produce. Those managers who are given similar inputs and responsibilities then have an opportunity to make a good impression by promising or producing better outcomes.

The boss can also check with his subordinates' subordinates, and if there is unqualified competition among all the bureaucrats the lower-level managers have an incentive to correct any erroneous information their superiors have given the boss in the hope of promotion and other rewards. Thus when there is bureaucratic competition among all administrators, each official must accordingly be cautious in under-reporting the potential productivity of the resources being allocated to him or in under-producing with the resources he is actually given. An astute superior can accordingly use competition among subordinates to exploit their more detailed knowledge and to draw out better estimates of potential production and better productivity than would otherwise be obtained. When there is full competition among subordinates, a leader can even allocate resources among his subordinates to those who make the best credible offers about how much output they will produce, so that, in effect, the resources are auctioned off to the subordinate managers who offer the highest "bids" or output-to-input ratios.

17. - Bureaucratic Collusion

The foregoing argument assumed that collusion of subordinates does not limit bureaucratic competition or reduce the information or power available to the center. For the early period of a Soviet-type economy (or a period after a purge, or a cultural revolution like the one Mao instigated, or other total shake-up of a society), this is a fairly realistic assumption. But, as earlier parts of the paper argued, in stable environments, collusion and other types of collective action increase over time. This eliminates the competition among subordinates that is the dictator's only source of information about what is actually happening in the factories, farms, and other enterprises. It also means that he cannot, as it were, auction the productive inputs off to the managers who promise to produce the most output, because managers will collude to offer less than they could have and then have surplus resources they can control themselves. Thus collusion or any kind of independent collective action among subordinates eliminates the competition that is the only thing that enables a Soviet-type economy to attain even modest degrees of productivity.

Subordinates have an incentive to collude at the expense of the center if they are not caught and punished for doing so. If, for example, all the managers of the enterprises in a given industry understate how much they could produce with given amounts of inputs, they can keep a surplus that each of them can control. If they all offer less than they can when a superior "auctions" inputs off to those who promise the greatest return, there is a surplus that they can keep. If the workers in a given setting collusively agree that they will only pretend to work, they are spared the effort that the foreman could have obtained from them had they remained in competition with one another. Such collusion is often feasible, since subordinates are the superior's main source of information about what is really possible.

The collusion normally begins at the level of the nomenklatura. There will normally be only a small number factory managers in any given industry or locality. Because the numbers involved are small, the managers in a given industry can collude in much less time than would be required for a large group to coordinate action in its common interest. The restraints on independent organization in a communist society – especially organization that weakens the control of the leader – require inconspicuous, informal, and secret collusion, and the need to proceed covertly makes collective action emerge much more slowly than it otherwise would. But small groups can typically collude secretly and somewhat larger groups that have sufficient trust in one another can also manage this.

Thus, as time goes on in a Soviet-type society, there will be opportunities for many groups – especially small groups of high-ranking administrators and enterprise managers in particular industries – to organize informally and covertly. As more time passes, subordinates of subordinates organize. In due course this small-group covert collusion can reach down even to coteries of senior workers in factories, mines, collective farms, and retail shops. In the fullness of time, even big state enterprises, individual industries, and subordinate levels of governments will, in effect, become organized coalitions that can discreetly and subtly cooperate in their common interest at the expense of the dictatorial center. Enterprises eventually become more nearly insider lobbies or organized special interests than productive enterprises. Ultimately even Republics in which language and ethnic loyalties facilitate collective action can become conspiracies at the expense of the center.

The foregoing accumulation of covert collective action would not be so damaging to the productivity of a Soviet-type society if each of the separate collusions, enterprises, and industry associations had a significant incentive to make the society work. But whereas the dictator or politburo at the center has an encompassing interest in the productivity of the society, the separate collusions and special-interest organizations do not. Their incentives are quite as perverse as those of narrow organized special-interests in the market democracies, and nearly as perverse as those of the individual criminal.

18. - Banding Together Against the Bandit

We earlier discussed the way in which market-contrary policies undermine law-abiding behavior and promote official corruption, because they create situations in which all of the parties involved have a common interest in evading the rules, keeping the evasion secret from the authorities, and corrupting the relevant officials. We know that the uniquely high rates of implicit tax collections in the systems of the Soviet-type implied great interference with markets and that this encouraged corruption under communism. But this market-contrary character of the Soviet-type systems does not adequately convey communism's corruption-inducing tendencies. This can best be understood by going back to our stationary bandit metaphor.

It should not be astonishing if the subjects of a stationary bandit feel morally entitled to withhold income that a stationary bandit wants to tax, or to take back some of the income he has taken from them. Thus exploitative autocracies may not benefit much from the common feeling in successful democracies that individuals should not cheat on their tax returns, much less steal public property. Probably the Soviet-type regimes suffered some losses because many of their subjects recognized that they were exploited, but we must be careful not to exaggerate this factor. The populations of these societies were form childhood exposed to education and propaganda designed to make them believe in the regime and to uphold the norms it required. Obviously the media in these societies contained nothing analogous to the complaints about high taxation and waste in government that are commonplace in democracies.

The most remarkable corruption-inducing feature of the Soviet-type systems becomes evident when one compares this system of implicit tax collection with the traditional types of autocratic tax-theft. The autocrat who leaves the productive assets and production of the society in the hands of his subjects has to fight tax evasion, but much of work of maintaining order is done by his subjects. Each subject tends to protect his property and this makes it possible for a traditional autocrat to keep theft among his subjects within bounds and also limits the exposure of his officials to bribery.

If, by contrast, an autocrat insists on obtaining 100% of the rents, profit, and interest earned by the natural resources and tangible capital of his domain, and also sets the wages of workers in order to maximize the implicit tax on labor, then there is almost no private property or privately managed production. There is also almost no property that subjects guard in their own self-interest. Both the fixed assets and the inventory of every significant enterprise belong to the autocrat and he is the only person who has an automatic incentive to guard this property. In order to maximize implicit tax collections, almost all production has to be under the control of the autocrat and his subordinates and so every manager is in part a tax collector.

The autocrat then has more property and more tax collection than any man can watch. So there must be watchers and also those who watch the watchers. If those who watch best and collect the most for the center are rewarded and those who lose property and collect least are punished, the competition among the watchers and the collectors means that everyone is watched and all the collections are passed on: the watchers and collectors watch and collect from each other. Though they all would gain from overthrowing the stationary bandit and keeping his exactions for themselves, this overthrow would be a collective good for millions and no individual has an incentive to share the costs of obtaining it.

But within small groups, the autocrat's subjects can, when they eventually develop sufficient trust in one another, safely conspire together in their common interest. It is in their common interest to skim off part of the red bandit's take. Whenever any diversion of production, any theft of state property, or any failure to work conscientiously is observed only within the small conspiring group, it will not be detected by the center. Whatever the autocrat cannot observe with his own eyes, he can learn about only through reports of those beneath him. Each individual in a small group will obtain a significant share of the yield of any collusion. So as time goes on more and more small groups explicitly or tacitly agree that they will do less work, allocate more of the resources under their control to their own purposes, and share more of the state property that they work with among themselves.

There are, however, limits to what any small group can take without being observed by someone outside the group. If the managers take too much, their subordinates may notice. If those in Department *A* take too much, those in Department *B* may be able to tell what is going on. So, if there is time for the manager and his subordinates, or Department *A* and Department *B*, to reach the point that they can trust each other with secrets, they can agree that more of the goods they produce and the assets they control will be kept for themselves. What happens in group after group and department after department becomes commonplace, and what becomes commonplace seems only natural and right. Eventually the enterprise, the industry, the locality, and even the ethnic or linguistic group come to agree, tacitly if not explicitly, that they can and should keep more for themselves. So as time goes on more and more of the central bandit's theft is taken back.

The center has those who watch the watchers: the higher officials, party cadre, police, secret police and other watchdogs whose job is to insure that none of the autocrat's property is stolen and that every enterprise, industry, locality, and ethno-linguistic group produces huge implicit tax collections for the center. But if no one except the center owns property, and if no one except the center has the legal right to claim the implicit tax receipts then everyone except the center has an incentive to induce these officials to become a part of the countless conspiracies to take back some of what the stationary bandit has stolen from them. If the watchdog officials can persuade the center they are doing a great job guarding the property and increasing the implicit tax collections of the center, then they are likely to be rewarded. Even a small share of the gains from a diversion of production or the theft of assets is, however, likely to be worth more than the extra salary that comes from a promotion. The best outcome of all for the official is to be promoted and then take a share of the implicit tax collections and state property over a wider part of the economy. Of course, the center has an interest in preventing this, but it has virtually no source of information on what is happening other than subordinate officials, all of whom have an interest in being part of a conspiracy to take back some of what the stationary bandit has stolen.

Ironically, it was Marx who coined the best phrase for describing a situation such as this. There is an "internal contradiction" in any system of the kind Stalin created. In such a system, the autocrat takes most of the economy's output for his own purposes and owns almost everything. But this means that almost everyone else has an incentive to be part of collusions to take back some of what the stationary bandit has stolen. If all of the autocrat's subordinates simply compete with one another to receive the autocrat's rewards and avoid his punishments, the system can work. But, in the fullness of time, as more and more coteries of subordinates collude in their own interests, the system not only loses efficiency and output but also becomes a web of counter-theft and corruption that ultimately leaves the center impoverished. If the harshest punishments are imposed on even the faintest suspicion, then the bureaucratic competition that is indispensable to the system can be preserved somewhat longer, so Stalinist purges can make the system work better. In the long run, nonetheless, the difficulties of covert collective action are bound to be overcome in more and more enterprises, industries, localities, and ethnic or linguistic groups. Thus it is a "law of motion" of Soviet-type societies that they must not only run down over time, but also become increasingly corrupt. Ultimately, it becomes, some say, "impossible to buy and easy to steal". More and more victims of the regime come to believe that he who "refrains from taking state property is robbing his family". That is, part of the population comes to have a visceral, intuitive sense that they are the victims of an extraordinarily rapacious stationary bandit and that it is only right that they should take something back.

In a sense, the system becomes fairer as time goes on: the stationary bandit's take is shared more widely.

It becomes fairer, but it cannot work. The stationary bandit who takes everything except the minimum needed to elicit the effort of his captives has an encompassing interest in the productivity of the society, so he does what must be done to make the society productive and thus better able to meet his needs. By contrast, each of the conspiring coteries, enterprise lobbies, industry associations, and local societies obtains so little of the society's output that each of them has only a narrow interest, i.e., little or no incentive to maintain the productivity of the society. As communism devolved, it was bound to collapse.

19. - The Cures for Corruption

Given the foregoing logic, there is nothing puzzling in the fact that Soviet-type regimes normally required state enterprises to make all payments through the state banking system and whenever possible tried to keep enterprises from using or holding currency, this facilitated extraction by the center and made retention of profits by the enterprise more difficult. The multiplication of private firms after the collapse of communism means that there are more enterprises that use significant amounts of currency. These private firms are subject to extortion by mafia gangs in ways that state-owned enterprises without cash were not. This consideration has probably helped make mafia-type crime increase in many countries after the collapse of communism. The disorganization attendant upon the collapse of the old order has probably worked in the same direction. The emergence of a free press has greatly improved the reportage of crime and made it more visible.

Considerations such as these have made some people assume that the market economy, private property, and democracy promote corruption and crime. The emergence of democracy and the market economy opened the curtains and made crime more visible. They probably also created inviting new targets for criminals and corrupt officials.

If the logic in this paper is correct, it was the inevitable devolution of the extractive system created by Stalin that is mainly responsible for the corruption and crime that many citizens of the post-communist societies are complaining about. The advance of market economies in the late 19th century was in most Western countries associated with the development of meritocratic civil services and higher standards of honesty in government than had prevailed in prior centuries. The rapidly growing market economies in West Germany and Japan after the defeat of fascism do not appear to have promoted crime and corruption.

When we take account of the ways in which the self-interest of the owners of private property makes them work to protect their property we see that a shift to private property tends to reduce theft. With private property, moreover, the net effect of the private sector incentives is normally to assist and encourage governmental efforts to combat theft. When there are market-contrary regulations, by contrast, those on both sides of the market gain from evading the law and cooperating to suborn the officials who enforce it.

Thus the diagnosis of corruption in this paper has strong and immediate implications about the therapy needed to cure the disease. One implication is that regulations, such as those that limit the export or control the price of oil and gas, that run against the incentives in the market, promote corruption. They create situations where all parties gain from evading the regulation and, when necessary, sharing the gains with officials who are supposed to enforce the regulation. To reduce corruption and crime, a country should have no government interventions in the market beyond those that meet both of the following conditions: 1) they are directed at what Western neoclassical economics defines as "market failures", and 2) the existing government, taking its shortcomings and the lobbying pressure that will be brought to bear on it into account, will come closer to generating a socially efficient and equitable outcome than the imperfect market.

Another practical implication is that the sooner the last vestiges of the extractive system Stalin created are eliminated, the less the dangers of crime and, especially, official corruption.

The foregoing diagnosis of the problem of corruption does not, however, imply that all that a society needs to do is "to let capitalism happen". In fact, corruption and crime cannot be properly controlled and a country's economic potential realized unless the government effectively performs a role that the private sector cannot perform. Some enthusiasts for markets, at least in the West, suppose that the only problem is that governments get in the way of the market and that private property is a natural and spontaneous creation. This view is unquestionably and drastically wrong. Though individuals may have possessions without government, the way a dog possesses a bone, there is no private property without government. Property is a governmentally protected claim on an asset, a bundle of rights enforceable in courts backed by the coercive power of government. The governments of the societies in transition have to perform the gigantic task of making and enforcing general rules that define property rights, providing for the impartial adjudication of disputes about ownership of property, and of cutting back drastically the domain in which the administrative of discretion of government officials can affect the value of property and contract rights. Better property and contract rights in the post-communist countries will not only help the economy immeasurably, but also mean that assets will be held by individuals and firms who have a secure and precisely defined interest in protecting them, and that will reduce corruption and crime.

20. - Fragmentation of Governments

The same red sclerosis that increased corruption in the communist societies also increased ethno-linguistic separatism and the devolution of power to regional and local governments. When the center is a system of extraction, it is only natural to want to escape it. To the extent that a group had a distinctive ethnic loyalty or language, it was better able to conspire and collude against the huge implicit taxes imposed by the center. Ethnic grievances and mutual trust within the group facilitate cooperation, and a separate language reduces the chances that the center will learn of a collusive discussion. This is one of several reasons why, though there was virtually no separatism resulting from the defeat of fascism, formerly communist countries like Yugoslavia, Czechoslovakia, and the USSR have broken down, and why there is separatism and devolution in various regions and localities of Russia.

Since is impossible to alter the past, the fissiparous tendencies must be recognized as realities that can only disappear as a result of mutually advantageous voluntary interaction in future years. The experience of various customs unions like the Common Market in

Europe and the North American Free Trade Area suggest that the gains from freer trade and outside investment in an area can be obtained without political integration. The exceptional prosperity of federalisms like Germany, the United States, and (especially) multilingual Switzerland suggest that large amounts of local governmental autonomy usually increase the efficiency and responsiveness of governments.

21. - From Economic Retardation to Economic Miracles

The most important effect of the covert collusions that emerged in Soviet-type economies was probably not their impact on corruption and the desire for political separatism, but their drag on economic growth. We recall that a Soviet-type system was dependent upon competition among subordinate officials both for information and for incentives for performance. Subordinate officials had an incentive covertly to collude to reduce the competitive pressures they imposed upon one another and to obtain surpluses that they could control. As time goes on there is additional covert collective action and eventually state enterprises and industry associations become powerful insider lobbies. Each insider lobby is a narrow rather than an encompassing interest and has virtually no incentive to care about the prosperity of the society. Because of this, the lack of information at the center, and the paucity of market incentives, the state enterprises in the later and more sclerotic phases of communism were ofrten extraordinarily inefficient. Some large state enterprises were so uneconomic that the value of the material inputs they used, when properly valued at world prices, exceeded the free market value of the outputs they produced. The size and the hierarchical character of these enterprises nonetheless meant that they had formidable lobbying power.

With the collapse of communism and the advent of democracy, the big state enterprises and industry associations could lobby openly for protection against imports, for other forms of government subsidies, and for nearly free loans and inter-enterprise credits that were ultimately financed by the creation of new money by the central bank. The relative political power of dinosaur enterprises was all the greater

UNIVERSITY
OF BRISTOL
LIBRARY

because newly created firms had not usually had the time to overcome the difficulties of collective action and were therefore unorganized. This meant the lobbying power in societies in transition is disproportionately held by precisely those enterprises that, in a vast number of cases, need to be replaced by new or foreign firms. This has greatly slowed down the adaptation and transformation of the formerly communist economies. The subsidized credits obtained by these firms have also been the main source of inflation in most of the societies in transition. Privatization can substantially reduce the lobbying power of these firms by denying them their insider status, but it by no means eliminates it.

As earlier parts of this paper showed, the economic miracles in West Germany, Japan, and Italy after the defeat of fascism owed a great deal to the fact that fascist governments and allied occupiers had largely eliminated their lobbies and cartels. After the defeat of communism, by contrast, the societies in transition from communism were dense with powerful lobbies of the large enterprises and industry associations inherited from the old regime. Red sclerosis had bequeathed these societies an especially virulent form of the "British disease". I believe that this is one of the most important reasons why economic peroformance has sometimes been even worse after communism was abandoned.

The therapy for this disease is easy to explain but difficult to implement. Each special-interest lobby, even if it consists of a gigantic firm or a major industry association, represents only a small minority of the population. Thus it will easily be outvoted whenever it demands special-interest favors if the public understands the matter. Indeed, most of the special-interests represent such a small part of the electorate that they are outnumbered even by the intelligentsia – even by that part of the population that does a lot of reading and is especially interested in public affairs. It follows that, if a better understanding of this problem and of western economics emerges in the societies in transition, the problem will largely be solved. It is not an easy thing to change public opinion, or even to obtain a more enlightened intelligentsia, but there is a little progress: a small but increasing number of people are coming to be aware of the problems that have been discussed in this paper. If there is enough of this progress, we can be confident that economic miracles akin to those that followed the defeat of fascism will follow in the post-communist societies.

22. - A Postscript on Italy and the West

There is no need to say anything more here about how the argument about economic growth in this paper relates to the West. This paper is an extension of the theory in my book on *The Rise and Decline of Nations*, which dealt mostly with economic growth in the West, and of other work dealing with this topic[20].

In view of the current concern in Italy about official corruption and the problem of mafia families, it may be useful to ask whether the foregoing argument about crime and corruption in the East could be elaborated and extended to cover Italy and the other countries of the West. Since the historical experience in Italy and other western countries is, of course, dramatically different from that of the former communist countries, the foregoing argument about corruption cannot be applied directly and without qualification to any Western country.

Yet I believe that the argument, if supplemented with other ideas and appropriately qualified, can illuminate the problem of official corruption and organized crime in the West. Though the governments of the West have obviously never imposed anything akin to the Stalinist system, nor even undertaken nearly as much market-contrary activity as most of the governments of the Third World, they have imposed quite a few market-contrary laws and regulations. Naturally, these market-contrary measures, in the West no less than in the East, give those on both sides of the market an incentive to evade the law and to cooperate when necessary in corrupting any officials aware of these evasions. In some western countries – and not least in Italy – there is also a considerable amount of property that does not belong to any individual or private firm, and thus the private sector has no

---

[20] Particularly «The Varieties of Eurosclerosis», in CRAFTS N. - TONIOLO G. (eds.), *Economic Growth in Europe Since 1945*, Cambridge, Cambridge University Press, 1996.

incentive to guard and protect this property. There are, of course, officials and employees of publicly-owned firms who have the responsibility of protecting this property, but they do not usually have such clear cut and strong incentives to protect it as private owners do. The management and career employees of these companies may eventually cooperate or collude well enough to form an effective lobby, and sometimes even acquire an informal quai-ownership of the public enterprise. Any such partial or informal ownership will increase their incentive to protect the enterprise's assets, and profitability capacity to use their partial control over the enterprise to enhance their own incomes and wellbeing.

Though there is much less market-contrary regulation and "state" owned property in the West than there was in the Soviet-type societies, the punishments for offenses are far less severe and the protection for defendants in the legal system incomparably more elaborate. Though it would be monstrous if Western societies adopted Stalinist – or even late Soviet period – punishments and prosecutorial abuses, it must also be recognized that the rule of law and civilized approaches to punishment also reduce the risk of engaging in illegal behavior. In areas, such as southern Italy, where there is a long history of ineffective foreign administrations and of weak government, the difficulties are greater than in areas with a heritage of efficient native administration and strong government.

From the perspective offered by this paper, the extensive subsidies and legislation designed to raise the South of Italy to northern levels of per-capita income also have a down side. To the extent that they increase the amount of market-contrary intervention and the proportion of assets that are not protected by their private owners, they tend to worsen the very pathologies that largely account for the lower level of economic development of the South. As the experience of the former Soviet countries shows, they can also bring about political fragmentation. When taxpayers believe that they are victims of tax theft by distant interests, those who are supposed to be the beneficiaries of this taxation can all too easily come to be regarded as aliens.

BIBLIOGRAPHY

[1] CHAN S., «Growth with Equity: a Test of Olson's Theory for the Asian Pacific-Rim Countries», *Journal of Peace Research*, vol. 24, n. 2, 1987, pp. 135-49.

[2] CHOI K., *Theories of Economic Growth*, Ames (IA), Iowa State, 1983.

[3] EASTERLY W. - FISCHER S., *The Soviet Economic Decline: Historical and Republican Data*, manuscript, 1993.

[4] ERSSON S. - LANE J.E., *Comparative political Economy*, New York, Pinter Publishers, 1990.

[5] GALLOWAY L. - VEDDER R., «Rentseeking, Distributional Coalitions, Taxes, Relative Prices, and Economic Growth», *Public Choice*, vol. 51, n. 1, 1986, pp. 93-100.

[6] GAMBETTA D., *The Sicilian Mafia*, Cambridge (MA), Harvard University Press, 1993.

[7] GATRELL P. - HARRISON M, «The Russian and Soviet Economies in Two World Wars: a Comparative View», *The Economic History Review*, vol. XLVI, n. 3, August 1993, p. 444.

[8] MCGUIRE M. - OLSON M., «The Economics of Autocracy and Majority Rule: the Hidden Hand the Use of Force», *Journal of Economic Literature*, vol. XXXIV, March, 1996, pp. 72-96.

[9] MCKINNON, «Taxation, Money, and Credit in a Liberalizing Socialist Economy», in CLAGUE C. - RAUSSER G. (eds.), *The Emergence of Market Economies in Eastern Europe*, Cambridge (MA) and Oxford (UK), Blackwell, 1992.

[10] MUELLER D.C. (ed.), *The Political Economy of Growth*, New Haven, Yale University Press, 1983.

[11] MURREL P. - OLSON M., The Devolution of Centrally Planned Economies, *Journal of Comparative Economics*, vol. 15, n. 2, June 1991, pp. 239-65.

[12] OLSON M., *Rise and Decline of Nations*, New Haven (CT), Yale University Press, 1982.

[13] ——, *Logic of Collective Action*, Cambridge, Harvard University Press, 1965.

[14] ——, «Dictatorship, Democracy, and Development», *American Political Science Review*, vol. 87, n. 3, September 1994.

[15] RAUCH J., *Demosclerosis*, New York, Times Books, 1994.

[16] SANDLER T., *Collective Action: Theory and Application*, Ann Arbor (MI), The University of Michigan Press, 1992.

[17] SHERIDAN J.E., *Chinese Warlord: the Career of Feng Yuhsiang*, Stanford, (CA), Stanford University Press, 1966.

[18] VARIOUS AUTHORS, «Mancur Olson: The Rise and Decline of Nations», *International Studies Quarterty*, special issue, vol. 27, 1983.

[19] ——, «Mancur Olson, The Rise and Decline of Nations», *Scandinavian Political Studies*, special issue, vol. 9, n. 1, March 1986.

[20] WEEDE E., «Catch-Up, Distributional Coalitions and Government as Determinants of Growth and Decline in Industrial Democracies», *British Journal of Sociology*, vol. 37, n. 2, June 1986, pp. 194-220.

Inflation, Central Bank Independence, Labour and Financial Governance: Some Evidence From OECD Countries[1]

Michele Bagella - **Leonardo Becchetti**
Università «Tor Vergata», Roma
Università «Tor Vergata», Roma
Linacre College, University of Oxford

1. - Introduction

Central bank (hereafter CB) independence is regarded by current economic literature as one of the most effective guarantees for the pursuit of price stability. A strong theoretical rationale for this assumption is that, in the context of intertemporal games between the government and economic agents, the delegation of monetary policy to an external agency attaching greater importance to price control in its utility function is considered to be an optimal way to avoid time inconsistency of announced antinfationary policies (Rogoff [49]).

The "CB independence approach" emphasises how the institutional framework – under the form of rules on the relationship among public institutions on monetary choices – is a key discriminant to judge perspective monetary policy consistency. This is because the declaration of the goal of price stability in *CB Constitution* is a

---

[1] The authors, M. Bagella, Director of the Department of Economics and Institutions, and L. Becchetti, Doctor of Research and M. Sc. London School of Economics, would like to thank S. Gorini, L. Paganetto, P.L. Scandizzo, F. Spinelli and other participants of the conference for thir valuable comments and suggestions. We are also gratefully indebted to S. Sacchi for her suggestions and precious collaboration. Although the paper is a collective work, Sections 2, 3 and 5 were written by M. Bagella and Sections 4, 6 and 7 by L. Becchetti.

N.B.: the numbers in square brackets refer to the Bibliography at the end of the paper.

necessary, but not sufficient, condition for the success of antinflationary policies. Other crucial conditions are the existence of «virtuous» relationships between the CB and the Treasury and between the CB and the government. The problem of consistency between rules and behaviour is measured with specific indicators whose methodological refinement is still in progress.

Even though the CB approach is a milestone in the analysis of structural determinants of inflationary performance, we wonder how much other institutional features matter. It is difficult in fact to neglect the role of labour market and capital market institutions in increasing or reducing inflationary pressures in the economy. In our opinion, these institutions represent crucial "side conditions" in allowing monetary institutions to pursue consistently their antinflationary aim.

This hypothesis is theoretically modelled by the most recent literature on CB independence (Lohman [34]; and Flood-Isaard [25]) demonstrating that the equilibrium of powers between government and CB is not once for all determined. In Lohman model the CB loses part of its independence when real variable shocks exceed a critical level. In the Flood-Isard model the government may act, under determinate circumstances, to suspend the CB independence. In this perspective when labour and capital market governance are not consistent with CB independence (for instance a too high NAIRU caused by poor labour governance) the government may have an incentive to reduce or suspend effective CB independence in order to avoid "politically" unsustainable levels of unemployment.

Given these considerations, the paper aims at: *(i)* updating and extending to a larger number of OECD countries the GMT (Grilli-Masciandaro-Tabellini) index of CB independence; *(ii)* estimating an index of labour market efficiency (labour governance); *(iii)* estimating an index of banking and financial market efficiency (financial governance); *(iv)* evaluating the joint and separate contribution of these two indexes together with the index of CB governance for 21 OECD countries in two different periods (1984-1988 and 1989-1994).

In particular, with regard to labour markets, the idea is that the national bargaining structure (centralised, decentralised at industrial or firm-level with one or two-tiers), the strength of unions and employers, the rules on wage indexation, the degree of union coverage and the procedures for the solution of disputes between employers and employees are crucial determinants of macroeconomic inflationary performance of OECD countries. All these elements influence in fact the country capacity of maintaining wage pressures within the limit of productivity increases (Layard, Nickell, Jackmann [33]) making easier the role of CB in controlling inflation.

With regard to financial markets, the idea is that an inefficient banking system increases transaction costs and interest rates generating an inefficient resource allocation with potential inflationary effects. In particular, the institution and the implementation of government bond markets increases the costs of unorthodox government debt policies leading to debt monetisation and to inflation and improves the capacity of securities market of absorbing public debt. The reduction of controls on the banking system increases the importance of monetary policy for the management of the economy. In the same way, the improvement of the efficiency of the banking system reduces investments costs that may be transmitted to final prices. The privatisation of state owned enterprises limits the future capacity of the government of generating debt through managerial inefficiency reducing the temptation and the necessity of using the "inflation tax" in debt management policies. The liberalisation of financial markets and the increase of capital market integration amplifies the sensitivity of the domestic financial system to external shocks in case of unorthodox economic policies reducing the scope for inflationary policies not consistent with those implemented by healthier economies.

We are aware in our attempt that: «when discussing the politics or the institutional conditions of economic policy, we are entering a field in which scientific experience is definitely still less advanced than in economics *stricto sensu*» and that «international cross-section regressions are notoriously exposed to errors due to omission of variables that have not been identified as potential explanatory factors» (Malinvaud [35]). For these reasons, the main goal of the paper, beyond the importance of the preliminary results obtained, is 1) of extending the scope of the analysis to new variables and 2) of collecting new data to provide more detailed pictures of the institutional features of examined countries.

The paper is structured in the following way. In the second section a survey of the literature on the effects of CB independence on real and financial variables is presented. In the third section, we propose to consider the contribution of labour and financial governance to enlarge the governance approach to the explanation of cross-sectional OECD inflation. To this purpose we present a Layard-Nickell-Jackman ([33]) index for labour governance and an original index of financial governance. In the fourth section, we analyse the main structural reforms occurred in the 1980s and at the beginning of 1990s and we update our indexes of labour governance. In the fifth section we present empirical evidence that confirms the significance of governance index in explaining not only the static distribution of OECD inflation rates but also its changes in the last years.

2. - A Survey of Central Bank Political and Economic Independence

A central bank is defined as politically independent when it formulates autonomously a monetary policy which is consistent with the aim of price stability. It is economically independent when it can choose policy instruments which are consistent with the established goals. The analysis of the degree of central banks' independence requires the definition of theoretically significant institutional indicators.

Political independence indicators are based on the following central bank's institutional features: *a)* rules over the appointment, term of office and composition of central bank's governing bodies, *b)* interactions of CB with the government and with the Parliament; *c)* goals of central bank's economic policy.

The structure of central bank's governing bodies is usually quite heterogeneous, even though in each CB three main common roles may be identified: 1) the Governor with legal responsibilities and representative power; 2) the Board of Directors with supervisory and general address tasks; 3) the Executive Committee, which is a direct expression of the Board of Director, with consulting powers.

CB monetary policy autonomy is likely to be influenced by the attribution of these powers. In all countries CB appointments are ratified by the government but the degree of CB autonomy will be higher if governing bodies are appointed by the CB itself and not by the government. A further reduction of CB autonomy occurs: *(i)* when a newly elected government has the right of appointing the new CB Board of Directors; *(ii)* when the terms of office are shorter or connected with the "political cycle"; *(iii)* when a member of the government is part of the Board.

The institutional interaction between the CB and the government is also fundamental for evaluating CB political independence, which can be reduced if CB policy has to be approved by the government and if the final responsibility on it rests on the government and not on the CB.

Institutional indicators of CB economic independence regard all those rules concerning the use of monetary policy instruments and in particular: *a)* budget financing instruments as direct credit facility to the government and open market operations; *b)* the determination of the discount rate.

CB control over monetary aggregates is in fact reduced if the government may determine rules to obtain CB credit, with negative effects both on monetary and fiscal policy. Countries allowing forms of CB direct credit to the government justify it with the necessity to cover temporary lags between government incomes and outcomes. Direct credit may be transformed, though, in a form of budget deficit money financing which reduced CB economic independence. The critical features, with this respect, are rules concerning the amount, the access to credit, its cost and terms of concession. CB may directly finance the Treasury by purchasing government bonds on the primary market. The degree of CB economic independence will vary, in this case, if CB access to government bonds primary market is compulsory, allowed or forbidden. Rules concerning CB government bond purchases on the secondary market through open market operations are also likely to affect the extent of CB economic independence. Finally, the power of determining the official discount rate obviously gives the CB more manoeuvre in controlling money aggregates and increases its economic independence.

Empirical literature used and refined concepts of CB political and economic independence in order to investigate over the effect of CB independence on the level and the variability of inflation, of interest rates and even of real variables such as output growth.

Parking and Bade [46] investigated the relationship between monetary policies and CB legislation in 12 OECD countries between 1972 and 1986 focusing on three main features: 1) the interaction between CB and governments in formulating monetary policies; 2) appointment procedures for CB senior members; 3) budget and financial relationships between CB and governments. On the basis of these features, they build an indicator of CB political independence that combines the following three variables: 1) the CB is the ultimate political authority; 2) non government members are present in the CB Committee; 3) more than half of the senior member appointments are independent from the government. They in particular observe that in all cases where the government is held responsible for monetary policy it also appoints all senior members. Given some limits in the possible combination of the considered variables and due to the simple unweighted sum used for the construction of the indicator, only four different types of central bank exist according to the Bode-Parking classification. The target variables considered in their analysis are the level of inflation and its variability (as a measure of political variability). The authors do not find any rank order correlation between the CB indicator of political independence and inflation variability. They instead find that countries (Japan, USA, Germany and Switzerland) with higher CB independence in the formulation of monetary policies and in the appointment of senior members have on average lower inflation rates.

Alesina-Summers [3] try to assess whether CB independence may affect not only the level of inflation, but also its variability and the level of real variables such as unemployment and real interest rates. According to Alesina-Summers, CB independence should reduce inflation rate variability as it reduces the links between monetary variables and country political events. In bipartisan countries, the alternance of left and right coalitions in power should positively affect inflation rate variability when CB is not independent, as right governments traditionally attach greater importance to the reduction of inflation and left governments to output and employment growth (Alesina [1]).

The arguments for supporting the hypothesis of a relationship between CB and real variables are as follows. First, a CB free from political pressures may insulate the economy from "political business cycle" manipulations and its more predictable behaviour may reduce interest rate risk premia (Nordhaous [42]; Rogoff [49]; Alesina [2]). Second, lower inflation rates in countries with more independent central banks reduce various types of economic distortions, rent seeking activities and excessively high risk premia, affecting the performance of real variables. On the other side, though, the opponents of this "optimistic" view argue that more independent CB are less likely to pursue expansive monetary policies leading to increases in output and reductions of unemployment (assumed that this latter is not structural as depending mainly on labour market rigidities). They also argue that tight monetary policies, ensuring low levels of inflation, are also responsible for high real interest rates producing negative effects on investments and growth.

Alesina-Summers [3] intend to verify the relative relevance of these two opposite views for the period between 1973 and 1988. Their index of CB independence is almost identical to the Bade-Parking index with the exception of the case of Italy, for which Bade-Parking do not consider the increase in economic independence occurred in 1982. This is because the additional variable used by Alesina-Summers is about the role of CB in absorbing short term excess supply of government bonds. Combining old and new criteria the authors create five CB typologies and find a strong cross-sectional inverse relationship between CB independence and, not only levels, but also variability of inflaction. No significant correlation is found instead for the relationship between CB independence and real variable performance for OECD countries (Switzerland is an example of CB independence but its rate of growth is lower than the OECD average). Results of CB independence effects on unemployment and real interest rates are also inconclusive.

Grilli-Masciandaro-Tabellini (GMT) [28] argue that CB power in choosing final goals of monetary policy depends on three elements: 1) the procedure for the appointment of CB senior members; 2) the interaction between the government and the bank board; 3) central bank legal responsibilities. They assume that credibility in the pursuit of the announced policy is the most important CB virtue and they classify on the basis of these elements the institutional monetary regimes of 18 countries.

The authors consider the following institutional attributes as indicators of higher CB political independence: *a)* CB governor not appointed by the government; *b)* Governor term of office for a period of more than five years; *c)* not all senior members appointed by the government; *d)* senior members' term of office for a period of more than five years; *e)* absence of a mandate of participation of a government representant on the CB board; *f)* no government approval required for the definition of monetary policy; *g)* goal of monetary stability explicitly mentioned in the CB constitution; *h)* rules for the solution of conflicts between the CB and the government. According to this classification, Switzerland, Germany, USA, the Netherlands, Canada and Italy are countries with a higher degree of CB political independence.

The authors then consider the following institutional attributes as indicators of higher CB economic independence: *(i)* non automatic concession of CB direct credit to the government; *(ii)* CB direct credit to the government at market interest rates; *(iii)* limits in the amounts of CB direct credit to the government; *(iv)* absence of CB purchase of government bonds on the primary market; *(v)* banking system surveillance not a task of the CB or the CB as the only responsible of the supervisory role.

GMT then separately evaluates the effects of the relationship between CB political and economic independence on the level of inflation finding the usual inverse relationship.

They then wonder if CB independence implies a cost in term of real variables performance but they do not find any systematic correlation between real growth and GDP, even though CB economic independence seems to be associated with lower rates of output growth.

Eijffinger-Schaling [24] construct a different indicator and identify in their paper CB typologies that are different from those of the previously examined authors. To them, CB political independence depends on the following attributes: 1) appointment procedures of CB board senior members; 2) interaction between the government and the CB in the definition of monetary policy; 3) CB formal repsonsibilities in the pursuit of the established monetary policy goals.

In particular they use the following criteria to determine CB independence: *a)* CB is the only ultimate responsible for monetary policy, or monetary policy responsibility is shared between CB and the government, or the government is the only ultimate responsible for

TABLE 1

CB INDEPENDENCE INDEXES

Countries	Parking-Bade [46]	Alesina-Summers [3]	GMT [28]	Eijffinger-Schaling [24]
Australia	1	1	9	1
Austria	—	—	9	—
Belgium	2	2	7	3
Canada	2	2	11	1
Denmark	—	—	8	—
France	2	2	7	2
Germany	4	4	11	5
Greece	—	—	4	—
Ireland	—	—	7	—
Italy	2	1.5	5	2
Japan	3	3	6	3
Netherlands	2	2	10	4
New Zealand	—	—	3	—
Portugal	—	—	3	—
Spain	—	—	5	—
Switzerland	4	4	12	5
Sweden	2	2	—	—
United Kingdom	2	2	6	2
USA	3	3	12	3

TABLE 2

CORRELATION MATRIX AMONG DIFFERENT INDEXES OF CB INDEPENDENCE

	Grilli *et* Al. [28]	Alesina-Summers [3]	Eijffinger-Schaling [24]
Grilli *et* Al. [28]	1.00	—	—
Alesina-Summers [3]	0.64	1.00	—
Eijffinger-Schaling [24]	0.47	0.82	1.00

monetary policy political authority; *b)* the government is not represented on the bank board; *c)* more than half of board appointments are independent from the government. From these criteria they identify 12 potential typologies of CB independence (some of them, though, cannot exist as that of a CB which is the only responsible in defining monetary policy but has government members on its board).

The authors do not use an unweighted average as they attribute two points to a CB which is the only responsible for defining monetary policy, are point if this responsibility is shared with the government, and zero points if it is attributed only to the government. In this way, giving single points to the other two criteria, the first criterion alone accounts for 1/2 of the overall index.

A critical survey of all previous contributions on the impact of CB independence and its impact on monetary and real variables is that of Swinburne-Castello-Branco [54]. The authors seriously question the validity of the empirical conclusions arguing that macroeconomic variables are extremely sensitive to changing values of the index and the contruction of the indexes often result to be too arbitrary. Such validity depends on the interpretation of national CB regulations and on the difficult distinction between purely formal or legal norms having a real impact on CB behaviour.

A comparison of the different indexes and their correlation matrix (Tables 1 and 2) shows that relevant differences exist among them confirming the importance of the subjective and arbitrary element in their definition.

The above surveyed studies, in spite of these critical considerations (Swimburne-Castelo Branco [54]), have the merit of highlighting the importance of the role of CB independence in determining structural conditions for lower inflation rates. They can be implemented in three main directions: 1) the extension from cross-sectional pictures (which give the illusion of a situation which is time invariant) to dynamic pictures analysing the effect of governance changes on financial variables. The relative position of a country, in fact, may change in the years and it depends, in turn, on past changes in country governance; 2) the improvement of data collection with both an increase of observed countries and an increase of the structural variable considered in order to reduce the measurement error bias; 3) the comparison of the relative weight of CB independence with that of other important structural factors determining both the dynamic and the structure of OECD inflation rates.

To this respect, the relative weight of at least other two variables should be considered in the analysis of the (time changing) structure of OECD inflation rates. These variables concern labour market governance (i.e. institutional rules on centralised/decentralised bargaining, union power and wage indexation) and financial governance (i.e. the degree of financial market openess and the degree of banking system liberalisation).

Finally, it is difficult to assess whether the finding of a correlation between CB independence and inflation variability depends more on the strong direct correlation between levels and variability of inflation or from the direct link between the index and inflation variability. Clowdury's [21] empirical results showing a strong correlation between levels and variability of inflation rates for 66 countries in the period 1955-1985 provide support for the first hypothesis.

Another controversial issue which has not been completely solved by past studies is the effect of CB exclusive or shared role in the surveillance of the banking and the financial system.

Some authors argue that a trade-off exists between the role of surveillance and that of maintaining a tight monetary stance. For this reason, they advocate a separation between them, supporting the proposal of a CB that delegates surveillance to other agencies maintaining, though, its role of lender of last resort (Bruni-Monti [13]). The CB should provide information and resources to the agency to which the role of banking surveillance has been delegated[2]. Several arguments have been supported in favour and against the presumed trade-off. The pursuit of banking system stability through surveillance may be in contrast with the CB antinflationary policy when, in order to avoid the risk of bankruptcy of financial intermediaries in a crisis, an excess growth of liquidity not consistent with the antinflationary stance is allowed. The likely effects of the concentration of the two

---

[2] In the Italian case SARCINELLI M. [51] explicitly recommends «a more distinct separation between the two roles of money governance and surveillance of the banking».

roles are lack of transparency in the pursuit of antinflationary stance, instruments misallocation and monetary policy inconsistency.

A stronger position is that supporting the existence of a structural trade-off between the two functions given that antinflationary policies tend to be anticyclical, while surveillance regulation policies tend to be procyclical (Goodhart-Shoenmaker [27]). The risk of trade-off is increased when, contemporary to the CB bank monopoly over surveillance, the large presence of the state in the banking sector makes it easier to pursue "non orthodox" policies on behalf of financial intermediaries. In this respect, we may observe that the institutional concentration of the two roles may, though, also have positive effects on monetary stability in that it allows the CB to reduce its information asymmetry with respect to financial intermediaries. This reduction may be profitably used to improve the efficacy of CB's antinflationary policies.

From the institutional point of view, the situation in the OECD countries is the following. The separation between the two roles of banking system surveillance and definition of monetary policy is one of the main guarantees of Bundesbank independence in Germany. In several other OECD countries CB has no monopoly power over the surveillance of the banking system (Belgium, Canada, Denmark, France, Finland, Japan, Norway, Spain and Sweden) while it has in others (Austria, Greece, Ireland, New Zeland, Portugal and United Kingdom).

The most common structure in OECD countries seems then to be a partial separation between the two roles, with the exception of most of the EEC members whose CBs retain monopoly powers over surveillance. For a given degree of CB independence, antinflationary performances of countries with partial separation of the two roles seem to be better than those of countries where CBs have surveillance monopoly power.

3. - The Index of Labour and Financial Governance and Their Role in Explaining OECD Inflation Cross-Sectional Distribution

Surveyed cross-sectional analyses explaining OECD inflation rates suffer from the defect of being based on only one structural aspect of the economy. They are based on theoretical approaches considering inflation essentially as a monetary phenomenon (Friedman-Schwartz [26].

More recent models consider that, even though inflation remains a monetary phenomenon, the CB independence and its power of resisting inflationary pressures depend not only by regulation on CB-government relationship, but also by regulation of labor and financial markets and by the extent to which this regulation induces labor and financial markets to behave in accordance with the antinflationary target (Lohman [34]; Flood-Isard [25])[3].

For this reason, we consider that the second and the third structural determinant that should be taken into account for their effects on inflation are the structure of labour and financial markets.

An influential ecletic approach to labour economics (Layard-Nickell-Jackman [33]) (hereafter LNJ) attributes to institutional factors a fundamental role in the determination of high and persisting rates of unemployment in OECD countries during the last two decades. A crucial role in the explanation of unemployment is based, according to these authors, on the institutional feature of the bargaining process in each country. But, at the same time, the LNJ wage-pressure based explanation of unemployment inevitably identifies in workers' wage claims a main source of OECD inflation as well as unemployment.

The indirect contribution of this approach to the analysis of the relationship between governance and inflation is that institutional features such as the rules for wage indexation, the degree of worker unionisation, the extent of co-ordination among employers and among different unions and the bargaining procedure are main structural explanations for the existing cross-sectional distribution of OECD inflation rates and for its past and future evolution. LNJ general rationale stems from a theoretical model where the NAIRU is determined, in absence of supply and demand shocks, by the parameters of a wage setting and a price setting equations. These two

[3] An interesting example of this is reported in G. Carli's 1994 book on Italian economic history where he affirms that, after the second oil shock, a refusal from him as a Central Banker to increase money supply in order to accomodate imported input and wage inflationary pressures would have been considered as a "seditious act".

equations are, in turn, the result of a maximising behaviour of different type of agents (employers and employees) whose objectives are in conflict. These parameter mainly express real and nominal wage rigidities which are, in turn, determined by the country labour governance structure. The NAIRU will then be relatively higher in a country with relatively poorer labour governance and this will increase government incentives to pursue inflationary policies to avoid "politically unsustainable" levels of unemployment (Phelps [47]). The possibility that the government might effectively do so is confirmed by the fact that CB independence is neither static nor irreversible and dynamically evolves according to macroeconomic conditions (Lohman [34]); Flood-Isard [25]. The inconsistency between the three governance indexes might then induce the government to act for a reduction of the effective CB independence.

With regard to the third structural determinant, the index of financial governance, we consider that the efficiency and the degree of internationalisation of the banking and financial systems affect important parameters in the model of the long-term relationship between central bank and government. A higher degree of internationalisation of the financial system increases government costs of reducing central bank independence when real shocks occur. This is because the negative reaction of domestic financial markets to "unorthodox policies" pursued by the government in constrast with the central bank is enhanced when these markets are open. Financial market internationalisation then indirectly strengthens the position of the central bank in its effective long-term relationship with the government, which is only partially defined by the norms of the "incomplete contract" included in constitutional rules on CB independence.

The decree of efficiency of the financial and banking system, affecting the cost of capital for investors, also plays an important role in the determination of domestic inflation rates. It is well known that asymmetric information between investors and financiers, inefficient rules on intermediaries reserve management and deposit insurance may create positive differentials between internal and external financing sources for firms (Becchetti-Bagella [8]; Becchetti [12]). Several theoretical and empirical contributions analysed this issue focusing on bank, stock market and venture capital financing. Apart from the negative effect on resource allocation caused by these inefficiencies, the increased cost of capital input may be translated by firms on prices.

4. - The Construction of the Index of "Labour" Governance

The arguments for the individual impact of each of these labour institutional features on inflation are the following: *(i)* in a centralised bargaining at national level workers care for the general level of prices and they internalise the negative inflation externality of individual wage claims. Industry-level bargaining generates more inflationary pressure than firm level bargaining when, as it is often the case, the elasticity of the demand for labour facing the industry is lower than that facing the individual firm (Calmors-Driffil [15]; LNJ [33]). As a consequence, centralised bargaining is less inflationary than firm level bargaining which is, in turn, less inflationary then industry level bargaining (and, more so, of a two-tier industry level bargaining); *(ii)* an increase in the percentage of unionised workers (coverage) strengthens, ceteris paribus, the union bargaining power increasing wage pressure and inflation; *(iii)* an increase in the level of union coordination has the same effect, while an increase in the level of employer co-ordination in resisting to wage pressure obviously reduces room for inflationary wage demands; *(iv)* the number of workers involved in strikes and the number of working days lost are an indirect measure of labour market instability and of the presence of wage-price spirals in the economy that can obviously determine high inflation variability; *(v)* wage contract flexibility is a crucial feature as the capacity of a country to reduce nominal wage inertia is obviously determined by it (LNJ [33]).

All assumptions on the five items composing the index of labour governance are theoretically supported by bargaining models in imperfectly competitive product markets.

On the basis of these considerations it is possible to construct a labour governance index that allows us to evaluate the relative role of "labour governance" compared with that of "monetary governance" in determining the existing cross-sectional distribution of OECD inflation rates (Table 3). The index is a simple re-elaboration of LNJ collection of statistical evidence on OECD labour institutions.

The considered variables are: the country bargaining structure, the percentage of unionised workers among the labour force, union

TABLE 3

THE INDEX OF LABOUR GOVERNANCE (1984-1988)

	Bargaining	Union coverage	Union coord.	Employer coord.	Wage contract flexibility	Degree of social harmony	Aggregate index
Belgium	0	1	2	2	2	2.5	9.5
Denmark	1	1	1	3	0	2.5	8.5
France	0	1	2	2	3	3	11
Germany	1	1	2	3	2	3	12
Ireland	0	1	3	1	4	2.5	11.5
Italy	0	1	2	1	4	1	7
Netherlands ..	1	1	2	2	1	3	10
Portugal	2	1	2	2	0	1.5	8.5
Spain	0	1	2	1	5	1.5	10.5
UK	0	1	3	1	4	2.5	11.5
Australia	0	1	2	1	0	2	6
N. Zealand ..	0	2	2	1	0	1.5	6.5
Canada	1	2	3	1	4	2	13
USA	1	3	3	1	5	3	16
Japan	2	2	2	2	2	3	13
Austria	2	1	1	3	2	3	12
Finland	2	1	1	3	3	1.5	11.5
Norway	2	1	1	3	2	3	12
Sweden	2	1	1	3	2	3	12
Switzerland ..	2	3	3	3	6	3	19
Greece	0	1	1	1	0	0	3

Legend,

Bargaining: 2 = centralised bargaining; 1 = firm-level bargaining; 0 = bargaining at industry level or two tier (industry and firm level) bargaining.

Union coverage: 1 = more than 75% of workers covered; 2 = a range of 25%-75% of workers covered; 3 = less than 25% of workers covered.

Union coordination: 1 = high; 2 = middle; 3 = low.

Employer coordination: 1 = high; 2 = middle; 3 = low.

Wage contract flexibility: 0-2 points for length of wage contracts (0 = 1 year or less; 1 = between 1 and 3 years; 2 = 3 years or more), 0-2 points for indexation in wage contracts (0 = if indexation is widespread, 2 = is there is no indexation), 0-2 points for synchronisation of wage contracts (2 = synchronisation; 1 = some synchronisation; 0 = no synchronisation).

Degree of social harmony: average points for workers involved in strikes (WIS) per annum (per of 100 workers) and points working days loss (WDL) per annum (per 100 workers); 1 = WIS higher than 20; 2 = WIS between 10 and 20; 3 = WIS lower than 10; 1 = WDL higher than 45; 2 = WDI between 20 and 45; 3 = WDL lower than 20.

Source, author's reelaboration on LNJ [33].

TABLE 4

INDEX OF FINANCIAL GOVERNANCE (1984-1988)

	Banking system efficiency	Banking system internationa-lization	Effciency in government debt management	Elasticity of domestic stock returns to US returns	Foreign firms listed in the domestic stock exchange %	Stock market capitalisation of domestic firms %
Belgium	5.3	110	7	0.171	42	49.3
Denmark	5.7	20.6	6.9	0.07	2.3	36.9
France	10.8	13	6.5	0.178	37.6	35
Germany	5	5	5.5	0.288	43.7	28
Ireland	5.1	51	7	0.08	0	10
Italy	7	0.9	5.6	0.17	0	20
Netherlands ..	4.7	20	5.5	0.18	49.5	48
Portugal	3	0.4	4.7	−0.02	0	5
Spain	4.3	10.2	6.2	0.03	0	27
UK	0.8	60	5.8	0.37	22.7	91
Australia	5.7	2.7	6.4	0.019	2.5	37
New Zealand	4.5	7.1	6	−0.08	35.9	30.9
Canada	1.9	8.1	3.3	0.55	5.55	59
USA	2.2	4	6.3	1	4.5	59
Japan	3.4	2	4.7	0.18	5	127
Austria	2.1	4.4	5.3	0.003	35.4	18.9
Finland	1.8	4	4.2	0.06	5	28.8
Norway	4.9	19.1	6	0.41	4.4	27.7
Sweden	4.3	0	6	0.33	6	65
Switzerland ..	1.4	110	3.9	0.48	57.6	92.5
Greece	5.3	35	–	0.08	0	20

Legend,

Banking system efficiency: interest rate spread between lending rate and deposit rate. For Austria money market rate instead of lending rate for the USA Certificates of Deposit rate and Commercial paper rate as a deposit rate: 3 = margin lower than 4; 2 = margin higher than 4 and lower than 7; 1 = margin higher than 7.

Efficiency in government debt management: (real average long-term government bond yields to maturity in per cent per annum). 3 = lower than 5; 2 = between 5 and 6.5; 1 = higher than 6.5.

Banking system internationalisation (cross-border deposits from non residents/national deposits) 3 = higher than 50%; 2 = between 25 and 50%; 1 = lower than 25%.

Elasticity of domestic stock returns to US returns: Domestic stock return-US stock returns beta coefficients. 3 = higher than 0.35; 2 = between 0.35 and 0.20; 1 = lower than 0.20. Stock market capitalisation: market value of listed domestic firms as a percentage on GDP; 4 = higher than 75%; 3 = between 50 and 75%; 2 = between 25% and 50%; 1 = lower than 254%.

Foreign firm participation to stock exchange: 3 = higher than 40%; 2 = between 20 and 40%; 1 = lower than 20%.

Sources, IMF; INTERNATIONAL FINANCIAL STATISTIC, FIBV, *Annual report* (various years); CONSOB, *Relazione annuale* (various years).

coordination, employer coordination, the degree of social harmony (including relative measures of the number of workers involved in strikes and of the amount of hours lost) and the wage contract flexibility.

The aggregate index is the sum of country values for the five considered institutional elements of the labour market. Given its crucial role in reducing inflationary pressures, wage contract flexibility has a double weight with respect to the other four partial indicators.

5. - The Construction of the Index of "Financial" Governance

The third element taken into account when considering structural variables affecting inflation rates is the efficiency and the internationalisation of a country's banking and financial systems ("financial governance") (Table 4).

The index of financial governance is based on the idea that the efficiency and the internationalisation of the banking system, government's ability in debt management and the capitalisation and the internationalisation of the stock exchange are structural determinants that positively affect country capacity in controlling inflation. The simple rationale for it is that the less regulated and more internationalised the financial and the banking system, the more difficult it is for the government to pursue "unorthodox" monetary policies because of the impossibility of insulating the system from subsequent market agents' negative reaction.

The five items of the financial index are: 1) the spread between lending rate and deposit rate as an indicator of banking system efficiency[4]; 2) the ratio between total bank (demand and time) deposits and non-resident deposits as an indicator of foreign investor's confidence and of the demand for domestic financial services; 3) the real average long-term government bond yield to maturity as an "indirect" indicator of government ability in debt management and in

[4] This spread may be result of several determinants such as bank's market power or translation of implicit reserve requirement costs.

its willingness to reduce state sector inefficiences[5]; 4) the elasticity of domestic stock returns with respect to US stock returns as an indicator of domestic stock exchange openness; 5) the ratio between foreign firms and domestic firms listed on the domestic stock exchange as an indicator of stock exchange internationalisation; 6) the domestic stock market capitalisation over the GDP as an indicator of the degree of country financial (non banking) development.

The choice of using an "indirect" governance index for financial governance comes from the consideration that, in this sector, the effective adjustment to institutional changes may be remarkably slower than in the two other sectors. While, for example, the effect of changes in wage indexation rules may have an immediate impact on prices, the decision to admit foreign firms to domestic stock market listing may not significantly change the composition between domestic and foreign firms listed for several years. Liberalisation and internationalisation of capital markets may then be better evaluated by "indirect" indicators measuring the effective enforcement of governance changes.

6. - Changes in the Cross-Sectional Distribution of OECD Inflation Rates in the Last Five Years: the Role of Monetary, Labour and Financial Governance

Contributions on CB independence surveyed in Section 2, the reelaboration of the LNJ index of "labour governance" and the creation of an index of financial governance refer to the situation of OECD countries in mid-1980s. Several changes have occurred since then with OECD countries adopting different speeds in the reform of financial, monetary and labour governance. The aim of this section is to show how these different speeds have crucially influenced the process of inflation changes between the end of the 1980s and the beginning of the 1990s partially modifying the cross-sectional pattern observed at the

[5] This financial indicator partially captures the impact of fiscal governance which is not explicitly considered in our approach. We assume in fact that real average long-term government yield is affected by changes in government capacity to repay debt which is, in turn, affected by changes in its fiscal structure.

TABLE 5

CB POLITICAL INDEPENDENCE
(1989-1994)

	1	2	3	4	5	6	7	8	aggregate index
Belgium							*	*	2
Denmark		*				*	*		3
France		*		*		*	*		4
Germany		*		*	*	*	*	*	6
Ireland		*				*	*		3
Italy	*	*		*	*	*			4
Netherlands		*		*		*	*		4
Portugal							*		1
Spain		*		*	*	*	*		5
UK					*				1
Australia		*					*	*	3
New Zealand		*		*			*	*	4
Canada	*	*					*	*	4
USA				*	*	*	*	*	5
Austria						*	*	*	3
Finland		*		*				*	3
Norway		*				*			2
Sweden	*	*			*			*	4
Switzerland		*			*	*	*	*	5
Greece			*		*	*		*	4

Source, author's reelaboration on GRILLI V. - MASCIANDARO D. - TABELLINI G. [28].

end of the last decade. The most significant changes in inflation rates have been achieved by those countries implementing the most significant reforms in labour, financial and monetary governance.

Our index of CB independence for the beginning of the 1990s is, as specified below, a revised and extended version of the Grilli - Masciandaro - Tabellini index described in Section 2.

We define a CB *politically independent* when it can pursue monetary policy targets independently from government goals. The main attributes of political independence are: 1) a CB governor not appointed by the government; 2) a term of office of CB govenor lasting more than 5 years; 3) a large part or all CB board appointments not decided by the government; 4) CB board terms of office lasting more than 5 years; 5) absence of a mandate for participation of a representant of the government to board meetings; 6) no government approval required for the definition of monetary policy; 7) explicit mention in the *CB statute* of the goal of monetary stability; 8) existence of procedures for the solution of controversies between the CB and the government.

The indicator of CB political independence then simply updates the GMT index to the period 1989-1994.

We define a CB *economically independent* when it has the power of choosing the most appropriate instruments for the pursuit of monetary policy goals. The main attributes of economic independence are: *(i)* concession of CB direct credit to the government; *(ii)* CB direct credit to the government at market interest rates; *(iii)* temporary CB credit to the government; *(iv)* limits in the amount of CB direct credit to the government; *(v)* absence of CB credit to the government; *(vi)* absence of CB purchase of government bonds on the primary market; *(vii)* CB determination of the discount rate; *(viii)* a situation in which bank surveillance is not a task of the CB or the CB is not the only to perform this function or the CB is in charge of surveillance but uses procedurally structured controls.

In the case of CB economic independence, our index presents several differences with respect to the correspondent GMT index. The attribute *(v)* takes into account that several countries, consistently with what prescribed by the art. 109 of the *Treaty for European Union*, abolished CB direct credit to the government increasing CB economic independence. The attribute *(viii)* considers that a CB with power of surveillance which is exerted within rigidly established and regulated procedures is in a better position to avoid government interference in the surveillance of the banking system and to avoid the possibilities of a trade-off between the role of surveillance and that of pursuing monetary stability. This is because, if surveillance procedures are regulated and rigidly established, a CB can commit ex ante to a surveillance behaviour which is consistent with monetary stability avoiding instrument misallocation, lack of transparencey and inconsistency in its antinflationary stance. We think that a CB with supervisory power but with explicitly regulated procedures is more economically independent than a CB not having the surveillance role as it can exploit the reduction of information asymmetry to improve its efficiency in the pursuit of monetary stability.

In order to update the labour governance and the CB independence index and in order to measure changes in financial governance, we summarise here the most relevant structural reforms occurred in OECD countries in the last fifteen years.

New Zeland has perhaps the most impressive record of structural reforms. In 1989 the *Reserve Bank Act* established the independence of the Reserve Bank from government and assigned to the CB the task of reducing inflation with a target of "price stability" (0-2% annual increase, by 1992-1993).

In 1990 the *Labour Relations Act* reduced the union power introducing competition between unions for new members and voluntary unionism. The *Act* also changed the previous complex three-tier bargaining system (with possible changes of centralised wage agree-

TABLE 6

CB ECONOMIC INDEPENDENCE
(1984-1994)

	1	2	3	4	5	6	7	8	aggregate index
Belgium					*****	*	*	**	9
Denmark		*				*	*	**	5
France					*****		*	*	8
Germany	*	*	*	*			*	**	8
Ireland............					*****		*		6
Italy						*	*	***	9
Japan	*		*			*	*	**	6
Netherlands			*	*			*	**	6
Portugal				*			*		2
Spain					*****	*	*	***	10
UK	*	*	*	*			*		5
Australia	*	*	*	*		*	*		6
New Zealand			*	*		*	*	***	7
Canada	*	*	*	*			*	**	7
USA	*	*	*	*		*	*	*	7
Austria............					*****	*	*	**	9
Finland	*	*	*	*			*	*	6
Norway	*	*	*	*				**	6
Sweden					*****		*	**	8
Switzerland........		*	*	*		*	*	**	7
Greece					*****		*		6

Source, GRILLI V. - MASCIANDARO D. - TABELLINI G. [28].

ments both at industry and at firm level) into a firm-level bargaining reducing structural components of wage-price claims. Several important reforms were also taken to liberalise the financial market: abolition of credit growth guidelines (1984), removal of quantity restrictions and entry barriers to the banking sector (1985-1986), removal of interest rate controls (1984), liberalisation of the stock exchange market (1986).

Australia's main reform was in labour governance with the *Prices and Income Accord* (1983-1987) which regulates and reduces indexation, and centralises wage-bargaining limiting possible firm-level wage increase within productivity improvements.

The Netherlands focus on structural reform was mainly aimed at improving stock market competitiveness with the abolition of the tax on stock exchange dealings and the strengthening of the position of market markers to increase market liquidity.

Sweden's main initiative was, in 1990, the change from a fully centralised bargaining system to a de facto two-tier system with industry level and firm-level bargaining. The liberalisation of financial markets started in 1978 and finished in 1986. The main steps were the liberalisation of private bonds' interest rates, of bank deposit rates, the abolition of liquidity quotas in the banking system, the introduction of the auction for government bonds (1984), the development of a secondary market for government bonds and the abolition of gross investment requirements for banks in priority bonds.

France has for certain respects a record parallel to that of Sweden, with important financial reforms starting in 1984 with the creation and the development of the MATIF (*Financial Future Market*).

Austria begins with the *Working Agreement* of 1987 a broad plan of privatisation which generated in the next two years net receipts from asset sales amounting to 20 billion Sch. The privatisation momentum lasted until 1990 when it stopped due to stock market weakness.

A significant structural change in the *USA* has been introduced by the *Federal Deposit Insurance Corporation Improvement,* 1991 which establishes procedures for "early intervention" of bank regulators. It goes in the direction of standardising the supervisory role of bank regulators avoiding discretionary suypervisory policies that may be in contrast with the role of controlling inflation rates. The attempt

TABLE 7

INDEX OF LABOUR MARKET GOVERNANCE FOR THE PERIOD 1989-1993

	Bargaining	Union coverage	Union coord.	Employer coord.	Wage contract flexibility	Degree of social harmony	Aggregate index
Belgium	0	1	2	2	4	2.5	11.5
Denmark	1	1	1	3	0	3	9
France	0	2	2	2	3	2.5	11.5
Germany	1	1	2	3	2	1	10
Ireland	0	1	3	2	4	3	13
Italy	0	1	2	1	4	1	7
Netherlands ..	1	1	2	2	1	3	10
Portugal	2	2	2	2	4	2.5	14.5
Spain	0	1	2	1	5	1	10
UK	0	1	3	1	4	1	10
Australia	2	2	2	1	2	2	11
New Zealand	1	2	3	1	2	3	12
Canada	1	2	3	1	4	1.5	12.5
USA	1	3	3	1	5	3	16
Japan	2	2	2	2	2	3	13
Austria	2	1	1	3	2	3	12
Finland	2	1	1	3	3	2	12
Norway	2	1	1	3	2	3	12
Sweden	1	1	1	3	2	2.5	10.5
Switzerland ..	2	2	3	3	6	3	19
Greece	0	1	1	1	0	0	3

Legend,

Bargaining: 2 = centralised bargaining; 1 = firm-level bargaining; 0 = two-tier bargaining at industry level and firm level.

Union coverage: 1 = more than 75% of workers covered; 2 = a range of 25% - 75% of workers covered; 3 = less than 25% of workers covered.

Union coordination: 1 = high; 2 = middle 3 = low.

Employer coordination: 1 = high; 2 = middle 3 = low.

Wage contract flexibility: 0-2 points for length of wage contracts (0 = 1 year or less; 1 = between 1 and 3 years; 2 = 3 years or more), 0-2 points for indexation in wage contracts (0 = if indexation is widespread, 2 if there is no indexation); 0-2 points for synchronisation of wage contracts (2 = synchronisation, 1 = some synchronisation, 0 = no synchronisation).

Degree of social harmony: average of points for workers involved in strikes (WIS) per annum (per of 100 workers) and points working days loss (WDL) per annum (per 100 workers); 1 = WIS higher than 20, 2 = WIS between 10 and 20, 3 = WIS lower than 10. 1 = WDL higher than 45, 2 = WDI between 20 and 45, 3 = lower than 20.

to prevent financial crises with more effective monitoring should in fact reduce the need of "lender of last resort" intervention in contrast to the monetary base control targets. In addition, early intervention is also intended to prevent one of the main causes of financial crisis, the adverse selection effect that induces financial intermediaries with inadequate capital to assume increasing investment risk.

With the *1984 Agenda, Canada* set an ambitious program of reforms which has been only partially implemented so far. The attempt of improving the bargaining system with national consultations on industrial relations was initiated and discontinued. More relevant steps have been made in deregulating the economy with the Implementation of the *New Competition Act* and of the *National Transportation Act* and with the completion of the first phase of financial deregulation relative to the securities industry. In 1991 more legislation on financial deregulation was approved breaking down barriers between banking, insurance, trust and loan companies and credit institutions. A significant privatisation policy led the government to privatise 23 public enterprises from 1984 to 1991.

The gradual financial market liberalisation is the most impressive feature of the governance record of *Japan* in the 1980s. among the various measures taken between 1980 and 1990, the most relevant are the introduction of long-term government bonds under private placement (1983), the establishment of the government bond futures market (1985), the access of foreign companies to the membership of Tokyo stock exchange, the introduction of public auction for 20-year government bonds (1987) and the introduction of futures transactions in 20-year government bonds. Between 1992 and 1994 the most relevant measures were the liberalisation of commissions on large equity transactions, the adoption of a rating system for issuers of commercial paper, the easing of rules for corporate bond issues and the complete liberalisation of interest rates on time deposits.

Denmark's policy for structural reforms was also mainly directed at financial market deregulation in the 1980s. The main measures were the abolition of lending ceilings and of controls on lending rate and prime rate deposit, the access of Denmark to the rest of foreign bond market (1983) and the dismantling of capital controls. Not particularly relevant structural reforms in labour, financial and monetary governance occur, though, in the period relevant for our analysis.

Ireland adopted in 1987 an important structural reform in labour governance with the *Program for National Recovery* which changed its bargaining system into a centralised one reducing space for industry-level and plant-level wage claims. Moreover, the coordination and bargaining strength of Irish employers was increased by the merger of the Federation of Irish Employers and the Confederation of Irish Industry to form the Irish Business and Employers Confederation, a single association dealing with economic and social issues in industrial relations.

Spain's approach to structural reforms in the 1980s was mainly directed toward the improvement of labour market governance. In 1992 the abolition of *Ordenanza liberal* significantly reduced the room for corporatist regulations weakening the power of sectoral unions. In 1993 the indexation for central government employees was discontinued reducing scope for nominal wage inertia. In 1992 an important step in the direction of improving monetary governance was the strengthening of the supervisory role of the Bank of Spain with a series of procedurally fixed controls that should avoid conflicts of interest between banking system supervision and monetary control.

Portugal has launched a vast privatisation program which since 1990 has implicitly reduced the need to finance ailing public enterprises. An important *Administrative Reform* in 1992 set rules for the reduction of state inefficiencies increasing labour mobility for civil servants. Financial liberalisation was particularly relevant in Portugal during the 1980s and led to the progressive growth of capital market that accounted in 1987 for 23 per cent of corporate financing against almost zero in 1984. From 1986 to 1987 alone the number of listed companies listed rose from 81 to 176. Interest rate deregulation has been steadily pursued since 1984.

The *UK* has an impressive record of labour market reforms, privatisations and tax reforms throughout all the 1980s. In ten years 44 major businesses were sold to privates and more than 90% of eligible employees have become shareholders in the privatised firm in which they work (OECD, *UK Survey*, 1991). Labour market reforms aim at weakening the monopoly power of trade unions and at deregulating the labour market with trade union membership falling from 56 per cent to 40 per cent from 1980 to 1989. Examples of this reform are, in 1988, the *Employment Act* which increased the accountability of union officials to their members and, in the 1990, the Employment Act which restricted the scope for unofficial industrial action.

The main steps of the financial reforms have been the abolition of foreign exchange controls (1979) and hire purchase controls (1982) and the "Big Bang" stock exchange reform. Another important step is the removal of Bank of England controls on the timing of new issues in the equity and bond market (Budget 1989).

The efficiency in the public sector increased since the beginning of the 1980s and, later on, with the introduction of the *Citizens' Charter* which demonstrated government commitment to public accountability of public-sector activities. One of the most extensive reforms in the public sector has been that of the National Health Service (NHS).

Since the beginning of 1987 *Greece* has embarked in a wide program of structural reforms involving the financial sector, the banking sector and the labour market. Interest rate controls on saving deposits and imposition of ceilings for loans to small-scale firms were gradually abolished from 1987 to 1993. Securities trading and bond issuance by commercial banks and investment banks, currency swaps by banks were allowed. The Bank's obligatory investment ratio in Treasury bills was cut from 40% of the increment in deposits to 30% in July 1991 and was completely abolished in 1993.

The Bank of Greece's supervisory role was implemented with periodic liquidity assessments aimed at preventing the insurgence of financial crisis. The Capital Market Commitee (having the role of supervision on securities markets) took action at the beginning of 1994 to promote greater transparency in transactions and stricter disclosure requirements. The results of the financial liberalisation are quite impressive with total capitalisation (including equities and bonds) passing from 8.7% of GDP to 22% and with bank pre-tax profits over asset passing from 0.3 in 1985 to 1.5 in 1991.

Italy's record presents several reforms on labour, financial and CB governance. A new banking law (September 1993) removed segmentation in the banking system transforming previously specialised intermediaries into "universal banks" that can compete among each other in any financial sector. The same law reduced discretionality in central bank's supervisory role fixing procedures for the surveillance of the banking system. In addition to it, Italy abolished central bank direct credit to the government in order to conform to *Maastricht* rules for European integration. Two main reforms occured in the financial system. In 1991 a reform of the stock exchange: *(i)* introduced and regulated brokerage activity of nonbanking financial intermediaries (SIM) on the Stock exchange; *(ii)* strengthened the role of supervisory bodies on the stock exchange (Banca d'Italia and CONSOB) and *(iii)* promoted the gradual passage from forward to spot transaction settlements. In 1992 a new law introduced the possibility of PPO.

The most important structural innovation introduced in the labour market was the government proposal for reduction of allowed degree of indexation in the "scala mobile" confirmed by referendum on 9 June 1985. Since then, the idea that employers might help to reduce inflation through wage moderation has become a structural element in the Italian bargaining system.

7. - Empirical Results

Empirical analysis based on the indicators of financial, labour and monetary governance confirms the significance of structural indicators in the explanation of the cross-sectional distribution of OECD inflation and its changes in the last ten years.

We do not try to estimate, as other authors did, the effect of governance on inflation variability. This is because higher inflation variability is not only the reflection of political variability in presence of a less independent CB. Given that CB independence is not a static concept, a passage from a lower level to an higher level of CB independence (the case of New Zealand), causing a sharp reduction in prices may also increase variance. The mix of thse two effects prevents the existence of an univocal negative relationship between CB independence and inflation variability.

The estimates in levels and in first differences of the separate and

TABLE 8

INDEX OF FINANCIAL GOVERNANCE (1989-1994)

	Banking system efficiency	Banking system internationalization	Efficiency in government debt management	Elasticity of domestic stock returns to US stock returns	Foreign firms listed in the domestic stock exchange %	Stock market capitalisation of domestic firms %
Belgium	5.5	150	6.2	0.18	49	41
Denmark	5.1	13	7.5	0.13	4.2	30
France	10	28.4	6.3	0.15	45	37
Germany	4.5	6	3.6	0.26	34.4	21
Ireland	5	40	5.7	0.19	14.4	425
Italy	7.3	1.3	4.6	0.20	2	15
Netherlands ..	7.2	23	4.6	0.32	47.7	62
Portugal	7.5	0.8	4.8	0.08	0	17
Spain	5.2	9	6.3	0.35	1	28
UK	7	35	4.9	0.38	26	129
Australia	6.2	4.4	5.5	0.10	4	71
New Zealand	4	3	5.5	0.10	23	51
Canada	1.3	13	3.8	0.48	5.9	60
USA	2	4	4.2	1	6.6	66
Japan	3.4	4	3	0.27	6	68
Austria	5.3	10.1	5	0.21	31.6	16
Finland	4.3	4	4.3	0.08	2	28
Norway	4.8	19.9	6.4	0.30	8.3	28
Seeden	7.2	0	4	0.32	6.25	64
Switzerland ..	−1	105	2.5	0.28	53.6	116
Greece	7.7	40	–	0.12	0	22

Legend,

Banking system efficiency: interest rate spread between lending rate and deposit rate. For Austria money market rate instead of lending rate for the USA Certificates of Deposit rate and Commercial paper rate as a deposit rate: 3 = margin lower than 4; 2 = margin higher than 4 and lower than 7; 1 = margin higher than 7.

Efficiency in government debt management: (real average long-term government bond yields to maturity in per cent per annum). 3 = positive and lower than 5; 2 = between 5 and 6.5; 1 = higher than 6.5.

Banking system internationalisation (cross-border deposits from non residents/national deposits) 3 = higher than 50%; 2 = between 25 and 50%; 1 = lower than 25%.

Elasticity of domestic stock returns to US returns: Domestic stock return-US stock returns beta coefficients. 3 = higher than 0.35; 2 = between 0.35 and 0.20; 1= lower than 0.20.

Stock market capitalisation: market value of listed domestic firms as a percentage on GDP. 4 = higher than 75%; 3 = between 50 and 75%; 2 = between 25% and 50%; 1 = lower than 25%. Foreign firm participation to stock exchange: 3 = higher than 40%; 2 = between 20 and 40%; 1 = lower than 20%.

Sources, INTERNATIONAL FINANCIAL STATISTICS, (various years), IMF; FIBV, *Annual Reports* (various years); CONSOB, *Relazione annuale* (various years).

of the joint explanatory power of labour, monetary and financial indexes of governance evidence the crucial role of these features in determining the inflation distribution across industrialised countries. This result supports the theoretical hypothesis that CB independence is neither static nor irreversible as it depends on other institutional features, such as those of labour and financial markets. With regard to the period 1984-1988 results from the correlation matrix and from one-regressor estimates show that labour governance has the highest explanatory power, while, in period 1989-1994 the result is reversed and financial governance has the strongest relevance.

The existence of a strong correlation between labour and financial governance generates some multicollinearity in multiple regression estimates with all three regressors. Indexes of monetary and financial governance changes (*DCB* and *DFIN*) tend to be collinear so that their joint effect (*DCB* + *DFIN*) is more significant than the combination of the two separate effects. The most significant estimate is when average inflation rates are regressed on the log composite index which is the sum of labour, financial and CB independence indexes (*LGTOT*84 and *LGTOT*89) (Table 9) (the scatter of the distribution of OECD countries with respect to average inflation and total governance in the two different periods is presented in Graphs 1 and 2). This result shows the elasticity of reductions in inflation rates for increases in the composite index is significant but diminishing for higher levels of ex ante total governance. The sum of the three indexes has its theoretical justification in the dynamic approach to CB independence, where "effective" CB independence is determined by "formal" CB independence (CB indicator), but also by the extent to which labour and financial governance reduces government temptation to restrict de facto CB independence.

An ispection of the data shows what is behind these simple econometric results (Table 8). Those countries which achieved more drastic structural changes (New Zeland, Portugal, Greece, Australia) have also the best performance in terms of inflation reduction. Some exceptions partially weaken the significance of the financial and monetary governance indexes: *(i)* Spain experienced serious reforms in the monetary governance but its antinflationary performance is modest; *(ii)* Japan has an impressive record of financial liberalisation,

TABLE 9

ECONOMETRIC RESULTS

$$INFL84 = 13.12 - 0.97\,CB84$$
(2.15) (0.25)
$R^2 = 0.43$

$$INFL84 = 15.10 - 0.90\,LAB84$$
(2.38) (0.21)
$R^2 = 0.49$

$$INFL84 = 13.76 - 0.76\,FIN84$$
(3.08) (0.27)
$R^2 = 0.29$

$$INFL84 = 9.03 - 0.53\,CB84 - 0.61\,LAB84$$
(3.21) (0.29) (0.25)
$R^2 = 0.56$

$$INFL84 = 15.60 - 0.08\,CB84 - 0.53\,FIN84 - 0.64\,LAB84$$
(2.70) (0.34) (0.29) (0.34)
$R^2 = 0.57$

$$INFL89 = 15.72 - 0.35\,CB89 - 0.26\,FIN89 - 0.39\,LAB89$$
(2.88) (0.19) (0.26) (0.22)
$R^2 = 0.49$

$$DINFL = 0.49 - 0.77\,DLAB - 0.19\,DBC - 0.25\,DFIN$$
(0.47) (0.19) (0.10) (0.21)
$R^2 = 0.37$

$$INFL84 = 15.89 - 0.56\,TOTG84$$
(2.51) (0.11)
$R^2 = 0.57$

$$INFL89 = 8.83 - 0.41\,CB89$$
(2.41) (0.22)
$R^2 = 0.14$

$$INFL89 = 10.87 - 0.55\,LAB89$$
(2.22) (0.18)
$R^2 = 0.31$

$$INFL89 = 11.79 - 0.62\,FIN89$$
(2.48) (0.21)
$R^2 = 0.31$

$$INFL89 = 14.91 - 0.40\,CB89 - 0.54\,LAB89$$
(2.77) (0.18) (0.17)
$R^2 = 0.45$

$$INFL89 = 15.64 - 0.36\,TOTG89$$
(0.08)
$R^2 = 0.49$

$$INFL89 = 43.43 - 11.41\,LTOTG89$$
(6.85) (2.01)
$R^2 = 0.62$

$$INFL84 = 35.06 - 10.34\,LTOTG84$$
(4.51) (0.11)
$R^2 = 0.70$

Variable legend,

INFL84: average inflation rate (1984-1988);
INFL89: average inflation rate (1989-1994);
LAB84: index of labour governance (1984-1988);
LAB89: index of labour governance (1989-1994);
FIN84: index of financial independence (1984-1988);
FIN89: index of financial independence (1989-94);
CB84: index of Central Bank independence (1984-1988);
CB84: index of Central Bank independence (1989-1994);
DINFL: *INFL89-INFL84*; *DLAB*: *LAB89-LAB84*; *DCB*: *CB89-CB84*; *DFIN*: *FIN89-FIN84*; *TOTG84*: *LAB84* + *CB84* + 84*FIN84*; *TOTG89*: *LAB89* + *FIN89* + *CB89*; *LTOTG84*: *LOG* (*TOTG84*); *LTOTG89*; *LOG* (*TOTG89*).

TABLE 10

CHANGES IN INFLATION AND IN REGULATION POLICIES BETWEEN THE TWO CONSIDERED PERIODS

	DINFL	*DLAB*	*DFIN*	*DCB*
New Zealand	−8.69	5.5	3	8
Portugal	−2.99	5	0	0
Australia	−2.91	4	3	0
Greece	−2.89	0	−1	3
Norway	−2.56	0	0	1
Denmark	−1.71	0.5	0	0
Ireland	−1.46	1.5	2	2
Spain	−1.16	−0.5	2	10
France	−0.87	0.5	2	5
Italy	−0.66	0	1	9
Finland	−0.64	0.5	1	0
Canada	0	−0.5	2	0
UK	0.52	−1.5	1	0
USA	0.54	0	3	0
Belgium	0.66	2	1	4
Switzerland	1.06	0	1	0
Sweden	1.15	−1.5	0	0
Netherlands	1.22	0	1	0
Austria	1.23	0	3	3
Japan	1.43	0	2	1
Germany	2.45	−2	−1	1

Variable legend,

DINFL: *INFL89-INFL84*; *DLAB*: *LAB89-LAB84*; *DCB*: *CB89-CB84*; *DFIN*: *FIN89-FIN84*.

but obviously, starting from a very low inflation rate in mid-1980s the elasticity of its antinflationary performance to these changes cannot be high. If we ignore the case of Japan then the effects of financial liberalisation on reduction tend to be much more significant than those registered by our estimates. This result is consistent with the idea of a nonlinear relationship between inflation rates and total governance.

Estimates in first differences, if significant, provide stronger evidence in support of the governance impact on inflation rates. In this case, changes in labour governance are significant, while changes in CB and financial independence have the expected sign but are not significant. This is not a result which disconfims the role of CB and financial independence, but, probably, evidence of the more lagged effects of CB independence changes on inflation rates.

8. - Conclusions

The aim of this paper is to evaluate the differing impact of structural features in affecting inflationary rates in OECD countries. The paper takes from the literature on CB independence the suggestion of considering a broader range of governance factors affecting macroeconomic stability and, for this reason, includes labour and financial governance together with monetary governance as structural determinants of inflationary performance. The theoretical support for these suggestions comes from the consideration that the equilibrium of powers between the government and the CB is not defined once for all and is not irreversible. "Politically unsustainable" levels of real variables generated by poor labour and financial governance may induce the government to act for the reduction of CB independence.

The sum of the three indexes has then its theoretical justification in the dynamic approach to CB independence, where "effective" CB independence is determined by "formal" CB independence (CB indicator), but also by the extent to which labour and financial governance reduces government temptation to restrict de facto CB independence.

In the light of these considerations, the paper simply explains two cross-sectional "pictures" of OECD inflation and the changes between the two pictures in terms of the three (labour, monetary and financial) governance indexes. It provides theoretical support for this method briefly describing the arguments explaining direct and indirect antinflationary effects of financial market and banking system liberalisation and of changes in union power, bargaining and wage indexation. The simple empirical description anticipates the results of strong significance of all the three governance indexes.

The most significant result is obtained when average inflation rates are regressed on the log of an index of total governance (the sum of labour, financial and CB independence indexes). This result shows that the elasticity of reductions in inflation rates for increases in the compositive index is significant but diminishing for higher levels of ex ante total governance. This means, in other terms, that antinflationary gains from improvement of the governance structure are dependent from the ex ante level of total governance and that countries with a relatively lower ex ante goernance index (the example of New Zealand) will benefit more from positive governance changes than countries with a relatively higher ex ante governance index (the example of Japan).

The results of this paper can be considered as a preliminary contribution for the determination of an "institution building" criterion that can be taken into account when discussing the institutional development of non-OECD countries. A further deepending of this approach along the lines here considered may help to design "average theoretical inflation rates" corresponding to a certain "governance maturity". In outlining this perspective for future development of governance studies we suggest that additional effort must be made in the direction of collecting relevant institutional information on structural determinants of OECD countries' financial performance.

BIBLIOGRAPHY

[1] ALESINA A., «Rules, Discretion and Reputation in a Two Party System», *Giornale degli Economisti e Annuali di Economia*, n. 1, January 1987.

[2] ——, «Macroeconomic Policy in a Two Party System as a Repeated Game», *Quarterly Journal of Economics*, n. 410, August 1987.

[3] ALESINA A. - SUMMERS L., «Central Bank Independence and Macroeconomic Performance: Some Comparative Evidence», *Journal of Money, Credit and Banking*, n. 2, May 1993.

[4] ALESINA A. - TABELLINI G., «Credibility and Politics», *European Economic Review*, n. 32, 1988.

[5] AMOROSINO S., *La funzione amministrativa di vigilanza sulle banche nel nuovo TU delle leggi in materia creditizia*, in CAPRIGLIONE F. [18], 1994.

[6] ANGELINI P. - PASSACANTANDO F., «Central Banks' Role in the Payment System and its Relationshipe with Banking Supervision», *Giornale degli Economisti e Annali di Economia*, 1993.

[7] ARTONI R., *Banca d'Italia e politica di sviluppo: un commento*, in RISTUCCIA - MASCIANDARO [46], 1988.

[8] BAGELLA M. - BECCHETTI L., «Finance, Investment and Innovation: a Review of the Literature and a Proposal for a Comparative Approach», CEIS, *Working Paper*, n. 46, 1994.

[9] BAGELLA M. - PAGANETTO L., «Proprietà e controllo nel sistema bancario italiano: punti di forza e punti di debolezza del nuovo ordinamento», *Economia e Diritto del Terziario*, n. 3, 1994.

[10] BALLING M., *Financial Management in the New Europe*, Blackwell, Oxford, 1993.

[11] BALTENSPERGER E., «Central Bank Policy and Lending of Last Resort», *Giornale degli Economisti e Annali di Economia*, n. 9, 1992.

[12] BECCHETTI L., «Finance, Investment and Innovation: a Theoretical and Empirical Comparative Analysis», forthcoming, *Empirica*, n. 3, 1995.

[13] BRUNI F. - MONTI M., «Autonomia della banca centrale, inflazione e disavanzo pubblico: osservazioni sulla teoria e sul caso italiano», *Quaderni del Centro Studi di Economia Monetaria e Finanziaria «Paolo Baffi»*, n. 52, October 1991.

[14] BRUNI F. - MASCIANDARO D., *Evaluating Central Bank Independence. Theoretical Issues and European Perspectives*, in RISTUCCIA - MASCIANDARO [46], 1988.

[15] CALMORS L. - DRIFFIL J., «Centralisation of Wage Bargaining and Macroeconomic Performance», *Economic Policy*, n. 11, 1988.

[16] CAPRIGLIONE F., «Le autorita di controllo dell'ordinamento finanziario», in CIS «*Le banche, regole e mercato*», 1995.

[17] ——, *Riforma bancaria e scenario economico. Spunti d'indagine*, in CAPRIGLIONE F. [18], 1994.

[18] CAPRIGLIONE F. (ed.), *Mercati e intermediari in trasformazione*, Roma, Futura 2000, 1994.

[19] CIOCCA P., *La moneta e l'economia: Il ruolo delle banche centrali*, Bologna, il Mulino, 1983.

[20] COMUNITÀ ECONOMICA EUROPEA (COMITATO DEI GOVERNATORI DELLE BANCHE CENTRALI DEGLI STATI MEMBRI), *Rapporto annuale*, April 1993.

[21] CHOWDRY A.R., «The Relationship Between the Inflation Rate and its Variability, the Issues Reconsidered», *Applied Economics*, n. 23, 1991.

[22] CUKIERMAN A. - EDWARDS S. - TABELLINI G., «Seigniorage and Political Instability», *The American Economic Review*, June 1992.

[23] DERMINE J., *European Banking in the 1990s*, Oxford, Blackwell Business, 1990.

[24] EIJFFINGER S. - SCHALING E., «Central Bank Independence in Twelve Industrial Countries», BNL *Quarterly Review*, n. 184, March 1993.

[25] FLOOD R.P. - ISAARD P., «Monetary Policy Strategies», Cambridge (MA), NBER, *Working Paper*, n. 2770, November 1988.

[26] FRIEDMAN M. - SACHWARTZ A.J., *Monetary Trends in the United States and United Kingdom*, Chicago, University of Chicago Press, 1992.

[27] GOODHART C. - SHOENMAKER, «Institutional Separation Between Supervisory and Monetary Agencies», *Giornale degli Economisti e Annali di Economia*, March 1993.

[28] GRILLI V. - MASCIANDARO D. - TABELLINI G., «Institution and Policies», *Economic Policy*, October 1991.

[29] GUARINO G., *Il ruolo della Banca d'Italia*, in RISTUCCIA - MASCIANDARO [46], 1988.

[30] HAAN J. - STURM J.E., «Argomentazioni a favore dell'autonomia delle banche centrali», *Moneta e Credito*, n. 179, September 1992.

[31] HARRIS L. - SMITH G., *Integration of European Capital Markets: Evidence from Cointegration Tests*, mimeo, 1995.

[32] ISTITUTO MONETARIO EUROPEO, *Rapporto annuale*, 1994.

[33] LAYARD R. - NICKELL S. - JACKMANN R., *Unemployment. Macroeconomic Performance and the Labour Market*, Oxford, Oxford University Press, 1991.

[34] LOHMAN S., «Optimal Commitment in Monetary Policy: Credibility Versus Flexibility», *American Economic Review*, March 1994.

[35] MALINVAUD E., «Comment to "Institutions and Policies" of Grilli V. - Masciandaro D. - Tabellini G., *Economic Policy*, October 1991.

[36] MANNING A., «An Integration of Trade Union Models in a Sequential Bargaining Framework», *Economic Journal*, n. 97, 1987.

[37] MASCIANDARO D., «Indipendenza della banca centrale, vigilanza bancaria e stabilità monetaria», *Moneta e Credito*, n. 184, December 1993.

[38] ——, «Modelli macroeconomici, politica *hazard*, indipendenza della banca centrale», *Giornale degli Economisti e Annali di Economia*, n. 1988.

[39] MICHELACCI C., «Central Bank Involvement in the Supervision of Banking System and of Financial Markets. A Comparative Analysis», Università L. Bocconi, *Quaderni del Centro di Economia monetaria e Finanziaria «Paolo Baffi»*, March 1993.

[40] MULLINEAUX A., *European Banking*, Oxford, Blackwell, 1992.

[41] NARDOZZI G., *Autonomia della banca centrale e istituzioni di governo: il caso della Banca d'Italia*, in RISTUCCIA - MASCIANDARO [46], 1988.

[42] NORDHAUS W.D., «The Political Business Cycle», *Review of Economic Studies*, n. 42, 1975.

[43] OECD, *«Country Surveys» (New Zealand, Portugal, Australia, Greece, Norway, Denmark, Ireland, Spain, France, Italy, Finland, Canada, UK, USA, Belgium, Switzerland, Sweden, Netherlands, Austria, Japan, Germany)*, 1984-1994.

[44] ONADO M., «Monetary Policy, Regulation and Growing Bank Risks. Comments», *Giornale degli Economisti e Annali di Economia*, March 1993.

[45] ONIDA V., *L'indipendenza delle banche centrali: tra politicità e neutralità*, in RISTUCCIA - MASCIANDARO [46], 1988.

[46] PARKING M. - BADE R., «Central Bank Laws and Monetary Policies: a Preliminary Investigation», *Rapporto della Banca d'Italia*, 1988.

[47] PHELPS E.S., *Inflation Policy and Unemployment Theory: the Cost-Benefit Approach to Monetary Planning*, New York, Norton W.W., 1978.

[48] RISTUCCIA - MASCIANDARO D., *L'autonomia delle banche centrali*, Milano, Comunità, 1988.

[49] ROGOFF K., «The Optimal Degree of Commitment to an Intermediate Monetary Target», *The Quarterly Journal of Economics*, November 1985.

[50] RONCI M. - TULLIO G., *Central Bank Autonomy, the Exchange Rate Constraint and Inflation: the Case of Italy, 1970-1992*, mimeo, 1995.

[51] SARCINELLI M., «Per un'ipotesi di legge delega», *Rapporto al Ministero del Tesoro del gruppo di lavoro per il riesame delle disposizioni in materia d'intermediazione finanziaria, bancaria e non bancaria*, 1991.

[52] SEPE M., *Prime note sul testo unico delle leggi in materia bancaria e creditizia*, in CAPRIGLIONE F., (ed.) [18], 1994.

[53] SPINELLI - FRATIANNI M., *Storia monetaria d'Italia*, Milano, Mondadori, 1991.

[54] SWINBURNE M. - CASTELLO BRANCO M., «Central Bank Independence: Issues and Experience», IMF, *Working Paper*, 1991.

Rules, Institutions and Crime: An Economist's Point of View

Fabio Gobbo *
Università di Bologna and Italian Antitrust Commission

Introduction

One of the most hackneyed comments which can be made when discussing the topic of crime is that it has much in common with economics. If we prescind from criminals' specific forms of "deviance", power and wealth are the true driving forces of both.

It would appear however that only recently has this latter observation received sufficient attention from economists, who are always very desirous to analyse ideal (and easily stylized) worlds but have little propensity for detailed investigation of the real workings of economics.

This nascent attention can be ascribed, on the one hand, to economic science's use of techniques which allow the complexity of the real-life phenomena to be better recorded and illustrated and, on the other hand and perhaps more strikingly, to an ever increasing awareness of the problems related to inequality and the explosion of the economy of crime.

The first essays to deal with these issues appeared in the 1970s; I remember those, for example, in Rottenberg [3], Andreano and Siegfried [1], Shelling [4], Stigler [5].

In Italy, attention began to be paid to the issues of the economics

---

* The author is Professor of Political Economy and a member of Italy's Authority for Competition and the Market. The author's opinions do not necessarily reflect those of said Authority.

N.B.: the numbers in square brackets refer to the Bibliography at the end of the paper.

of organised crime only in the early 1990s. They were analysed at a meeting of the Italian Society of Economists in 1992 specifically dedicated to the issue (the acts of the meeting were published in Zamagni [6], and at the 1993 Forum organised by the Parliamentary Anti-Mafia Commission chaired by L. Violante the proceedings of which were published as *The Economy and Crime* in Rome in 1993.

Economists' lack of interest in this problem, with the exception of a handful of pioneers in the United States who combined economic and sociological methodologies as early as the 1920s, is all the more culpable because, starting from the 1930s and the studies on the imperfect working of the market economy, all the available empirical evidence has demonstrated the importance of the interconnections between crime and the economy.

Economists could therefore have played an important role in preventing and limiting serious criminal activities.

As far as I know, the institutions specifically charged with combating crime have also done little in this field. Once again, only a handful of pioneers have implemented those cognitive, interpretative and monitoring tools which could have proven themselves to be very useful. And, in this regard, we cannot even use the fact that in some sporadic cases fiscal tools were used to incriminate and neutralise criminals as an example.

It is therefore even more incomprehensible that those tools of intelligence and economic evaluation which have proved so effective for confronting (and in some cases disputing with) other countries have not been appropriately brought into play in the fight against organised crime.

I refer in particular to the tools used to evaluate a country's economic might, the organisation of its production and trade systems, the material and immaterial resources, whether available or "dormant", etc.

1. - Size and Characteristics of the World Economy

One consequence of the recent "globalisation" of the world economy has been a considerable increase in trade and financial flows and the size of companies. This has furnished a considerable stimulus to the development and consolidation of crime, with the result that even the most knowledgeable crime fighters are often ill-prepared to combat phenomena of such size and extent.

But what has been seen of late is probably merely a foretaste of the developments that can be expected in the coming decades when all the industrialised countries become fully-fledged members of the "information society".

They will be flanked by two other groups of countries: one, the most numerous, comprising the intermediate developed nations of Asia, Latin America and, at least in part, the Mediterranean basin and east Europe, while the second will embrace those countries which today appear to have lost all hope of catching up with the more developed countries and be largely composed of African, Asian and Latin American nations.

For some decades now, economists have spoken of the "international division of labour"; I believe we can now speak of the "international division of crime". Each of the three areas outlined above has its own level of development and will have its own specific role in this scenario.

1.1 *Some Structural Data*

I do not intend to define in detail the development paths of this "international division of crime", nor do I have the technical tools for doing so, but this overall vision of the problem allows us to introduce some data illustrating the present situation, which can, at least to a certain measure, give an idea of the characteristics of the international economy. The data refers to the early-1990s and gives rise to complex problems of monetary conversion.

The richer countries have an average per capita income of between $20,000 to $30,000 per year, the poorer ones of less than $100 per year. Important, populous countries, such as Turkey with 60 million inhabitants, have an average per capita income of less than $2,000 and hence a GDP (which can to a certain extent be likened to the turnover of a company) of less than $120 billion per year.

By way of comparison, Luxembourg has less than 400,000 inhabitants yet its GDP is just under one-tenth that of Turkey. Italy has a population similar to Turkey yet its GDP is ten times bigger.

Many of the poorest countries in Africa, which have big populations of 10 million or more, have a GDP of less than $1 billion.

The trade in– and outflows of the bigger and more industrialised countries are often larger than the GDP of other medium–sized countries: for example, the imports and exports of the USA, Japan or Germany are worth some $400-500 billion per year, a figure which is three or four times Turkey's GDP.

1.2 *The World's Major Companies*

In order to fully appreciate this data, it is worthwhile comparing it to that of the world's major manufacturing companies; comparison with the leading international financial companies is possible (with even more astonishing results) but the specific characteristics of these companies make the analysis too complex.

The size (from all aspects) of the world's major companies means that they can be compared to countries with a medium level of development and population. Turkey's GDP, $120 billion, is less than turnover at General Motors, the world's leading manufacturing company, and roughly similar to turnover at the world's second-ranking manufacturing company, Ford.

Turnover at Daimler Benz, the world's tenth-ranking manufacturing group, is five or six times greater than the GDP of Luxembourg and slightly less than that of Greece, an EU state which has more than 10 million inhabitants.

These few, rough figures give a clear, albeit superficial idea not only of the range of income, both individual and national, which exists from country to country, but also, and above all, of the characteristics of the world economy and the power relations between the single countries and big companies.

It is the nature of these big multinational companies to operate according to logics which we can define as "global" just as we have defined the economy as "global".

This means that they diversify the location of their legal, administrative, and financial offices and production sites, locating them in those countries where it makes economic sense to do so, with regard to both their general objectives and their individual operative needs (thence the concept of "international division of labour").

If these objectives are coherent with the general rules of economic behaviour no difficulties arise, but it is obvious that this fragmentation of the company's various operations can make it difficult for an outsider to reconstruct the logics of the behaviour of the single units.

When instead there is wide-spread managerial incompetence or, even worse, bad faith, this freedom of behaviour for companies can engender costs for the international community, individuals or other companies, as was recently demonstrated by events at one of the UK's leading financial institutions which choose to concentrate its business in two countries with lax financial controls.

1.3 *Crime Trusts*

The figures for the "turnover" of crime are huge, especially if evaluated in terms of "overall economic cost", but difficult to quantify. Crime in Italy has a "turnover" of an estimated 10-15% of the country's GDP, i.e., $150-200 million per year. This figure includes all criminal activities, thefts, drug trafficking, money-lending, the illegal disposal of waste and the prevention costs engendered.

It is estimated that the world's drug traffic is worth a total $500 billion, only part of which derives from exports from producer countries: in the case of Colombia, exports are worth $2-3 billion per year.

It is much more difficult to estimate crime's "turnover" not by sector (drugs, prostitution, extortion, etc.) but by "business". Just like industrial multinationals, organised crime tends to increase its organisational dimension and operate in different countries and differentiate its activities in all sectors of the economy, both legitimate and illegal.

The Italo-american mafia and the Japanese yakuza are excellent examples of this evolution and they generate turnovers (or overall economic costs) which can be estimated in tens of billions of dollars per year.

Some claim these figures are exaggerated and overestimate the criminal economy, justifying their convinction with the observation that there is a wide-spread interest in impressing public opinion. This may be true, but the figures, even if halved, are such as to fully justify the observations below.

The first is that these figures are fully comparable to those regarding the GDP or trade flows of a nation or the turnover of a big international company.

The second, which derives from the observations above, is that these criminal trusts increasingly resemble big, multinational companies and hence espouse such companies' logics, namely locating their activities in different countries according to "global" strategies and the "international division of labour".

One consequence of all this is that criminal trusts are finding it increasingly easy to control big countries or nations, even those of medium size which have attained a modest level of development.

2. - Institutions and Rules for the Economy

The conclusion to be drawn from the above observations is that rules are needed for the economy and in the economy. These rules have still, by and large, to be codified but it is already clear that they should be founded on a fabric of closely interrèlated national and international institutions which can gather and exchange information and ensure timely intervention, each in its specific field of competence.

2.1 *A Historical Perspective*

The problem of rules for the economy is quite old, for example around 2,000 B.C. the Assyro-Babylonians tried to impose authoritative price control mechanisms.

Similar attempts were repeated numerous times in the following centuries but always with disastrous results. In 313 B.C. for example, Diocletian issued an edict which sought, with little success, to regulate price and tariffs for most goods and services in both the East and West of the Roman Empire.

Other attempts were made more recently, for example in the recent 1970s when many Western countries introduced measures specifically designed to regulate prices in the wake of the first oil shock.

The results of 4,000 years of attempts to control prices have been disastrous because price controls contrast with the very nature of the economy for two reasons, firstly because the system for gathering and managing information has always been proved inefficient and secondly because the institutions which are charged with the task been generally incapable of acting effectively.

Administrative price control systems have always given rise not only to widespread evasion but also speculation, hoarding, unlawful enrichment and serious inequality for the weaker sections of society.

2.2 *Which Rules and Which Institutions*

This historical overview leads us to the core of our reflection: namely, that what are needed are coherent rules managed by institutions which have all the necessary information available and can implement all the appropriate decisions in a timely and transparent manner. Furthermore, the provisions, both general and abstract (laws), and specific and concrete (rulings and administrative measures), should be respected. In other words, they should be made efficacious by the establishment of a sanctionary apparatus which acts as a suitable deterrent to behaviours which violate it.

This is the only way to furnish a functional response to the needs engendered by the development of crime as a phenomenon increasingly linked to the economy which is used by gang bosses and criminals as both a means and an end.

The question should not, however, be confined to the rules, but also be extended to the institutions.

From this viewpoint, the increasingly significant presence of independent bodies charged with applying the rules which take over the role of the ministries should be seen as a step forward towards ensuring the transparency of commercial transactions and the creation of conditions which attribute players with direct responsibilities in the working of the market.

Rules and institutions should therefore be placed in conditions to operate which encourage the correct functioning of the economy and should be equally applicable to the economic behaviour of nations, companies and also that of the individual.

These rules should be valid both internally and externally. In the former case it should be possible to codify and make available all information which permits the verification of the ownership and trade and financial flows of nations and companies (for example, a company's legal, accounting, financial and commercial records).

In the case of external rules, it should be possible to establish a set of behavioural norms which nations and companies should respect in their dealings with other nations and companies. Within this set of rules, the norms concerning international trade, capital transfers, the protection of competition and fiscal behaviours should be broadened.

The establishment of institutions specifically charged with upholding the rules complete this picture; these institutions, just like the rules, may be either national or supranational.

2.3 *An Example: The Protection of Competition*

The rules and institutions which already exist and are charged with protecting competition are an example of how it is possible to set up a system which, while having its own specific objectives, can also be used in the fight against crime. As noted by the then Prime Minister Carlo Azeglio Ciampi during the *Forum on the Economy and Crime* organised in 1993 by the Parliamentary Anti-Mafia Commission: «there is both conceptual and substantial incompatibility between the principles of competition – which are closely linked to policies ensuring transparency and protecting the weak contracting parties – and the methods of the mafia, which are characterised by systematic recourse to intimidation, abuse of power and violence.

The method of the mafia is to negate the freedom of entrepreneurship, competition, transparency of information, right of access to markets; it generates distortions which have negative consequences on the price formation mechanism, on the exercise of company ownership rights and on the labour market».

The strict and conscious application of measures for protecting competition is therefore an instrument for endowing the economy with transparency and discipline.

On this matter, it is worth noting the results of a study carried out in 1993 by the Department of Economic and Social Sciences of the Federico II University in Naples. The results allow us to state that there is a close interdependence between underdevelopment, organised crime and market structure.

The study was carried out in all the regions of Italy and shows that there is a high degree of correlation between crime levels (murders, attacks and extortion in proportion to the population) and markets which are protected and without competition, such as that for public works. In particular, the three regions in southern Italy with the highest level of crime (Campania, Calabria and Sicily) have three characteristics in common, namely, a low per-capita income, a level of high economic dependence and a significant percentage of protected markets.

Sector without competition allow organised crime to prosper from two points of view: firstly because the players can bear the so-called crime tax (the costs of extortions and enjoined supplies) as they can be passed on to the buyers or the public administration without losing market share as would be the case for example for entrepreneurs who operate in markets with competition.

The "completely ordinary and clean company" into which the profits from criminal activities are reinvested differs in at least one aspect from the normal company of a normal entrepreneur: it is relatively indifferent to costs. Hence, it can penetrate the market targeted with greater ease as it is backed by superprofits which do not derive from a normal economic activity and which give it additional muscle and thus a net competitive advantage vis-à-vis other players.

This shows how opening hitherto protected sectors in which the institution charged with ensuring observance of the rules intervenes incisively and with determination can be an important economic policy tool for combating organised crime.

The first application of norms to protect competition can be traced back to more than a century ago, when the problem of excessive economic power and the respect of individual freedom, the risks of abuse of market power by large commercial and oil trusts and the survival of democracy clearly emerged in the US.

Detailed provisions were passed to prevent agreements contrary to competition and the abuse of a dominant position and specific institutions (both administrative and jurisdictional) created for the task of implementing these provisions.

The results achieved over the past one jundred years have not always been those hoped for, nonetheless, other countries have adopted this useful model as a foundation for their provisions. First the Uk and Germany, then the European Community and gradually all the other leading industrialised countries have equipped themselves with rules and institutions for protecting competition: among the last, and very recently (1990) also Italy.

Even the countries of Central and Eastern Europe, which have only recently changed their institutional set-up and discarded the centralised economy have decided to equip themselves with similar provisions. Nonetheless, and I mention this only in passing as it is not directly related to the issue under discussion here, there countries can apply the provisions only with much travail, and in an indecisive and haphazard manner as a result of internal difficulties.

The existence of norms and institutions which protect only national competition has been a formidable obstacle to the real integration of economies as such norms and institutions tend not to be co-ordinated amongst themselves and sometimes jealously guard their own prerogatives.

This logic has still to be completely discarded: the first steps were made by the states of the European Union which are striving to harmonise their national rules on competition with the contents and aims of the Community provisions and from this point of view Italy, one of the laggards as regards the introduction of such provisions, has at least had the merit or bringing its normative system into line with that of Europe.

The problem of differentiated rules arises on two levels. In the relation between intervention by the Community bodies and the national bodies and in the relation between the single national interventions of the various member-states of the European Union. The globalisation of the economy has not been followed by a globalisation of the rules and powers of those bodies charged with applying them.

As regards the relation between the Community and national institutions, the *Maastricht Treaty* introduced the principle of subsidiarity under which for those matters that did not specifically lie within its jurisdiction, the Community would intervene only if the objectives of the envisaged action could not be adequately achieved by the single member states and could therefore, by virtue of the dimension and effects of the intervention in question, be better realised at Community level. Thus there exists a principle of allocation of competences which envisions the division of powers between the Community and national levels.

The problem of the transnational nature of economic transactions obviously cannot be treated in the same manner when we are talking about defining the relations between the Commission and the member states, but rather between the single legislations. In this case the only solution is that of bilateral agreements.

The problem is very complex, so much so that the European Union and the United States have just concluded negotiations aimed at identifying coherent models of reciprocal coordination for competition protection policies. At the same time, however, the US is threatening to apply its own provisions also to non-American companies which break its rules anywhere, even outside US territory.

The latest step towards greater order in international trade and in the behaviour of businesses is represented by the recent, and definitive signing of the treaty which has given birth to the World Trade Organization, the heir to the provisional GATT (so provisional that 40 years were needed to agree on its successor!).

At the same time, competition issues are receiving in-depth attention from other bodies, such as special agencies of the United Natins, central banks and their coordination bodies, and the OECD.

All these bodies, which are charged with verifying and gathering information on lawful behaviour, can also unearth and report the unlawful behaviours.

Conclusions

The globalisation of the economy and the globalisation of crime require increasingly coherent rules and behaviours.

This entails creating, at both national and international level, rules and institutions which, while respecting others' field of competence, can interact in an effective manner, above all as regards the gathering and exchange of information.

As the Secretary General of the United Nations stated at the International Conference on Crime held recently in Naples: «all market economies see regulation as a fair counterweight to prevarication and abuse. But now the market is global and without a legal regulatory framework it becomes little short of a jungle. And from the jungle arises the mafia».

To prevent the mafia arising from the jungle what is needed are rules, and also mechanisms within the institutions charged with applying the rules which guarantee transparency and control of their actions by the public authorities. These mechanisms should be entrusted to national or international technical authorities or by bodies which are subordinate to the political and administrative apparatus which should move at the same speed as the economic phenomena they are charged with overseeing. In other words, the rules should not act as a brake on economic growth and, above all, should not represent additional unjustified costs for the production system as do for example Italy's state accounting rules, which date from 1924 and are one of the main burdens on Italy's public administration and the Italian economy even to this day.

On this matter, the studies of Douglas C. North on institutions' influence on economic phenomena show the importance in terms of conditioning the factors of production, and the role played by legal and regulatory provisions, etc.

The rules disciplining economic phenomena aimed at controlling the ciminal economy should basically take account of the changed relationship between authorities and freedom, ensuring greater efficiency on the part of the public authorities while respecting the economy's production funcion.

The wise legislator, whether national or international, should therefore aim to ensure greater efficiency for a lean state whose actions are transparent.

I conclude with the concept of transparency because this is the most important guarantee for the economy.

BIBLIOGRAPHY

[1] ANDREANO R. - SIEGFRIED J.J. (eds.), *The Economics of Crime*, Cambridge (Mass.), Schenkman Publishing Co., 1980.

[2] COMMISSIONE ANTIMAFIA, *Forum su economia e criminalità*, Roma, Camera dei deputati, 1993.

[3] ROTTEMBERG S. (ed.), *The Economics of Crime and Punishment*, American Enterprise Institute for Public Policy Research, Washington, 1973.

[4] SCHELLING T.C., *Choice and Consequence*, Cambridge, Harward University Press, 1984.

[5] STIGLER G.J. (ed.), *Chicago Studies of Political Economy*, Chicago, University of Chicago Press, 1984.

[6] ZAMAGNI S. (ed.), «Mercati illegali e mafia, l'economia del crimine organizzato», *Atti della società italiana degli economisti, 1992*, Bologna, il Mulino, 1993.

Economic Development, Reciprocity and Industrial Growth

Luigi Paganetto - Pasquale Lucio Scandizzo *
Università «Tor Vergata», Roma

1. - Introduction

The elusive nature of the concept of economic development is not only semantic. Although difficult to define, the intuitive concept of a society that grows both in quality and quantity would be sufficient to satisfy our desire to be precise, if we knew also with some certainty the ingredients necessary to achieve such a condition. The definition of these ingredients, however, is most problematic: some societies grow under conditions that seem totally different from others. Convergence in economic growth, a happy prediction of neoclassical economic theory, does not seem to occur except perhaps in a time so long to make it irrelevant. A project for development appears to be as difficult as the recipe of a complicated and unknown high cuisine dish: no economic engineering or chemistry seem to be able to help.

Perhaps the most elusive aspect of the development process is linked to its non intentional character. Far from being the predictable consequence of planned activities, economic and social growth of a country seems rather the secondary effect of a condition of harmony, which remains largely mysterious. Individuals, institutions and the other "active" subjects appear to move together, in a state of communion, spontaneous and intense. As in a dance driven by an

---

* Luigi Paganetto is Dean of the Faculty of Economics and P.L. Scandizzo Professor of Political Economy at the University of Rome "Tor Vergata".

N.B.: the numbers in square brackets refer to the Bibliography at the end of the paper.

unknown music, the societies of success emerge from the background, with seductive moves, which can diminish and hide even the most serious flaws. Without this benevolent cover, the societies that are unsuccessful in their strive to join the dance of economic development, reveal instead their weakest sides in all the squalor and the drama of the situations that stagnate, the lack of improvement, the incapacity to escape the infinite vicious circles of underdevelopment and poverty.

We formulate the hypothesis that underlying the root of all this is the phenomenon of institutional reciprocity, that is the creation of social structures capable of endering a flow of voluntary exchanges of benevolent or malevolent actions on the basis of mutual expectations of response. As the foundation of any social life, reciprocity is the intangible element that allows the construction of the networks that link the economic actors in the web of implicit contracts. The components of these networks are always acts of exchange, often benevolent, sometimes malevolent, with reciprocal expectations of immediate or delayed retribution.

As many studies on Italian industrial growth have shown (Piore and Sabel [10]; Best [3]; Goodman [7]; Pyke, Beccattini, Sengenberger [12]), the so called model of "new competition" relies on cooperation and informal exchanges among small and medium firms. The industrial district, locus of privilege for myriads of families, enterprises and individual relations, flowered in an historical environment where the network of favourable relations happened to be specially well developed, as a consequence of the local government of the Comuni and the Signorie (Putnam [11]). Today, it appears to be the key to understanding the successful performance of the Italian industry in the transition from the production of final goods to the manufacture of specialized machinery.

In the 1970s and 1980s the model of industrial development adopted by Italy appeared to be helplessly impaired by the choice of the export sectors (see, for example, Nomisma [9]). «Mature» consumption goods, like textiles or food, with low level of technological content and mediocre growth prospects for demand, characterized the specialization pattern of Italian industry. This condition led many economists to advocate an industrial policy aimed at restoring some balance in this pattern so heavily skewed in favor of sectors without future, through a public intervention capable to promote the growth of the so-called strategic sectors.

While most of the attempts that followed this quest for strategic behavior failed in the helpless enterprise of artificial industries, the links among active subjects of the industrial districts appear instead to have performed an ongoing miracle. Italian firms producing machinery are world leaders for the sectors where Italy used to be confined to the production of final goods: food, textiles, furniture, shoes, ceramics. From a mere producer of final goods with low level technology, Italy appears to be evolved toward a more robust and diversified productive base for its industrial system (Belussi [1]; Blim [2]; Camuffo-Comacchio [5]; Camuffo [4]).

What is the secret of this success story, that engenders both wonders and regrets, as we seem to be unable to reproduce it where, as in the Mezzogiorno (CNR [6] p. 41), it would be mostly needed? The two crucial elements seem to reside in the two characteristics of non intentionality and intensity of the links that tie the economic agents in the success areas.

Within the set of informal ties among the subjects of an industrial district, non intentionality implies that the exchanges of know-how and technology are entirely voluntary and, at the same time, not driven by any ulterior motive except the interest arising from the two components of exchange: its direct «gift-like» component and the expected return. Any external effect of more general nature is thus entirely non intentional. The exchanges of favors and the expectations of reciprocal treatment, within a general predisposition to good relations, appear essentially opportunistic: they respond to the opportunities that rational agents see as interesting at each specific time (Locke [8]).

The opportunism and the lack of far-sighted plans however, go hand in hand with an intense activity of relations, that allows to experiment with continuity and impetus new forms of new initiatives, and, with them, of exchanges of information and experience. As it is typically the case for non hierarchical structures, where horizontal coordination prevails, the economic projects are examined by individuals, adopted by some and rejected by others, without having to go through the bureaucracy of centralized institutions or dominant firms. An intense activity of successful and unsuccessful enterprise creation thus characterizes the district network, which narrows or enlarges itself around a myriad of economic events, led by single individuals, but shared by many in their informational content and in the *pathos* of their performance.

On all the economic activities, reciprocity extends its veil. This quality has nothing to do with altruism, even though the behavior originating from it may not be distinguishable from what altruism would command. It consists in the fact that each subject performs a certain number of actions in the reasonable expectation that he will receive in exchange a response, material or immaterial, from the subjects involved in the same actions. If reciprocity concerns productive inputs, it is potentially capable of creating a virtuous circle between social action, production and growth: *a's* input may be used by *b* to produce something that may in turn be used by *a*. This virtuous circle may be the engine of endogenous growth, that is of a growth pattern that continually constructs the base for a new leap forward.

2. - Gift Giving, Reciprocity and Communication

The simplest case of an exchange economy based on reciprocity can be outlined imagining two actors, each endowed with a different utility function over two sets of goods. The first set represents the goods that the actor can directly provide through his work or through the market, while the second set includes all goods that can be obtained only by receiving them as a gift. Because gift giving is voluntary, each actor cannot control the second set of goods, for which he has to depend entirely on the initiative of the other actors. The principle of reciprocity, however, suggests that he may indirectly influence the gift giving in his favor by giving gifts to his counterpart. If the gifts received are a positive function of the gifts given, each actor can try to maximize his satisfaction not only by choosing the level of consumption that he can directly provide for himself, but also through the exercise of his faculty of giving gifts.

More specifically, consider the constrained maximization problem for the *i*-th agent:

$$\text{(1)} \qquad \text{Max } U^{(i)} = A_i \, c_{ii}^{\alpha i} \, c_{ji}^{\beta ji}$$

subject to: $$Y_i = c_{ii} + c_{ij} \qquad i, j = 1, 2$$

$$c_{ji} = F^{(j)} \, (c_{ij})$$

where: c_{ij} = consumption of the self-provided goods for the *i*-th agent;
c_{ji} = consumption of the goods given as a gift by agent j to agent i;
c_{ij} = consumption of the goods given as a gift by agent i to agent j;
Y_i = endowment of agent i

$c_{ji} = F^{(j)} \, (c_{ij})$ = the reaction function of agent j with respect to agent i, from the point of view of the latter, i.e. the estimate agent i makes of the return that will follow from his gifts to agent j. This function has a positive first derivative and depends both on agent j's behavior and on agent's i estimate.

Substituting the two constraints in the utility function, we obtain a maximization problem where the sole control variable is the level of gift giving c_{ij}:

$$\text{(2)} \qquad \underset{c_{ij}}{\text{Max}} \; U^{(i)} = A_i (Y_i - c_{ij})^{\alpha i} \, c_{ji}^{\beta ji}$$

$$\text{(3)} \qquad \frac{\partial U^{(i)}}{\partial c_{ij}} = -\frac{\alpha_i \, U^{(i)}}{Y_i - c_{ij}} + \beta_{ji} \frac{U^{(i)}}{c_{ji}} \, \frac{\partial c_{ji}}{\partial c_{ij}} = 0$$

$$i, j = 1, 2$$

where $c_{ij} = F^{(j)} \, (c_{ij})$ is the reaction function of agent j in response to gifts of agent i.

Equation *(3)* is a system of two differential equations in the functions $c_{ij} = F^{(i)}(c_{ji})$ and $c_{ji} = F^{(j)}(c_{ij})$. Because we assume that both agents are not motivated by altruism in their exchange giving, it must be that $F^{(i)}(0) = F^{(j)}(0) = 0$. This suggests a functional form of the type $F^{(j)}(c_{ij}) = B_i\, c_{ij}^{\eta_{ji}}$ $(j,\ i = 1,\ 2)$. Substituting into *(3)*, and solving yields:

$$c^*_{ij} = \frac{\beta_j\, \eta_{ji}}{\alpha_i + \beta_i\, \eta_{ji}}\, Y_i \qquad (4)$$

$$i, j = 1, 2$$

where c^*_{ij} denotes the optimizing value of the voluntary exchange for each of the two agents.

Equation *(4)* is the main condition regulating the flow of voluntary exchange in a network. It states that the gifts from the *i*-th to the *j*-th agent are a share of *i*-th income (or capacity to give). Such a share is higher, the higher the relative preference for the goods provided by the other agent (β_i) and the higher the response that can be expected from the same agent.

Equation *(4)* can be immediately generalized to the case of more than one agent:

$$c^*_{ij} = \left(\frac{\alpha_i\, \beta_{ji}\, \eta_{ji}}{\alpha_i^2 + \prod_{k \neq j}^{n} \alpha_i\, \eta_{ki}\, \beta_{ji}} \right) Y_i \qquad (5)$$

$$i = 1, 2 \ldots n$$

Expression *(5)* states the intuitive result that in a network of more than two agents, the amount given by agent *i* to agent *j* will be lower, the higher is his preference for the goods provided by the *j*-th agent and the more responsive are the other agents to gift giving. With respect to equation *(4)*, this simply adds that the amount of gifts (or voluntary exchange) that an agent will receive will depend on his relative reputation, i.e. on his responsiveness to gifts as compared to the responsiveness of each other agent.

Graph 1 shows how the Nash equilibrium is reached in the case of two agents. In order to have a stable equilibrium in $c^* = (c^*_{ij})$, it is sufficient that both reaction functions have slopes below unity and that the constants respect the relations obtained by combining the reaction functions with the equilibrium equations in *(4):*

Solving the system given by such a combination readily yields:

$$\log \beta_i = (1 - \eta_{ij}\,\eta_{ji})\ [g_i\,\eta_{ij} - g_j\,\eta_{ji}] \qquad (6)$$

$$i, j = 1, 2$$

Graph 1

REACTION AND EQUILIBRIUM FUNCTIONS

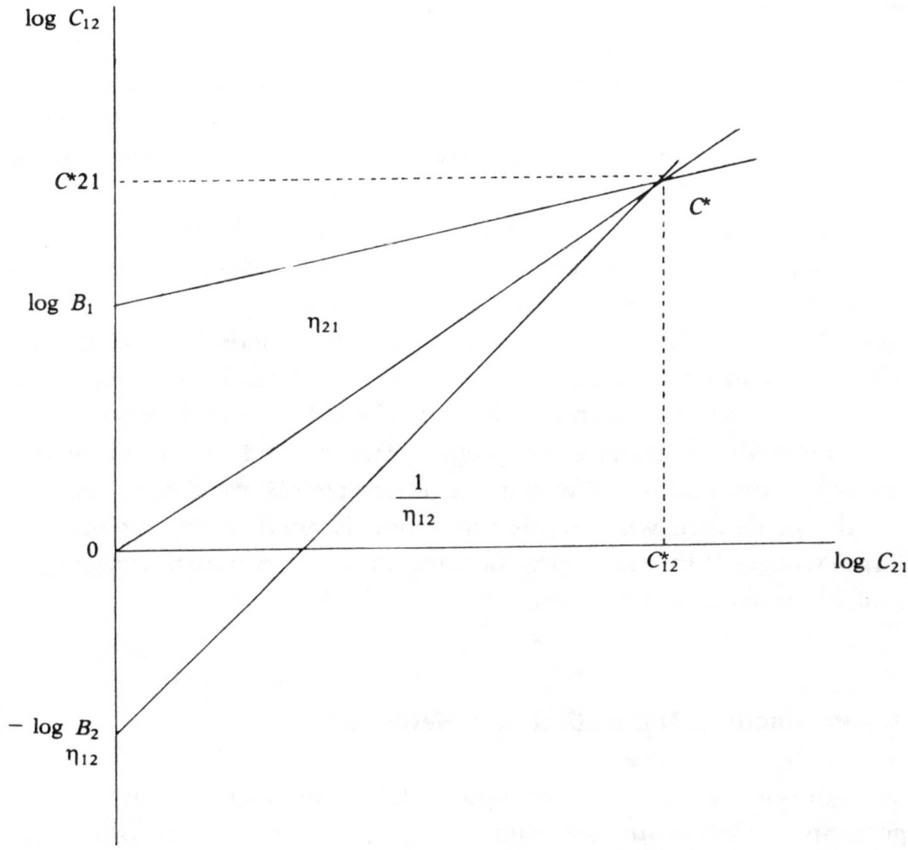

where: $g_i = \log c^*_{ij}$ $(i, j = 1, 2)$ as defined in *(4)*.

Substituting *(5)* into the utility function *(1)* generalized to many agents, we obtain the expression of the utility index at equilibrium:

$$(7) \qquad U^{(i)} = A_i^* Y_i^{\alpha_i} \prod_{j=1}^{mi} Y_j^{\beta_{ji}};$$

$$A_i^* = A_i \left(\frac{\alpha_i}{\alpha_i + \sum_{k \neq j}^{n_i} \eta_{kj} \beta_{kj}} \right)^{\alpha_i} \prod_{j=1}^{m_i} \left(\frac{\alpha_j \beta_{ij} \eta_{ij}}{\prod_{k \neq j}^{m_i} \alpha_i \eta_{ik} \beta_{ij}} \right)^{\beta_{ji}}$$

where n_i is the number of people to whom the *i*-th agent has given gifts, while m_i is the number of agents that give gifts to him. In a rational expectation equilibrium where all expectations are perfectly fulfilled $n_i = m_i$, but in general, it is possible that an individual may give to more people than he is receiving from, if he expects such a gap to be filled over time or, alternatively, if his liberality towards some may convince others to reciprocate in advance.

In this perspective, the utility function in *(2)* can be entirely explained as an index of independence and reputation. The first term in square parenthesis, in fact, measures the extent to which the individual can afford to rely on own provided goods for satisfaction. This term can be high if the agent considers particularly valuable the goods he is endowed with or, alternatively, if he sees the other agents as potentially ungrateful recipients. The second term, viceversa, measures the extent to which the other agents may consider him worthy of dealing with. If his reputation is good, many agents, (m_i large) will give him many gifts, because of the high returns (large η_{ij}'s) that his reputation promises.

3. - Production, Innovation and Networks

Consider now the case where the exchange of gifts is not performed by consuming agents but by producers. If producers produce inputs that can be complementary, but cannot be exchanged for a price either because of their intangible nature or because no acceptable market relation exists, a constrained maximization problem analogous to *(1)* can be formulated:

$$\text{(8)} \qquad \underset{Q_{ij}}{\text{Max}}\, \Pi_i = G_i X_i^{\Theta i} Q_{ji}^{1-\Theta i} - Q_{ij}$$

subject to: $\quad Q_{ji} = h^{(j)}(Q_{ij}) \qquad i, j = 1, 2$

where:

X_i = resource endowment of the *i*-th producer
Q_i = quantity produced of the *i*-th good
$Q_j i$ = the amount of good produced by j given to i;
$Q_{ji} = h^{(j)}(Q_{ij})$ = the reaction function of producer j to the transfer of output of producer i.

The homogeneity condition $h\ (0) = 0$ again suggests that the level function $h^{(j)}(\cdot)$ be of the form $H_i\, Q_{ij}^{\varepsilon ji}$, so that the optimum level of Q_{ij} turns out to be:

$$\text{(9)} \qquad Q^*_{ij} = \left[(1 - \Theta_i)\, \varepsilon_{ji}\, G_i\, H_i^{(1-\Theta i)}\, X_i^{\Theta i}\right]^{\frac{1}{1-\varepsilon_{ji}(1-\Theta_i)}}$$

$$i, j = 1, 2$$

where equilibrium requires that the elasticities ε_{ji} meet the complementarity condition:

$$\text{(10)} \qquad \log \varepsilon_i = (1 - \varepsilon_{ji}\, \varepsilon_{ij})\,(q_i\, q_{ij} - q_j\, \varepsilon_{ji})$$

$$i, j = 1, 2$$

where: $q_i = \log Q^*_{ij}\ (i, j = 1, 2)$ as defined in *(9)*.

In the case of a production economy, the possibility of exchanging inputs thus implies quite a different condition from that of pure exchange. The amount of inputs exchanged may be uneven, as in the case of pure exchange, but the unequal partnership entails exponential differences. The more one of the parties finds the other responsive to transfers of his output, the more he is motivated to transfer a larger amount of the same output. If one of the two parties is a producer of machinery, for example, while the other can only transfer know-how, as in the case of the innovative technologies experimented by the food or the textile industry in Italy, a strong relationship can develop among producers, even though very little exchange seems to occur between producers of machinery and producers of food or textiles. The techniques of production that are transferred by the food producers to the machine producers are intangible and hard to observe, while the machines produced may be increasingly used by the original producers who have inspired them.

To see more clearly how the elasticities of response are linked to each other in a reciprocal relationship, consider again the problem in *(8)* and solve it as a system of equations:

$$(11) \qquad \frac{\partial \Pi_i}{\partial Q_{ij}} = (1 - \Theta_i)\, G_i X_i^{\Theta_i}\, Q_{ji}^{-\Theta_i} \frac{\varepsilon_{ji}}{Q_{ij}} - 1 = 0$$

$$i, j = 1, 2$$

Taking logarithms and solving for log Q_{ij} ($i, j = 1, 2$) yields:

$$(12) \qquad q_{ij} - \Theta_i\, q_{ji} = \log \varepsilon_{ji} + \Theta_i X_i + \log(1 - \Theta_i) + g_i$$

$$i, j = 1, 2$$

where lower case letters indicate logarithms.

Solving the system in *(12)*, we find:

$$(13) \qquad q_{ij} = \frac{[\log\varepsilon_{ji} + \Theta_i X_i + \log(1-\Theta_i) + g_i] + \Theta_i\,[\log\varepsilon_{ij} + \Theta_j X_j + \log(1-\Theta_j) + g_j]}{1 - \Theta_i \Theta_j}$$

which corresponds to the gravity model:

(14) $$Q_{ij} = (\gamma_{ij} X_i^{\Theta_i} X_j^{\Theta_i})^{\frac{1}{1-\Theta_i\Theta_j}}$$

$$i, j = 1, 2$$

where: $$\gamma_{ij} = \varepsilon_{ij} G_i (1 - \Theta_i) (\varepsilon_{ji} G_j (1 - \Theta_j))$$

Substituting *(14)* into *(8)*, we finally obtain:

(15) $$Q_i = G_i^* X_i^{\Theta_i \frac{2-\Theta_i\Theta_j}{1-\Theta_i\Theta_j}} X_j^{\frac{\Theta_i\Theta_j}{1-\Theta_i\Theta_j}}$$

$$i, j = 1, 2$$

where:

$$G_i^* = G_i \gamma_{ij}^{\frac{1}{1-\Theta_i\Theta_j}}$$

Because resources and response elasticities may change over time, on the other hand, it is also useful to state the growth rates corresponding to *(14)* and *(15)*:

(16) $$\frac{\dot{Q}_{ij}}{Q_{ij}} = \frac{1}{1-\Theta_i\Theta_j} \left[\frac{\dot{\varepsilon}_{ji}}{\varepsilon_{ji}} + \Theta_i \frac{\dot{\varepsilon}_{ij}}{\varepsilon_{ij}} + \Theta_i \left(\frac{\dot{X}_i}{X_i} + \Theta_j \frac{\dot{X}_j}{X_j} \right) \right]$$

(17) $$\frac{\dot{Q}_i}{Q_i} = \left(\frac{2-\Theta_i\Theta_j}{1-\Theta_i\Theta_j} \right) \Theta_i \frac{\dot{X}_i}{X_i} + \frac{\Theta_i\Theta_j}{1-\Theta_i\Theta_j} \frac{\dot{X}_j}{X_j} + \left(\frac{1-\Theta_i}{1-\Theta_i\Theta_j} \right) \left(\frac{\dot{\varepsilon}_{ji}}{\varepsilon_{ji}} + \Theta_i \frac{\dot{\varepsilon}_{ij}}{\varepsilon_{ij}} \right) \qquad i, j = 1, 2$$

Expressions *(16)* and *(17)* both suggest that in a society where some voluntary exchange of inputs occurs as a consequence of a positive expectation of reciprocation all agents will grow at a higher rates. Furthermore, an increasing confidence in each other (i.e. an increasing anticipated response to voluntary exchange) will accelerate growth both of all the agents directly and indirectly experiencing the exchange.

4. - Some Preliminary Conclusions

While all activities of exchange have a reciprocal character, institutional reciprocity can be regarded as the capacity to engender exchange on the basis of mutual expectations. As such, reciprocity is a property of the social structures, rather than of the pure rationality of agents' behavior, and responds more to the characteristics of agents as potential providers of goods or favors, than on the actual supply of such goods.

The models of voluntary exchange that we have sketched in this paper appear to provide some interesting insights in the process of formation of "structures of reciprocity" among agents. Assuming selfishness and rational behavior, the possibility of exchanging goods or bads, with expected resource, is sufficient to create a network of relations among agents. Even though this network in some respects resembles the flow of goods and services in a market, its characteristics go beyond the barter economy, in that each agent becomes committed, through the parameters of mutual expectations, to his partners of exchange. Once the web of commitments is developed and stabilized, the agent is characterized by a utility function which has become an indicator of social integration, i.e. an indicator of costs of liberality (the cost of giving to others) and of benefits of reputation (the benefit of receiving from others).

The Nash equilibrium reached in this voluntary exchange regimes has some interesting properties. It is: *(i)* cooperative, *(ii)* it displays network externalities and, because of *(i)* and *(ii)*, it is not necessarily dominated by a command economy equilibrium. This suggests that network integration may be preferable to vertical integration when cooperation and network externalities are sufficiently large to outweigh the decrease in transaction costs and the improvement in resource allocation achieved by verticalization.

When we consider the case of a production economy, these results are strengthened. In a two sector economy where factors can be exchanged between firms, all firms grow faster than they would if they were produced in isolation. Network externalities arise as in the pure exchange case and, depending on the size of the network, may outweigh any economy from vertical integration. Each production function, as in the consumption case, becomes an indicator of the degree of network integration of the economy.

BIBLIOGRAPHY

[1] BELUSSI F., «Benetton Italy; Beyond Fordism and Flexible Specialization to the Evolution of the Network Firm Model», in MITTER (ed.), *Information Technology and Women's Employment: The Case of the European Clothing Industry*, Berlin and New York, Springer Verlag, 1989.

[2] BLIM M.L., «Economic Development and Decline in the Emerging Global Factor: Some Italian Lessons», *Politics and Society*, vol. 18, n. 1, March 1990, pp. 143-63.

[3] BEST M., *The New Competition*, Cambridge, Harvard University Press, 1990.

[4] CAMUFFO A., «L'evoluzione del Gruppo Marzotto: imprenditorialità e management», Venezia, Università Cà Foscari, *Working Paper*, February 1993.

[5] CAMUFFO A. - COMACCHIO A., *Strategia e organizzazione nel tessile-abbigliamento*, Padova, CEDAM, 1990.

[6] CNR, «Progetto strategico-ISPE, "cambiamento tecnologico e sviluppo industriale"», *Le medie e piccole imprese tradizionali napoletane, Working Paper*, January 1995.

[7] GOODMAN E., «The Political Economy of the Small Firm in Italy», in GOODMAN - BAMFORD - SAYNOR (eds.), *Small Firms and Industrial Districts in Italy*, London, Routledge, 1989.

[8] LOCKE R.M., *Remaking the Italian Economy: Policy Failures and Local Successes in the Contemporary Policy*, forthcoming, Ithaca, (NY) Cornell University Press, 1996.

[9] NOMISMA, *Rapporto sull'industria italiana*, Bologna, il Mulino, 1992.

[10] PIORE M.J. - SABEL C.F., *The Second Industrial Divide*, New York, Basic Books, 1984.

[11] PUTNAM R.D., *Making Democracy Work: Civic Traditions in Modern Italy*, Princeton (NJ), Princeton University Press, 1993.

[12] PYKE F. - BECATTINI G. - SENGENBERGER W. (eds.), *Industrial Districts and Inter-Firm Cooperation in Italy*, Geneva, International Institute for Labor Studies, 1990.

Regulation of Capital Flows and Exchange Rate Volatility. Preliminary Results on the Italian Experience

Andrea Berardi - **Alberto Dalmazzo** - **Giancarlo Marini** *

Banca Commerciale Italiana, Milano and London Business School

Università di Siena

Università «Tor Vergata», Roma

1 - Introduction

The consequences of excessively efficient financial markets have been lucidly described by James Tobin on more than one occasion (Tobin [29]). In particular, perfect capital mobility may be highly undesirable when there are rigidities in labour and product markets. The stabilising effect of speculation illustrated by Friedman [13] can occur when exchange rate fluctuations mostly reflect market fundamentals. Complete deregulation has increased, however, the scope for destabilising short-run speculations, which are unrelated to longer period economic fundamentals. Speculative bubbles slow to burst are likely to create political tensions and may in the end endanger the correct functioning of federal European programs. Different degrees of chronical nominal inertia do not seem to be compatible with the

---

* The authors, A. Berardi – researcher at Banca Commerciale Italiana and the London Business School, A. Dalmazzo – researcher at the Department of Political Economy, and G. Marini – professor at the Department of Economics and Institutions, would like to thank Andrea Calamanti and their discussants, Vittorio Grilli and Massimo Tivegna, for their valuable suggestions.

N.B.: the numbers in square brackets refer to the Bibliograpy at the end of the paper.

increased efficiency of capital markets. It may thus be necessary to reduce such an efficiency, as proposed by Tobin.

Measures must be designed to reduce the welfare losses along the transient path: a tax on short-run capital movements would leave virtually unaffected longer term capital flows (preserving their stabilising effectiveness *a la* Friedman) while deterring the search for easy gains. Interest equalisation taxes to eliminate the wedge between domestic and foreign interest rates or dual exchange rate regimes, as proposed by Dornbusch [6], are but two examples of possible forms regulation could take.

The case against the (re-)imposition of capital controls mainly rests on the argument that governments would feel less pressure to enact the required structural corrections. Deregulation in itself, however, does not seem to be of much help in enhancing the credibility of countries in trouble.

The desirability of controls is arguably an important theoretical issue. The more relevant policy question is, however, whether (and to what extent) regulation is effective[1].

The present paper attempts to provide some preliminary evidence for the Italian experience on capital coontrols. In particular, we investigate whether exchange rate variability has been dampened as a result.

The scheme of the paper is as follows. Section 2 briefly restates the case for and against regulating capital flows. The question of controls' effectiveness is addressed in Section 3. The empirical evidence on the effectiveness of controls for the Italian experience is discussed in Section 4. Section 5 concludes.

2. - The Desirability of Capital Controls

2.1 *The Case for Controls on Capital Movements*

Controls on capital movements may be desirable for at least two

---

[1] Many authors would, in fact, question the very feasibility of biting controls in the light of financial innovation.

reasons: 1) command on monetary policy and interest rate determination and, 2) limitation of exchange rate volatility.

1) A main argument is that, by artificially reducing the degree of capital mobility, controls allow for a greater autonomy in the conduct of the monetary policy, without generating, at the same time, intolerably strong effects on the exchange rate (Eichengreen, Tobin and Wyplosz [10]). Governments could thus refinance a large public debt at «reasonable» conditions. Controls might then be a device to insulate the domestic financial market from foreign interest rates.

2) By constraining capital mobility, controls may limit the responsiveness of exchange rates to shocks and reduce exchange rate volatility. Hence, in case of realignments in fixed exchange rate regimes, national authorities can negotiate the new parity with their foreign counterparts without undergoing excessive turbulences on the forex market. Controls may also discourage rational «self-fulfilling» expectations of devaluation (Obstfeld [23]) and Eichengreen and Wyplosz [11])[2]. Eichengreen, Tobin and Wyplosz [10]) argue that measures which penalise high-frequency capital flows may force speculators to concentrate more on fundamentals rather than «market sentiment». Finally, higher stability in exchange rates may reduce the uncertainty faced by national firms which actively trade abroad. In fact, while the exchange rate risk on ordinary import-export activity can be easily eliminated by hedging operations, a firm planning to adopt export-oriented productions (or import-oriented technologies) will find it more difficult to buy insurance against such risks. It can then be argued that, whenever controls are a device to reduce exchange rate volatility, firms can be more willing to search for new opportunities abroad. In this perspective, controls may be important since they make a system of pegged exchange rates more credible and easier to manage: according to Kenen [20], this scope was successfully reached in the times of the «old» EMS. The main advantage which the current debate attributes to reduced volatility, however, is to facilitate the transition to the European Monetary Union (Eichengreen, Tobin and Wyplosz [10]).

---

[2] Such a view is supported by the empirical findings of Ghosh A.R. [15], according to which fundamentals alone cannot justify the observed volumes of capital mobility.

2.2 *The Case Against Controls on Capital Movements*

Controls such as a compulsory deposit requirement at zero interest rate must have a broad coverage in order to be effective. With regard to the September 1992 *Peseta*'s crisis, Garber and Taylor ([14], p. 176) note that controls did not only hamper speculative attacks but also limited financial operations and risk hedging related to foreign trade. Hence, measures aimed at maintaining a fixed exchange rate system may, in the short run, end up exposing domestic firms to greater exchange rate risks. Analogous considerations apply to the «Tobin tax»[3].

According to Kenen ([20], p. 189), a small transaction tax is unlikely to deter speculation. However, when the tax is not small, it is likely to affect also ordinary foreign trade. If Kenen's argument is correct, then, the presumption that the Tobin-tax hits mostly «high-frequency» traders, identified with speculators, may not be right. A very large tax might be necessary to discourage massive speculative attacks like the ones of 1992.

Another main argument against controls is that the more effective they are, the more they allow national governments to keep lax monetary and fiscal policies. According to Eichengreen, Tobin and Wyplosz ([10], p. 168), there are credible instruments, in the European context, to penalise this kind of government's moral hazard. However, as emphasised by Alesina, Grilli and Milesi-Ferretti [1], controls seem to have widened the scope of governments' action and increased the role of seigniorage. In particular, the governments of countries with a large public debt may have an incentive to create inflationary pressures, in order to reduce the real value of debt repayments. The experience of the 1970s suggests that the advantages for public debt financing might translate into negative real interest rates hitting mainly small savers and, in general, those who are less capable of evading controls.

The argument that taxes and controls on capital movements inevitably reduce exchange rate volatility may not be correct. Vol-

---

[3] Also, a Tobin tax or other measures increasing transaction costs would hamper the daily inter-dealer trading aimed at balancing inventory positions. According to CHEN Z. [4] then, controls would reduce the risk-sharing role of the market.

atility can increase if, for example, controls happen to discourage «informed» trading relatively more than «noise» trading (Hakkio [17], p. 22). Also, measures which reduce participation can raise volatility by making the market less liquid[4].

3. - The Effectiveness on Controls of Capital Movements

The crucial question about controls is whether they are effective in curbing speculative capital flows. Johnston and Ryan [19][5] argue that controls implemented by industrial countries significantly affected their capital movements. According to them, however, restrictions were particularly effective in diminishing international investment flows, such as foreign direct and portfolio investment. A more skeptical view about controls' effectiveness is taken by Garber and Taylor [14]: they argue that controls, especially when they are introduced by a single country, have the main effect of moving the forex market offshore. Evaluating Italy's and France's experience, Gros and Thygesen ([16], Ch. IV) conclude that controls neither affected significantly the size of capital flows, nor insulated (or reduced) domestic interest rates in the long-run. At most, controls succeded in protecting domestic interest rates only in the short-run. Even Eichengreen, Tobin and Wyplosz ([10], p. 163) recognize that the effectiveness of restrictions is likely to decrease over time. Further, as noticed by Kenen [20], the progressive integration of European financial markets in the most recent phase of the EMS has already moved abroad a large share of the trading of domestic assets denominated in the home currency.

The view that controls tend to be ineffective, if not harmful, is not supported by a recent empirical work of Alesina, Grilli and Milesi-Ferretti [1] on 20 OECD countries for the period 1950-1989. According to

---

[4] For a formal model relating participation, market liquidity and volatility see, among others, PAGANO M. [28]. CHEN Z. [4] p. 5, reports that «the [Spanish] forward market almost completely died due to the lack of liquidity», after the introducton of zero-interest compulsory deposit requirement during the 1992 Peseta crisis.

[5] JOHNSTON B. - RYAN C. [19] use data drawn from 52 countries for the period 1985-1992. On the limited effectiveness of controls on the degree of monetary independence, see also MATHIESON D.J. - ROJAS-SUAREZ L. [21].

these authors, capital controls tended to be imposed by governments which had a relatively high power on the conduct of monetary policy and succeded in keeping interest rates artificially low. This fact has obvious implications for countries characterised by high public debt, such as Italy or Belgium (see Section 2 above).

Alesina, Grilli and Milesi-Ferretti do not report any significant relation between controls and real GDP growth rate. They also find that *a)* controls are more likely to be introduced in a regime of pegged or managed exchange rates (as it was in the early stages of the EMS) and, *b)* fixed/managed exchange rates are associated with higher growth. The relevant implication is that, if controls strengthen a system of fixed exchange rates, then they can indirectly stimulate growth.

One of the few uncontroversial points is that controls are more likely to be effective when they are imposed multilaterally: if a country alone imposes some restrictions on capital movements, the forex market will likely tend to move abroad. There are, however, very different costs in reducing capital mobility across countries. For example, in the UK, where the City has a big direct and indirect weight on the British GNP, the financial market segmentation generated by restrictions would be against the interests of a relevant part of the public, who would lobby not to adhere to such a mutual agreement[6]. On the other hand, capital restrictions would favour high public debt countries, since it would be easier to manage interest rates. Moreover, the volume of home-currency denominated assets traded in the domestic financial market would be artificially increased. Contrasts of interest among countries, by preventing credible international cooperation, are then a major factor reducing the power of controls.

4. The Italian Experience on Controls: Some Preliminary Evidence

Italy experienced extensive controls on capital movements in the 1970s and in the first half of the 1980s. These controls were mainly

[6] On this point, see also HAKKIO C. [17], p. 26.

aimed at constraining financial outflows, in order to limit the depreciation of the Lira and the loss of foreign currency reserves. Several measures, both permanent and temporary, were adopted[7]: notably, compulsory deposit requirements for all residents were in effect between 1973 and 1987, a double forex market was in place in 1973, firms' hedging operations were put under strict constraints until 1986, loans to non-residents were forbidden and the overall foreign exchange position of banks was subject to stringent limits.

4.1 *A Reference Model for Exchange-Rate Volatility*

The underlying theoretical framework can be based on simple prototypical rational expectation models, where exchange rate volatility is driven by exogenous shocks (Driskill and McCafferty [9] and Flood [12]). In Driskill and McCafferty [9] for instance, the exchange rate level is determined by monetary and real trade balance shocks on the forex and the money market. As a result, the variability of the exchange rate turns out to be a linear and positive function of the variability of both money supply and trade balance. A peculiar result of this model is that, if controls can be represented as a reduction of the degree of capital mobility, they should decrease the component of exchange rate variability due to monetary shocks and increase the component arising from real shocks. In the empirical implementation we will try to deal also with aspects that cannot be adequately considered in simple exchange rate models of this type.

4.2 *Data Description*

We use monthly data from January 1971 to October 1994. We consider two measures of the Lira nominal exchange rate[8]: 1) Lira-USA dollar, 2) Lira-Deutschmark. In order to construct the nominal

---

[7] See Cotula F. - Rossi S. [5] and Banca d'Italia [2].

[8] The analysis of nominal exchange rates is justified by the EMS membership. According to Gros D. - Thygesen N. [16], however, nominal and real exchange rate volatilities present similar dynamics.

shock components, we use the M1 aggregate for Italy, Germany and the USA. The real shock on the foreign exchange market is built on the volume of net exports in real terms. We also consider the spread between the Italian long-term yield on Treasury bonds and the corresponding yields on German and US bonds, so to account for depreciation expectations.

We model the impact of (permanent) controls on capital movements by a dummy variable[9] (*CCM*), taking value one when a zero-interest compulsory deposit requirement was operative (July 1973-April 1987)[10]. The presence in the EMS is represented by a dummy (*EMS*), which is equal to one between March 1979 and August 1992.

4.3 *Empirical Results*

A preliminary assessment of the quantitative importance of controls on exchange rate volatility is provided by a 12-month variance decomposition analysis obtained through a VAR system which includes as endogenous variables the differences[11] of: 1) the logarithm of the Lira-Dollar exchange rate (*EXUS*), 2) the annual growth rate of *M*1 for Italy (*M*1*I*), 3) the annual growth rate *M*1 for the USA (*M*1*U*), 4) the annual growth rate of real net exports (*RNX*) and 5) the spread on the long-term yields of Italian and USA bonds (*SIU*). We break the sample into two sub-periods (1973-1987 and 1987-1994) in order to measure the relevance of controls (1973-1987) in insulating exchange rate volatility from exogenous monetary and real shocks. As shown by Graph 1, in the first period the percentage of the volatility of the exchange rate which is explained by the other variables amounts to about 10%. Once the controls were removed (1987-1994), the volatility of the exchange rate turns out to be explained in a larger

[9] On the use of dummy variables to capture the effect of controls on capital movements see also Dooley M. - Isard P. [8].

[10] As mentioned before, this measure was just one among the several restrictions on capital movements adopted in the 1970s. We take it to represent the government's general attitude on capital movements.

[11] We use logarithmic differences of the series since the unit-root tests do not allow us to reject the null hypothesis of non-stationarity for the original series.

GRAPH 1

PERCENTAGE OF 12-MONTH FORECAST ERROR VARIANCE
OF *EXUS* EXPLAINED BY INNOVATIONS IN
M1I, M1U, RNX, SIU

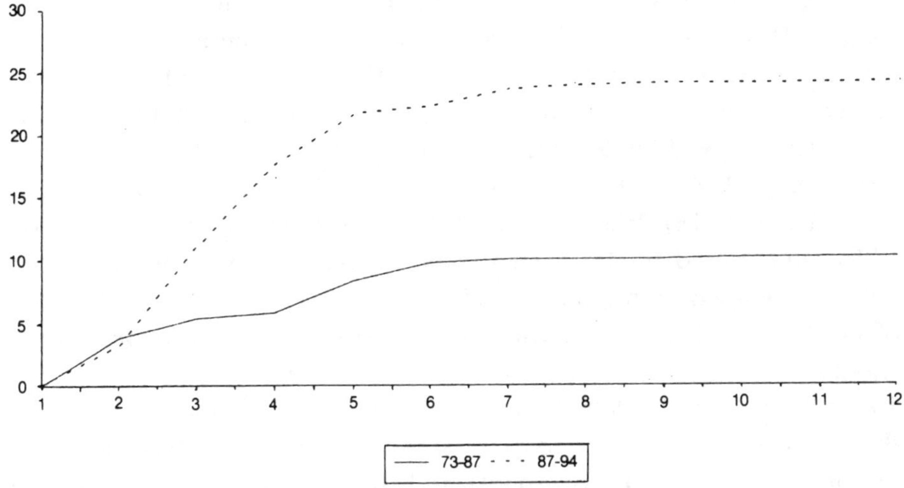

GRAPH 2

PERCENTAGE OF 12-MONTH FORECAST ERROR VARIANCE
OF *EXGE* EXPLAINED BY INNOVATIONS IN
*M1I, M1*G, *RNX, SIG*

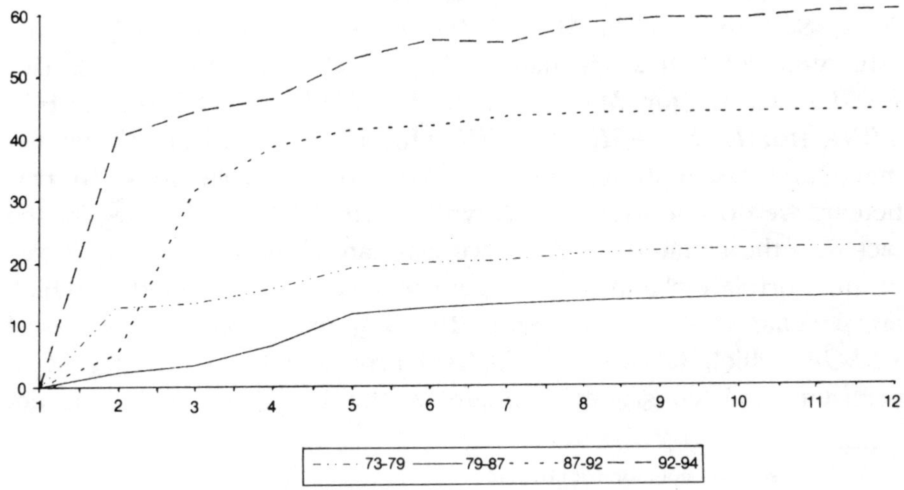

proportion (25%) by the other variables. This evidence suggests that controls were relevant to limit the impact of monetary and real shocks.

A similar analysis is adopted to study the joint effect of the EMS and capital controls on the Lira-Dm exchange rate (Graph 2). We replace *M1U* with the difference of the annual growth rate of *M1* for Germany (*M1G*) and the spread on the yields is calculated with respect to the German *Bund* (*SIG*). We divide the sample in four sub-periods: 1973-1979 (controls and no EMS), 1979-1987 (controls and EMS), 1987-1992 (no controls and EMS) and 1992-1994 (no controls, no EMS). With respect to 1973-1979, the introduction of the EMS contributed to diminish the percentage of exchange rate variability explained by monetary and real shocks (1979-1987). The lifting of controls in 1987 made the Lira-Dm volatility more responsive to shocks and, in particular, to the German monetary policy (1987-1992). Once the Lira left the EMS, the share of volatility explained by the other variables rose above 50%. Hence, both the implementation of controls on capital movements and the presence of the EMS seem to have largely «insulated» the Lira-Dm volatility from monetary and real shocks.

Time-series estimates of the volatility of the variables under analysis over the whole sample period (January 1971-October 1994) are obtained from the squared residuals derived from two *VAR* specifications including as endogenous variables *EXUS, M1I, M1U, RNX, SIU* and *EXGE, M1I, M1G, RNX, SIG,* respectively[12]. The estimated volatilities are named *VEXUS* (for *EXUS*), *VEXGE* (for *EXGE*), *VM1I* (for *M1I*), *VM1U* (for *M1U*), *VM1G* (for *M1G*), *VRNX* (for *RNX*), *VSIU* (for *SIU*) and *VSIG* (for *SIG*). We do not make any assumption about the form of the volatilities. In particular, we do not adopt *ARCH*-type parametrisations because of the fact that the squared residuals we estimate show a very low degree of autocorrelation and do not seem to possess the properties which are peculiar of *ARCH* processes. The only exception is the series of *VEXGE*, which follows an *ARCH*(2) process with a low degree of persistence. A consistent estimate of the Lira-Dm volatility is ob-

[12] We use orthogonalised innovations.

GRAPH 3

LIRA-DM VOLATILITY: ANNUAL AVERAGE VALUES

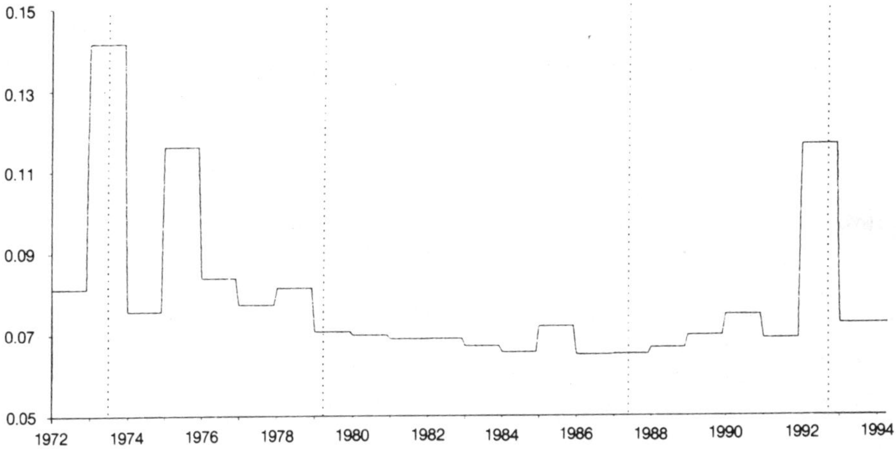

tained by using the two-step estimator suggested by Pagan and Schwert [26][13].

Graph 3 illustrates the estimated time series of *VEXGE*: the introduction of controls on capital movements seems to have significantly reduced the average value of the Lira-Dm volatility which, after the 1973-1974 and 1976 crises, declined sharply in spite of the several and large devaluations of the Lira between March 1981 and April 1986. After the lifting of compulsory deposit requirements in May 1987, volatility started to rise and reached its maximum level in September 1992. With regard to the Lira-Dollar volatility, we obtain that its average value over the 1973-1987 period is about 19% lower than the value between May 1987 and October 1994[14].

We use the estimated volatility measures to construct impulse response functions. With this procedure, we try to capture the impact

[13] A similar procedure has been adopted, for example, by DOMOWITZ I. - HAKKIO C. [7].

[14] With regard to the real effects of exchange rate variability, we obtain that the Lira-Dm volatility exhibits a small but statistically significant negative correlation (−0.16) with the industrial production index. Instead, the correlation between industrial production and Lira-Dollar volatility is not statistically different from zero.

of both capital controls and the EMS on exchange rate variability. In particular, we obtain the response of the exchange rate volatility to a

GRAPH 4

IMPULSE RESPONSES OF *VEXUS* TO SHOCKS IN *CCM*

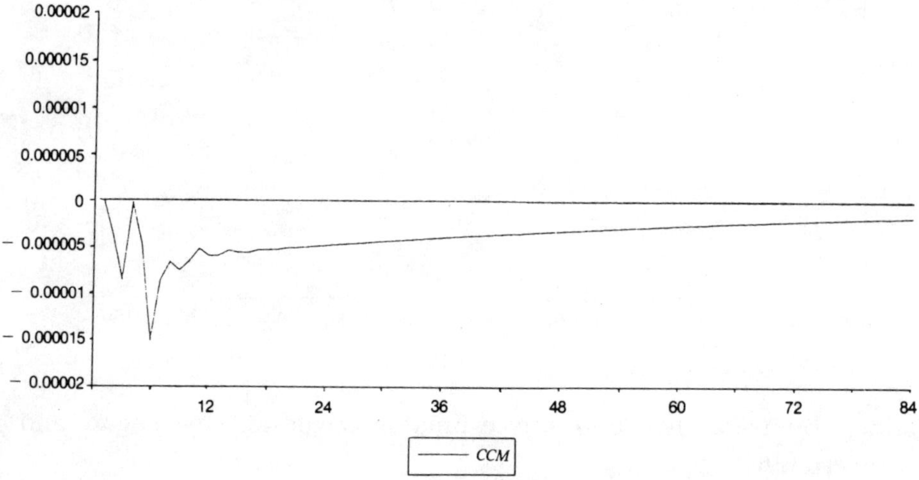

GRAPH 5

IMPULSE RESPONSES OF *VEXGE* TO SHOCKS IN *CCM* AND *EMS*

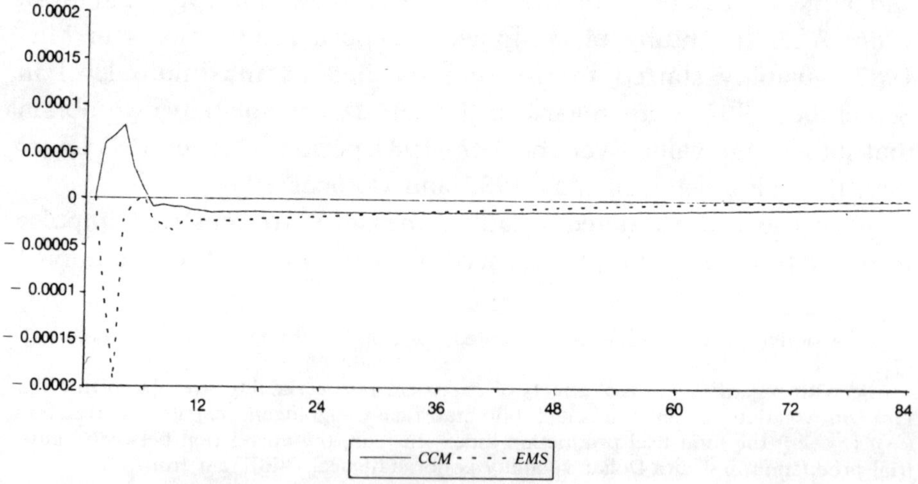

one-standard deviation shock due both to capital movements restrictions and the «tightening» of the EMS. Graph 4 shows that the Lira-Dollar volatility tends to be persistently reduced by controls: it is worth noting that, even if the magnitude of the effect is rather small, the controls' impulse takes about 5-6 years to die out. This conclusion contrasts the common view that controls' effectiveness decays fast over time (mostly due to financial innovations).

Graph 5 shows that Lira-Dm volatility is mainly reduced, in the short-run, by an impulse which can be interpreted as a «tightening» of the exchange rate agreements. The negative effect of a stiffening of controls on the Lira-Dm volatility displays its effects after 6 months and persists for quite a long period.

In order to test whether controls on capital movements affect the exchange rate variability in a significantly negative way, we start by estimating the following equation:

$$(1)\qquad \begin{aligned} VEXGE_t = {} & \alpha_1 + \alpha_2\, CCM_t + \alpha_3\, EMS_t + \beta_1\, VM1I_t \\ & + \beta_2\,(CCM \times VM1I)_t + \beta_3\,(EMS \times VM1I)_t + \\ & + \gamma_1\, VM1G_t + \gamma_2\,(CCM \times VM1G)_t + \gamma_3\,(EMS \times VM1G)_t + \\ & + \delta_1\, VRNX_t + \delta_2\,(CCM \times VRNX)_t + \delta_3\,(EMS \times VRNX)_t + \\ & + \eta_1\, VSIG_t + \eta_2\,(CCM \times VSIG)_t + \eta_3\,(EMS \times VSIG)_t + \varepsilon_t \end{aligned}$$

for the Lira-Dm volatility and

$$(2)\qquad \begin{aligned} VEXUS_t = {} & \alpha_1 + \alpha_2\, CCM + \beta_1\, VM1I_t + \beta_2\,(CCM \times VM1I)_t + \\ & + \gamma_1\, VM1U_t + \gamma_2\,(CCM \times VM1U)_t + \\ & + \delta_1\, VRNX_t + \delta_2\,(CCM \times VRNX)_t + \\ & + \eta_1\, VSIU_t + \eta_2\,(CCM \times VSIU)_t + \varepsilon_t \end{aligned}$$

for the Lira-Dollar volatility.

Since the equations *(1)* and *(2)* contain residual-generated regressors, an error in variables problem arises. This implies that ordinary least squares estimators turn out to be inconsistent and, therefore, an instrumental variable technique must be used[15]. We obtain consistent estimates of the model parameters by applying the generalised method of moments (*GMM*) technique[16]. In the set of instruments which enter the orthogonality conditions various conditional moments of the rates of change of the original variables are included. The number of orthogonality conditions imposed by the *GMM* procedure exceeds the number of parameters to be estimated, and it allows us to over-identify the parameters of the model. A chi-square statistic enables us to test the null hypothesis that the over-identifying restrictions of the model are valid.

We expert a positive sign for the coefficients relate to the volatilities (β_1, γ_1, δ_1, η_1), and a negative sign for the coefficients of the terms in which the volatilities are multiplied by the dummies, i.e., (β_2, γ_2, δ_2, η_2) and (β_3, γ_3, δ_3, η_3).

We also estimate two different specifications, which use the differences between the countries' annual money growth rates. In particular, in the Lira-Dm regression, *VDMIG* (the volatility of *M1I-M1G*) replace *VM1G* and *VM1I* and, in the Lira-Dollar regression, *VDMIU* replace *VM1U* and *VM1I*. These two specifications are then:

$$\text{(3)} \qquad VEXGE_t = \alpha_1 + \alpha_2\, CCM_t + \alpha_3\, EMS_t +$$
$$+ \rho_1\, VDMIG_t + \rho_2\,(CCM \times VDMIG)_t + \rho_3\,(EMS \times VDMIG)_t +$$
$$+ \delta_1\, VRNX_t + \delta_2\,(CCM \times VRNX)_t + \delta_3\,(EMS \times VRNX)_t +$$
$$+ \eta_1\, VSIG_t + \eta_2\,(CCM \times VSIG)_t + \eta_3\,(EMS \times VSIG)_t + \varepsilon_t$$

for the Lira-Dm volatility and:

$$\text{(4)} \qquad VEXUS_t = \alpha_1 + \alpha_2\, CCM_t +$$
$$+ \rho_1\, VDMIU_t + \rho_2\,(CCM \times VDMIU)_t +$$

[15] In particular, the fact that the volatility measures are generated from the residuals of the VAR specification implies that the error terms in *(1)* and *(2)* are not uncorrelated with the regressors. On these problems, see PAGAN A.R. [25], BOWDEN R.J.-TURKINGTON D.A. [3] and PAGAN A.R. - ULLAH A. [27].

[16] See HANSEN L. [18]. In the empirical estimation, we use the NEWEY W.K. - WEST D.W. [22] correction to account for autocorrelated disturbances.

$$+ \delta_1 \, VRNX_t + \delta_2 \, (CCM \times VRNX)_t +$$

$$+ \eta_1 \, VSIU_t + \eta_2 \, (CCM \times VSIU)_t + \varepsilon_t$$

for the Lira-Dollar volatility. Obviously, we expect ρ_1 to be positive and both ρ_2 and ρ_3 to be negative.

The results of the estimation of equation *(1)* show that all the volatility coefficients, and the associated dummies, exhibit the expected sign, apart from that of real trade balance volatility[17] (Table 1). Hence, the Lira-Dm volatility is, in general, positively associated with the other volatilities and both capital controls and the EMS seem to have reduced the impact of monetary and long-term yield randomness

TABLE 1

LIRA-DM VOLATILITY: *GMM* ESTIMATES

VEXGE	Equation *(1)*		Equation *(3)*	
	Parameter	Std. error	Parameter	Std. error
C	0.00052	0.00009	0.00055	0.00005
CCM	0.00005	0.00007	0.00006	0.00003
EMS	− 0.00012	0.00009	− 0.00016	0.00005
VM1I	0.29398	0.28353		
CCMx VM1I	− 0.30001	0.26870		
EMSx VM1I	− 0.21033	0.23289		
VM1G	0.53940	0.11431		
CCMx VM1G	− 0.09134	0.12361		
EMSx VM1G	− 0.53881	0.11416		
VDMIG			0.11656	0.06582
CCMx VDMIG			− 0.12147	0.06111
EMSx VDMIG			− 0.11445	0.06591
VRNX	− 0.01566	0.00564	− 0.00636	0.00353
CCMx VRNX	0.01277	0.00561	0.00524	0.00313
EMSx VRNX	0.00398	0.00262	0.00101	0.00170
VSIG	8.89851	2.72543	11.72652	3.55267
CCMx VSIG	− 0.49015	0.22306	− 0.76354	0.30977
EMSx VSIG	− 8.64564	2.68286	− 11.1111	3.57275

[17] However, the fact that the dummies associated with real volatility show a positive sign can be consistent with DRISKILL R. - MCCAFFERTY S. [9] model, in the case that controls reduce the degree of capital mobility.

TABLE 2

LIRA-DOLLAR VOLATILITY: *GMM* ESTIMATES

VEXUS	Equation *(2)*		Equation *(4)*	
	Parameter	Std. error	Parameter	Std. error
C	0.00048	0.000111	0.00033	0.00005
CCM	0.00016	0.00007	− 0.00011	0.00013
VM1I	0.29868	0.13312		
*CCM*x*VM1I*	− 0.32585	0.14120		
VM1U	0.78139	0.57848		
*CCM*x*VM1U*	− 1.22267	0.61965		
VDMIU			0.40139	0.26753
*CCM*x*VDMIU*			− 0.43503	0.27853
VRNX	− 0.01484	0.00356	− 0.04652	0.01566
*CCM*x*VRNX*	0.01481	0.00378	0.05312	0.01717
VSIU	8.51297	0.25735	11.04105	0.70063
*CCM*x*VSIU*	− 8.10435	0.49763	−10.54410	0.86335

(i.e., *VM1I*, *VM1G* and *VSIG*) on the exchange rate variability. Very similar results are obtained by estimating equation *(3)*, where the spread in the money growth rate between countries is considered: the coefficients related to it exhibit the expected sign and, statistically, are highly significant. In both cases, the chi-square statistic for testing the validity of the over-identifying restrictions of the model allows us not to reject the null hypothesis at the 30% significance level.

Similarly, the over-identifying restrictions of equations *(2)* and *(4)* for the Lira-Dollar volatility are not rejected at the same significance level. In these cases also, all the coefficients are statistically significant and take the expected sign, with the exception of those related to the real trade balance volatility (Table 2). In general, the coefficients of these regressions seem to confirm the hypothesis that controls have significantly reduced the volatility of the Lira-Dollar exchange rate.

To sum up, the estimation of equations *(1)-(4)* yields the following results: 1) the volatility associated with the domestic and foreign monetary policy is positively related to the exchange rate volatility; 2) both capital controls and the EMS reduce the impact of monetary shocks on the exchange rate variability; 3) the same conclusions as for 1)-2) are obtained when considering the spreads between long-term yields; 4) the trade balance variabilities display the «wrong» (negative) sign, and the dummies associated with them have a positive sign.

Even if the evidence presented is to be considered as preliminary, the extensive use of controls undertaken by the Italian authorities between 1973 and 1987 seems to have reduced the exchange rate average variability by partially insulating it from exogenous shocks. This empirical result is rather relevant since there are sound theorical arguments suggesting that controls might actually increase variability (Section 2.2 above).

As suggested by the variance decomposition analysis, exogenous shocks became much less influential in explaining both the Lira-Dollar and Lira-Dm variability when controls were in effect. Also, controls seem to have persistently reduced exchange rate volatility. These deductions are corroborated by the *GMM* regression analysis we developed. In particular, controls seem to have reduced the impact that the domestic money supply randomness and the volatility of the spread on long-term yields had on exchange rate volatility.

5. - Discussion and Conclusions

The excessive volatility of exchange rates is one of the most debated issues in current international economic theory and policy design. The increased sophistication of deregulated financial markets accompanied by rigidities in the real sector may in the end cause serious output losses. It might thus be necessary to throw sand in the gears of foreign exchange markets during the adjustment path. On the other hand, it is often argued that the shelter of capital controls could relax the pressure exerted by market forces on «wet» governments.

The skeptical attitude towards the imposition of capital controls mainly rests on their alleged ineffectiveness. Our evidence, based on the Italian experience over the period 1971-1994, indicates that the measures adopted by the authorities have indeed been quite successful in dampening exchange rate volatility. However, our empirical results may not be used to suggest that capital controls would surely be effective also in current days. European financial markets have become much more integrated and sophisticated and, in Italy, the

Central Bank's ability to monitor foreign currency transactions has become much more limited. We must then conclude that the case for new and (possibly) more sophisticated forms of regulation of capital flows is not very strong, especially if restrictions were to be imposed by a single country.

However, in this particular phase both countries with weak and strong currencies have high incentives to find some form of international cooperation in order to «stay in Europe» and reduce current account deficits, respectively. In the absence of effectively coordinated monetary policies, the introduction of multilateral controls might be an obvious instrument to reduce exchange rate volatility, prevent the possible occurrence of trade wars and give new impetus to the process of monetary integration.

BIBLIOGRAPHY

[1] ALESINA A. - GRILLI V. - MILESI-FERRETTI G.M., «The Political Economy of Capital Controls», *NBER Working Paper*, n. 4353, 1993.

[2] BANCA D'ITALIA, *Bollettino Economico* (various issues), Roma.

[3] BOWDEN R.J. - TURKINGTON D.A., *Instrumental Variables*, Cambridge, Cambridge University Press, 1984.

[4] CHEN Z., «Speculative Market Structure and the Collapse of an Exchange Rate Mechanism», London, Financial Markets Group, London School of Economics, *Discussion Paper*, n. 202, 1995.

[5] COTULA F. - ROSSI S., «Il Controllo amministrativo dei flussi finanziari in Italia», in COTULA F. (ed.), *La politica monetaria in Italia*, vol. II, Bologna, il Mulino, 1989.

[6] DORNBUSCH R., «The Theory of Flexible Exchange Rate Regimes and Macroeconomic Policy», *Scandinavian Journal of Economics*, n. 78, 1976, pp. 255-75.

[7] DOMOWITZ I. - HAKKIO C., «Conditional Variance and the Risk Premium in the Foreign Exchange Market», *Journal of International Economics*, n. 19, 1985, pp. 47-66.

[8] DOOLEY M. - ISARD P., «Capital Controls, Political Risk, and Deviations from Interest-Rate Parity», *Journal of Political Economy*, n. 88, 1980, pp. 370-84.

[9] DRISKILL R. - MCCAFFERTY S., «Exchange-Rate Variability, Real and Monetary Shocks, and the Degree of Capital Mobility under Rational Expectations», *Quarterly Journal of Economics*, n. 95, 1980, pp. 577-86.

[10] EICHENGREEN B. - TOBIN J. - WYPLOSZ C., «Two Cases for Sand in the Wheels of International Finance», *Economic Journal*, n. 105, 1995, pp. 162-72.

[11] EICHENGREEN B. - WYPLOSZ C., «The Unstable EMS», *Brooking Papers on Economic Activity*, n. 2, 1993, pp. 51-143.

[12] FLOOD R., «Explanations of Exchange Rate Volatility and Other Empirical Regularities in Some Popular Models of the Foreign Exchange Market», *Carnegie-Rochester Conference Series on Public Policy*, n. 15, 1981, pp. 219-50.

[13] FRIEDMAN M., «The Case for Flexible Exchange Rates», in FRIEDMAN M., *Essays on Positive Economics*, Chicago, University of Chicago Press, 1953.

[14] GARBER P. - TAYLOR M., «Sand in the Wheels of Foreign Exchange Markets: A Skeptical Note», *Economic Journal*, n. 105, 1995, pp. 173-80.

[15] GHOSH A.R., «International Capital Mobility Amongst the Major Industrialised Countries: Too Little or Too Much», *Economic Journal*, n. 105, 1995, pp. 107-28.

[16] GROS D. - THYGESEN N., *European Monetary Integration*, London, Longman, 1992.

[17] HAKKIO C., «Should We Throw Sand in the Gears of Financial Markets?», *Federal Reserve Bank of Kansas City Economic Review*, n. 79, 1994, pp. 17-30.

[18] HANSEN L., «Large Sample Properties of Generalised Methods of Moments Estimators», *Econometrica*, n. 50, 1982, pp. 1029-54.

[19] JOHNSTON B. - RYAN C., «The Impact of Controls on Capital Movements on the Private Capital Accounts of Countries' Balance of Payments: Empirical Estimates and Policy Implications», *IMF Working Paper*, WP/94/78, 1994.

[20] KENEN P.B., «Capital Controls, The EMS and EMU», *Economic Journal*, n. 105, 1995, pp. 181-92.

[21] MATHIESON D.J. - ROJAS-SUAREZ L., «Liberalisation of the Capital Account: Experiences and Issues», Washington, *IMF Occasional Paper*, n. 103, 1993.

[22] NEWEY W.K. - WEST D.W., «A Simple, Positive Semi-Definite, Heteroskedasticity and Autocorrelation Consistent Covariance Matrix», *Econometrica*, n. 55, 1987, pp. 703-8.

[23] OBSTFELD M., «Rational and Self Fulfilling Balance of Payment Crises», *American Economic Review*, n. 76, 1986, pp. 72-81.

[24] ——, «The Logic of Currency Crises», *NBER Working Paper*, n. 4640, 1994.

[25] PAGAN A.R., «Econometric Issues in the Analysis of Regressions with Generated Regressors», *International Economic Review*, n. 25, 1984, pp. 221-47.

[26] PAGAN A.R. - SCHWERT G.W., «Alternative Models for Conditional Stock Volatility», *Journal of Econometrics*, n. 45, 1990, pp. 267-90.

[27] PAGAN A.R. - ULLAH A., «The Econometric Analysis of Models with Risk Terms», *Journal of Applied Econometrics*, n. 3, 1988, pp. 87-105.

[28] PAGANO M., «Trading Volume and Asset Liquidity», *Quarterly Journal of Economics*, n. 104, 1989, pp. 255-74.

[29] TOBIN J., «A Proposal for International Monetary Reform», *Eastern Economic Journal*, n. 4, 1978, pp. 153-9.

Transaction Cost Politics and Economic Policy: A Framework and a Case Study

Avinash Dixit *
Princeton University, Princeton (NJ)

1. - Introduction

The paper critizes the conventional normative (social welfare maximizing) and positive (public choice) frameworks for the study of economic policy. It argues that the process of policy-making should be seen from a perspective that closely parallels transaction cost economics, and can be termed transaction cost politics. This approach emphasizes various limitations on information and actions, and sees the policy process as an ongoing effort to cope with these problems. The outcomes of such a process are found to exhibit low-powered incentives, path-dependence, and contain surprises for some or all of the participants. The framework is developed, and then illustrated using as a case study an account of the evolution of the GATT [1].

Economists usually think about and analyze economic policy in one of two frameworks, the normative approach based on the maximization of a Bergson-Samuelson type social welfare function, and the public choice or contractarian approach developed by

---

* The author is Professor of Economics.

N.B.: the numbers in square brackets refer to the Bibliography at the end of the paper.

[1] This paper is based on my *Munich Lectures in Economics*, 1994; the lectures will be published in full by the MIT Press (DIXIT A. [23]). I thank David Bradford, Bengt Holmström, Anne Krueger, Mancur Olson, Edmund Phelps, Hans-Werner Sinn, Oliver Williamson, and the conference discussants for valuable comments.

Buchanan and traced back to Wicksell. In this paper I will argue that each of these approaches has important defects. I will suggest a third perspective, based on the concepts adapted from the transaction cost economics pioneered by Oliver Williamson. This is to view economic policy-making as a dynamic process that tries to develop rules and organizations to cope with various limitations on the participants' information and actions. North [35] has considered some aspects of this idea, and labelled it transaction cost politics; I will develop it much farther, although limitations of space will force me to be brief. I will outline the main points, show how some of the burgeoning literature on political economy fits into the transaction cost politics framework, and then illustrate the ideas using as a case study the evolution of the GATT in the decades after the Second World War.

I begin by considering the two familiar approaches to economic policy analysis.

1.1 *The Normative Approach*

The normative approach views policy-making essentially as a control engineering problem, maximizing a social welfare function subject to various constraints. In its original form, the constraints were purely those of resource availability and technology. The resulting optimum was the first-best, and could be achieved in an idealized world with a compete set of perfectly competitive markets. Therefore policy intervention came to be seen as a remedy for various market failures. This was followed by the gradual recognition that policy has limits of its own. First came some constraints on the policy instruments, for example the impossibility of lump-sum taxation, which led to theories of second-best optimum commodity taxation and Ramsey pricing. Limits on the information possessed by the planner, and the need to elicit this from private agents, were examined next, and led to a rich theory of incentive schemes. Despite these limitations, it was found that the constrained optimal policy could generally improve upon a market outcome (Greenwald and Stiglitz, 1986), Stiglitz ([41], p. 28).

However, all through these developments, the assumption of a single maximizing policy-maker remained. This left out a crucial aspect of actual economic policy-making, namely the political process. To make a crude but effective caricature, normative policy analysis began by supposing that policy was made by an omnipotent, omniscient, benevolent dictator. The work on the second-best removed the omnipotence. That on information removed the omniscience. However, the assumptions of benevolence and dictatorship have remained. In fact there is no such dictator, and economic policy is the outcome of a game of strategy in which various affected persons and groups are the players. Many important features of policy in reality can only be understood in this way.

This recognition has gradually spread in the economics profession, and the last dozen years have seen many models of political economy that study equilibria of such games involving voters and political parties, regulators and lobbies, administrations and central banks, and so on. I will attempt to unify these into a transaction cost framework.

1.2 *The Public Choice Approach*

The longest-standing and best-known alternative to normative policy analysis is the public choice or contractarian framework of Buchanan and others; see Mueller [33] for a recent survey and exposition. Buchanan emphasizes the distinction between the constitution that governs the whole policy process, and individual instances of policy-making within this constitution. Each such instance, which I will call a policy act, is the outcome of a play of a game whose rules are set by the constitution. At the level of policy acts, we can conduct positive analysis that helps us understand the game, but there is no scope for normative analysis. Any normative considerations must be applied to the issues of constitution design. Moreover, Buchanan claims that individuals behind a Rawlsian veil of ignorance will be able to design the constitution on a basis of unanimity.

However, closer inspection reveals some weaknesses. If constitutions are contracts, they are very incomplete ones. They do not spell out the rules and procedures to be followed in every conceivable instance in precise detail. They leave much to be interpreted and determined in specific future eventualities. The reasons for this are basically the same as the reasons why most business contracts are incomplete, namely 1) the inability to foresee all the possible contingencies, 2) the complexity of specifying rules even for the numerous contingencies that can be foreseen, and 3) the difficulty of objectively observing and verifying contingencies so that the specified procedures may be put into action. In fact, constitutions last much longer, and they cover many issues, and more complex issues, than typical business contracts. Therefore their incompleteness is much greater and has more consequences. Interested participants can opportunistically manipulate the incomplete rules and procedures to their own advantage, and such games are of the essence in the making of individual policy acts.

Nor are constitutions made behind a veil of ignorance. The framers know very well the positions they will occupy, at least for the first several years of operation of the rules, and therefore try to write the rules so as to favor themselves. Thus constitution design is almost as political as policy acts.

It may be useful to draw a distinction between two functions of constitutions, setting specific rules for future actions, and laying down dispute-settlement procedures that are to be followed when faced with situations that are not covered by the rules. My observations apply with particular force to the first function; the drafters of the constitution have very clear stakes in specific substantive areas. The second function, however, may be more amenable to constitutional treatment. To borrow a term from the theory of the firm, it is tantamount to specifying residual rights of control, or asset ownership. As in that theory, there are sometimes good and commonly acceptable efficiency reasons for assigning these rights in particular ways.

On the other side of the picture, many policy acts have long-lived effects. They create facts, expectations, organizations, new interest groups, and even institutions, whose subsequent momentum and inertia gives them some of the same durability as a constitution itself. Therefore policy acts can often outlive their usefulness; there is a "politics of Qwerty" just like David's [10] economics of Qwerty.

1.3 *An "Evolutionary" Synthesis*

Thus the distinction between constitutional rules and policy acts is one of degree rather than one of kind. Rules are subject to erosion and reinterpretation, while acts can create durable facts and institutions. Therefore the policy process must be seen as dynamic, or even evolutionary, in its view of policy rules and acts. it should treat policy-making as a process in "real time", one that evolves and constantly combines some features of rule-making with some of individual acts, in varying degrees. Correspondingly, there is not a clear distinction between normative and positive analyses: there are some degrees of freedom at the level of policy acts for normative considerations, and there is a political game that needs to be studied positively at the level of constitutional design.

Stated thus, the view is very reminiscent of Williamson's "transaction cost economics", and with good reason. That approach builds upon the idea that economic transactions are beset by a number of costs arising from limitations on the participants' information and action, difficulties of observing some aspects of the goods or services being exchanged, difficulties of commitment, difficulties of carrying out perfect calculations in a complex environment, and so on. Perhaps even more importantly, it recognizes that the participants will anticipate this, and will try to design economic institutions and organizations in such a way as to cope with the transaction cost problems. The suggestion here is that the political process is beset by similar transaction costs, perhaps to an even greater degree, and that constitutions and policy acts contain mechanisms to cope with these costs. Therefore this view of the policy process can be called "transaction cost politics". Indeed, North [35] has done precisely that, and focussed on one specific kind of transaction cost, namely limited rationality. I will develop the idea in greater generality.

My aim is limited one. I am not concerned with politics or governance as a whole, only the operation of political mechanisms in the matter of making economic policy. Therefore I take for granted the background requirements of governance, such as the ultimate sanction of coercion, which Olson [36] has stressed. Also, as Williamson ([44], p. XII) himself recognizes, the transaction cost approach should be used in conjunction with, not instead of, other modes of analysis.

2. - The Transaction Cost Politics Perspective

Williamson [44] gives an excellent review and synthesis of the literature on transaction cost economics (TCE). He identifies some important forms of transaction costs, and methods and problems in dealing with them. I will group these costs into three, and will argue that each is present to an even greater degree in transaction cost politics (TCP). But first we should note some general points.

1) Each party to an economic contract thereby agrees to do something that benefits the others. Problems arise in specifying, monitoring, and enforcing compliance. Political contracts are similar agreements to convey benefits in return for political considerations like votes or contributions, and suffer similar problems to an even greater degree.

2) When a contract cannot lay down the actions to be taken in all the complex future contingencies, it must contain some provision for resolution of disputes, including the allocation of residual rights of decision-making. Since political contracts are less formal, and are rarely enforced by an outside authority like a court, such provisions are often more difficult.

3) It is pointless to contrast the outcomes of the process to some hypothetical ideal and declare them to be inefficient. We must ask whether any realistic mechanisms exist by which the process could better cope with the difficulties. Williamson [45] calls this the criterion of "remediableness".

4) We should recognize that parties to a relationship where mutually advantageous deals are thwarted by transaction costs will search for ways to get around the obstacles and thereby achieve better outcomes. Many seemingly puzzling contracts and institutions can be seen, upon closer examination, as just such methods for coping with transaction costs.

2.1 *A Taxonomy of Transaction Costs*

2.1.1 Bounded Rationality

TCE recognizes that the possible states of the world are so complex, and knowledge of the workings of the world so imperfect, that all feasible contracts are necessarily incomplete. Therefore ex post institutions (dispute settlement mechanisms) are very important. But the very complexity of nature makes these mechanisms less than perfect; the state of the world may not be observable ex post, or even if observed by the parties to the contract, may not be verifiable to an outsider whose job is to enforce it.

In TCP the uncertainty is even more pronounced. Explicit contracts that make political promises contingent upon various international developments, domestic shifts of opinion etc., would be impossibly complex. In many instances explicit contracts of this kind between economic interests and politicians or bureaucrats might be tantamount to bribery and therefore simply illegal, and imperfect informal substitutes for them would emerge. Dispute settlement mechanisms are even less effective because they must be internal to the process (e.g. election or impeachment). For all these reasons, political contracts are even less complete than economic ones, and bounded rationality has more serious bite.

2.1.2 Information-Impactedness

This term was introduced by Williamson to capture all aspects of limited and asymmetric information. It has a close parallel in the work of Stiglitz and others in information economics, where the corresponding concept is split into three different aspects: 1) a pre-contract informational advantage for one of the parties (adverse selection, leading to signalling and screening costs), 2) non-observability of the agent's action (moral hazard, leading to costs of monitoring or incentive schemes), and 3) non-verifiability of information to outsiders (leading to auditing costs or the costs due to misrepresentation when an audit is too costly).

In TCP, if there are no outside dispute settlement mechanisms anyway, then nothing further is lost by the lack of verifiability. It still inflicts costs on the transaction, because parties will take actions anticipation of this lack of verification; for example, underinvest. Other kinds of information asymmetries, namely adverse selection and moral hazard, are often more prevalent and more serious in TCP; for example political parties' true intentions are often hidden behind their publicly announced platforms. The voters must then try to infer the truth from observations of actions. Banks [4] treats signalling and screening models of this kind in politics.

2.1.3 Opportunism

In TCE, when actions of agents are unobservable, they are subject to moral hazard. The need to control it implies the need for suitable *ex ante* mechanisms (monitoring schemes and incentive payment contracts) as well as *ex post* (auditing and penalties, or similar other safeguards) ones.

Opportunism is particularly important in relationships that require one or both parties to invest in some assets specific to the relationship. This is because such an investor, having less good or no alternative uses for the asset, becomes vulnerable to expropriative demands of the other to renegotiate the terms of the contract, and anticipation of this danger will lead to underinvestment. There are similar aspects of asset specificity within the political process itself, but more importantly, these also interact with the performance of the economy. Thus: 1) Economic investments in specific assets may be deterred by fear of political hold-up (policy switch). 2) Politicians with specific assets (in locations, industries etc.) and their pivotal supporters with economic specific investments (human or physical capital specific to an industry) may together conspire to cause lock-in of policy.

Agency relationships in TCP are also more complicated. There are frequent occurrence of multiple agency, both horizontal (cabinet government, decentralized jurisdictions) and vertical (electorate, politician and civil servant, federal, state and local etc.). Similarly, there is frequent common agency (politicians beholden to, or bureaucrats answerable to, multiple interest groups). Monitoring of some branches (legislative and judiciary) is constant in the media, but that of others (executive, especially many of its agencies) is much harder. Wilson [46] has emphasized this multiplicity and complexity of agency relationships in politics and public administration. An open democratic system allows all interested parties to observe and influence the decision procedure of policy-making agencies. Therefore common agency is in a sense *the* essential feature of such a system.

It is the quintessential way political relationships differ from economic ones. I will argue that it leads to a severe weakening of the power of incentives that can be used in politics.

2.2 *Mechanisms to Cope with Transaction Costs*

2.2.1 Commitment and Delegation

Since opportunism generally arises from the freedom to take an action *ex post* in contravention of the contractual agreement, an obvious way to control it is to make a precommitment that limits this freedom. The device of commitment is probably the one most discussed in theoretical analyses of transaction cost politics, as well as the one most attempted in practice. Of course, a commitment must be credible if it is to have the desired effect. To be credible, in turn, the commitment must be 1) clear and observable to all *ex ante*, and 2) irreversible *ex post*. In practice, credibility is not an all-or-nothing matter, just as the dichotomy between constitutions and acts is not a clear binary choice. There are degrees of credibility, and the success of each commitment device depends on the degree it can achieve.

The two most commonly discussed devices of this kind are 1) taking an irreversible action in advance that locks one in and prevents future opportunistic deviation, 2) delegating the future action to someone who lacks the motives or opportunities to deviate. (For more general discussions of commitment devices, see Schelling [38] and Dixit - Nalebuff [14], Chapter 6).

Commitments carry a cost, namely the sacrifice of flexibility. In principle one could make a commitment to a contingent rule, which will specify the precise actions to be taken in all future eventualities, but this is often too complex to be feasible. This necessitates a trade-off between commitment and flexibility.

Theoretical analysis of problems of time-consistency and commitment began in the arena of macroeconomic policy with the famous article of Kydland and Prescott [26], and has developed into a large literature, dealing with commitments to control inflation, capital taxation, government debt, and so on. Persson and Tabellini [37] contains several prominent contributions, and an introduction by the editors. This material is sufficiently well-known that I need not spend any time on it, except to point out that it finds a natural and prominent place in the general scheme of transaction cost politics.

The literature on macroeconomic political economy has not previously made much contact with the work of Williamson and others. Analyses of regulatory policy are of course explicitly based on transaction cost ideas. The creation by the United States Congress of autonomous agencies to regulate industries is a commitment to refrain from politically motivated intervention in their future operation. However, these agencies are then subjected to numerous constraints, and subsequent attempts by Congress to micro-manage their functioning. These ideas are developed and illustrated in Noll ([31], pp. 1278-81), McCubbins, Noll and Weingast [30], Wilson ([46] pp. 242-3), Levy and Spiller [28].

2.2.2 Repetition and Reputation

The emergence of cooperation through repetition of plays in games like the *Prisoners' Dilemma* has long been known in game theory. To give a crude summary, cooperation is more likely 1) the longer the horizon of the relationship, 2) the more patient the players, in the sense that they do not discount future payoffs too much in relation to immediate ones, 3) the more quickly and more accurately a deviation is detected, and 4) the higher the cost inflicted by the punishment on the initial deviator. A thorough treatment of this theory is in Fudenberg and Tirole ([17], Chapters 4, 5).

A closely related idea is that of reputation. In a repeated relationship, each participant can stand to benefit by acquiring and preserving a reputation concerning his intentions or future actions. This leads to signalling games; (Fudenberg and Tirole, [17] Chapter 9).

Once again, these ideas have been well explored by researchers in the political economy of macroeconomic policy, for example in connection with sovereign debt; (Persson and Tabellini [37]). I will examine the aspect of international trade agreements below.

Moe [31] examines how the uncertainty of power in a democracy causes political parties to reach accommodations of various kinds. Policies that are enacted, and bureaucracies that are formed to implement them, embody some concessions to the current losers – fragmented authority, checks and balances, delays, and procedures that give the opposition opportunities to participate and influence the results. Moe argues that the result is delay, ineffectiveness and failure of decision-making. Tirole ([42] p. 17) also observes that political uncertainty stops governments from committing policies for the long term, but argues that when the government in power at any time is likely to be biased toward a particular group, letting it lock in policies that favor this group may be socially detrimental, so the checks and balances serve a good purpose.

2.2.3 Incentive Schemes

Next I consider the class of transaction costs that arise because of information asymmetries, where one party to the transaction does not know another's attributes like skill or tastes (adverse selection), or cannot observe another's actions like effort (moral hazard). The economist's standard answer to such problems is to design an appropriate incentive scheme. Indeed, if the better-informed party (the agent) is risk-neutral, then giving it all the rights to make decisions in return for a fixed fee, thus in effect selling the whole operation, will yield an ideal or first-best outcome. Here the agent keeps 100% of the marginal return to his effort or skill, and therefore has the full incentive to deploy skill. More generally, the need to share risk makes it optimal to give the agent some sure income but less than 100% of the marginal return. These second-best incentive schemes are therefore said to have lower power.

The theory of such schemes is very well advanced. Laffont and Tirole [27] is a thorough and masterly treatment; Armstrong, Cowan and Vickers ([1], Chapters 2, 3) give a compact but valuable exposition. By contrast, explicit use of such theory-based schemes in regulatory policy is almost unknown. The (*RPI-X*) schemes in the United Kingdom are perhaps the exception, and their theoretical basis is much simpler and intuitive.

Most importantly, it is observed that incentive schemes in the economic policy arena have very low power. Wilson [46] comments on this in connection with bureaucracies, and attributes it to two factors: government agencies have multiple tasks, and are answerable to multiple principals. He offers no formal analysis, but separately conducted formal modelling backs him up on both counts, particularly the latter.

Holmström and Milgrom [20] have developed a model of multitask agencies. They find two important results: 1) If the result of one task is very poorly observable, then the incentive scheme for a competing task must have lower power in order to avoid excessive diversion of effort away from this task to more observable ones. 2) If some tasks are primarily of value to the agent, and can be controlled in an all-or-nothing fashion, then it may be desirable for the principal to simply prohibit these, rather than try to give extra incentives for others. This point is especially important if the incentives for other tasks must be low-powered in conformity with the first result.

Tirole ([42], pp. 6-7) develops this idea further. He points out that when output of the agent's effort is an "experience good" whose quality will be revealed only with a delay, then the immediate incentive scheme must be low-powered so as not to destroy the incentive to maintain quality.

Dixit ([13], Appendix) shows how multiple principals (common agency) can dramatically reduce the power of incentives. The intuition is that each principal tries to free ride on the incentives provided by the others.

Suppose two principals *A* and *B*, are trying to influence the agent, who controls two tasks *a* and *b*. Principal *A* is primarily interested in the outcome of *a*, and principal *B* in that of *b*. The amount of effort the agent devotes to the tasks is not observable, but the outcomes are commonly observable to all.

Since the agent's time or effort is scarce, more spent on *a* will necessarily mean less spent on *b* and vice versa. Therefore principal *A* will offer an incentive scheme that responds positively to *a*-output and negatively to *b*-output, that is, gives the agent a marginal reward for producing more *a* and a marginal fine or penalty for producing more *b*. The scheme also has a constant term, or a sure payment, whose level can be adjusted to make sure that the agent is willing to work, that is, satisfy the agent's participation constraint. Similarly, principal *B* offers a scheme that rewards the agent for producing more of *b* and penalizes him for producing more of *a*.

Now suppose principal *A* offers a high-powered scheme, that is, one with larger marginal reward for producing an extra unit of *a*. When the agent responds by making more effort on task *a*, he gets more money from principal *A*; but because principal *B* employs a negative marginal payment for this task, the agent pays more to principal *B*. In other words, some of *A*'s money passes to *B* via the agent. Recognizing this, principal *A* will not find it desirable to offer such a high-powered scheme. The leakage of one principal's money to the other is less than one-for-one, so each principal continues to find it desirable to offer some incentives to the agent; but in the final outcome of the whole calculation, that is, the Nash equilibrium of the game of strategy between the principals, the overall power of the incentives received by the agent is quite low.

In the mathematical model, the outcome is very simple: the equilibrium with n principals is exactly as if there is just one hypothetical principal with an objective function which is the sum of all the separate principals' objectives, but the agent's risk aversion is multiplied n-fold. Remember that the more risk averse the agent, the lower the power of the incentive scheme. Thus the Nash equilibrium incentive scheme with n principals has, roughly speaking, only $(1/n)$-th the power of the second-best that would be offered by one truly unified principal.

Thus one must distinguish different levels of efficiency in the outcomes. The hypothetical ideal with observable efforts and Coasian bargaining between all principals and the agent would be the first-best. Respecting the information asymmetry, but allowing all principals to get together and offer a combined incentive scheme would give the second-best. If the principals cannot be so united, their Nash equilibrium is in general a third-best. See Bernheim and Whinston [5] for the exact relationships among these. In these formal terms, the result above says that the third-best outcome that is achieved has very low-powered incentives.

Tirole ([42], p. 4) offers yet another explanation for the low-powered incentives in policy-making. If there are several agents performing similar tasks and subject to common risks, then each agent's performance can be compared with that of the others to get a better estimate of his effort or skills which were not directly observable. Therefore an incentive scheme based on comparative performance, or "yardstick competition", can be effective and high-powered. In politics and bureaucracy, such competition is often limited or even non-existent; therefore incentives must have lower power. In some cases, for example provision of some urban services, competition can exist or even be created for the specific purpose of allowing better incentive schemes. We increasingly observe examples of this in garbage collection, mail delivery, and even in policing and prison management; Britain has recently set up an internal market mechanism in its National Health Service. However, the multi-task nature of these activities often precludes the use of such devices to their full extent; there exist other "principals" who are more interested in other dimensions of these agencies such as equity and accountability, and their influence limits the use of competition to promote efficiency; (Wilson [46], Chapter 19).

Finally, it was pointed out above that dispute resolution and safeguards must be largely internal to the political process. So must incentives. This can make it harder to sustain them, especially if the system is prone to a short-term outlook and therefore finds it difficult to develop or sustain a reputation, which requires a longer horizons.

It was argued above that the ability of several principals to exert simultaneous influence on agencies' actions is an essential feature of an opern democratic system. We see that it by itself causes a great diminution of the power of incentives, and also reinforces the other reasons (multiple tasks, lack of competition, and short-termism) for the weakness of incentives.

3. - A Case Study: The GATT

In this section I will examine the evolution of the GATT as case study through the transaction cost politics lens. It neatly illustrates how various transaction costs in the signatory countries' domestic politics as well as in their international trading relationships, and efforts to cope with these costs, influenced the design and the constitution of the organization, and its subsequent operation and evolution.

I focus on one key point of political tension, namely the *Prisoners' Dilemma* in maintaining a cooperative liberal trading regime, which generated repeated shifts in rules and procedures as the countries tried to manipulate the system in their own favor. The format combines a narrative of the developments, and some informal conceptual discussion of the role played by transaction costs in the story and how the actors in the drama attempted to cope with these costs. The treatment is brief, as befits the lecture in which the studies were first presented. The approach is neither formal theoretical modelling, nor formal statistical testing, nor detailed historical or institutional analysis. My sole aim is to highlight the transaction cost aspect of the situation, hoping thereby to convince the reader that these costs are significant in policy issues of major importance, and that the transaction cost politics framework is likely to be useful in more detailed studies of economic policy-making. The work should be regarded as suggestive, not definitive; but at that level I believe it serves well to illuminate the concepts by illustrating them.

There are several excellent histories and analyses of the GATT. From the legal and historical perspectives, Diebold [12], Dam [9], Jackson [23], and Hudec [21], [22] are noteworthy. Staiger [40] gives a detailed description of several GATT rules and procedures in connection with his survey of the theoretical literature on international trade agreements. Baldwin [3] also focuses on the economics, while Moser [32] analyses the political economy of the GATT from a public choice perspective. Bhagwati [6], Hathaway [18] and Snape [39] consider various aspects of GATT reform. Evans and Walsh [16] and Collins and Bosworth [8] are early studies of the structure and the likely economic effects of the new GATT or WTO. Destler [11] focuses on the politics of United States trade policy. I have drawn on all these studies, although I will not always cite them individually.

The key political conflict in international trade is a *Prisoners' Dilemma* for the group countries seeking to agree to a more liberal trading regime. Each country wishes to restrict its trade, sometimes because it wants to exert some national monopoly or monopsony, sometimes because it wants to pursue a strategic industrial policy that is at least in principle in its national interest, sometimes because trade barriers are thought to counter some domestic market failure, but mostly because some interest group powerful in its domestic politics wants protection from foreign competition. If all countries give way to this pressure, all will be losers. Therefore they have an incentive to get together and exchange credible promises of retaining open trade regimes. Of course, each retains an incentive to renege on such an agreement, and then to try and prevent others from doing the same. The story of the GATT is a playing out of these tensions. It is particularly interesting in its demonstration of how quickly a supposedly clean slate gets dirty in the political process.

3.1 *The Founding of the GATT*

The end of the Second World War was as good a time for making a completely new start, and laying down new rules and institutions for an international political and economic order, as there has ever been. A few major powers had unchallenged ability to impose their will; even after the rift between the Soviet Union and the Western powers, the latter had the freedom for several years to shape all economic arrangements outside the Soviet bloc. They had much experience to draw on; in particular, they could avoid the disastrous mistakes made at Versailles after the end of the First World War.

Three international economic institutions emerged from this endeavor, the International Monetary Fund (IMF), the International Bank for Reconstruction and Development (the World Bank), and the General Agreement on Tariffs and Trade (GATT). The last is in some ways the most interesting from the perspective of transaction cost politics. It was shaped by many unanticipated events, it evolved in ways quite different from those foreseen, and has a record of important successes as well as failures in its mission. It demonstrates very well the importance of politics and history in shaping economic policy. It carries some important lessons for the attempts to establish the new World Trade Organization, and some implications for its future. From the large and complex history of the GATT, I will pick just a few episodes that illustrate the forces and the effects of transaction costs.

The GATT was a strange constitution for world trade. It was made by countries with strong perceptions of their economic interests and their domestic political imperatives. In fact, although unbeknown to them, they were behind a veil of ignorance. The economics of world trade shifted faster than GATT did. This produced many surprises, only some of which could be remedied by a change in procedures to bring them into conformity with the changed political realities.

The GATT was not meant to be a permanent organization at all. It was an interim arrangement that was supposed to be replaced by a more powerful body, the International Trade Organization (ITO). This never came into being, because the United States, after playing a leading role in the negotiations that culminated in the *ITO Charter*, failed to ratify it. The reasons were a curious mix of domestic and international politics. The American business community did not support the ITO, some for the usual protectionist reasons, and others for perfectionist ones, they wanted an even more perfect free trade agreement and opposed the exceptions and escape clauses that were placed in the *ITO Charter* at the insistence of one country or another in the negotiations. Other interest groups in the United States, including labor unions, were halfhearted in their support. The Truman administration lacked support in Congress, and was unwilling to use up its political capital when more important issues such as the

Marshall Plan and the military build-up for the cold war demanded more attention. Facing defeat, President Truman withdrew the *ITO Charter* from Congress. In 1950 it was inconceivable for the world to proceed to an international trade agreement without the United States. Therefore the ITO was abandoned, and the GATT was allowed to continue. Diebold [12] describes and analyzes this episode.

This led to some strange consequences. GATT was not a treaty, although most countries regarded it as such. The results of negotiating rounds had to be given effect in US law by legislation that went the usual route through both Houses, and not by ratification in the Senate as would be the case for a treaty. Also, the countries in GATT were formally not members, but "contracting parties". A better term used by some economists is "signatories". The usage "members" is common except in GATT's formal documents, however.

3.2 *Enforcement Mechanisms*

Given its temporary purpose, GATT did not set up any effective enforcement procedures. These evolved gradually, under constant resistance by some member countries, and therefore remained weak, but it is not clear whether better mechanisms would have survived the political imperatives brought to the scene by the economically most powerful countries.

The procedure was roughly as follows. If country *A* violated some GATT agreement, another country *B* that suffered some economic consequences of this violation could bring a complaint to GATT. A panel was established to examine the complaint, and made a recommendation. This could include authorization for country *B* to take some retaliatory measure. The report of the panel was considered by the whole GATT. Its approval could in principle be by majority vote, but since 1959 the custom had been to require unanimity.

The weaknesses of this are numerous and obvious[2]. First, there were long delays in setting up the panels, although panels seemed to

[2] The following account is based on HUDEC R.E. [22], COLLINS S.M. - BOSWORTH B.P. [8] and EVANS P. - WALSH J. [16].

report in reasonable time once constituted. Second, when a panel's report was considered by the whole GATT, country *A* had the de facto ability to veto an adverse ruling. This wa like putting the accused on a jury that required unanimity. Third, if a country chose to ignore a ruling, or stalled in its compliance, there was not much that GATT can do. International opprobrium was no match for substantial domestic economic interests. Punitive measures by third countries, which would be much more effective, were explicitly ruled out in the GATT framework[3]. Fourth, if country *A* restricted some imports from country *B* in violation of its GATT obligations, then *B* was typically authorized to restrict some other imports from *A*. What this did was to hurt some innocent third parties in country *A*, not those import-competing interests in *A* who were politically powerful enough to obtain the protection, in violation of *A*'s GATT obligation, in the first place. Thus the punishment hit the wrong group in *A*, and was therefore less effective in securing *A*'s compliance (Moser [32], p. 34). Fifth, the whole process could be bypassed, as the case of voluntary export restraints discussed below reveals. Finally, the whole process was loaded in favor of the larger economic powers and against the smaller ones. The average compliance with panel rulings was quite good (over 80%), but the record of the more important larger countries was much worse. (Hudec [22] p. 362).

In the new WTO, panel reports are to be accepted automatically unless they are appealed by one of the parties and reversed under an established procedure, but the other weaknesses remain. In particular, it is difficult to see how the WTO can prevent voluntary bilateral deals among sovereign countries, particularly if they are the larger economic powers. Attempts to strengthen procedures will have little success unless they are backed by the political desire to make them succeed. In world trade such determination is weakened by the pressure of domestic interests.

Since an effective dispute settlement procedure is an important part of the mechanisms to cope with incomplete contracts, moral hazard, and opportunism, any international trade organization whose

---

[3] See Maggi G. [29] for a theoretical model that brings out the importance of multilateral punishments in sustaining cooperative trade agreements.

powers in this dimension are restricted must remain weak in its ability to deal with these important transaction costs.

3.3. *Safeguards or Loopholes?*

An important principle of the GATT is "tariff binding", whereby a trade-liberalizing tariff reduction once agreed cannot be reversed. Exceptions are allowed, however, to cope with sudden surges in imports that inflict serious harm on domestic import-competing industries, and in some other such instances. These are called "Safeguards" or "Escape Clauses". Non-tariff barriers are essentially prohibited in theory, although they are tolerated in practice, and were even officially recognized in a "code of conduct" that was part of the Tokyo Round of GATT negotiations.

These may seem blatant licenses to violate or bypass the founding principles or practices of the GATT, but it has been argued that they stem from a recognition of the inherent political weaknesses of the dispute settlement mechanism, and provide a safety valve that prevents a catastrophic failure. In a repeated *Prisoners' Dilemma* where the conditions are changing from one play to the next, there may be identifiable occasions when the advantages of cheating are larger. Unless the agreement allows some such actions, it cannot be sustained in equilibrium. In the case of trade liberalization, recessions or import surges in a country create large pressures for protection in its domestic politics. The Escape Clause allows temporary measures to relieve this pressure, and thereby helps hold together the rest of the agreement. Thus the loopholes may be a reasonable attempt to cope with the transaction costs of the complicated game of domestic and international politics unfolding over time. A theoretical analysis of this comes from Bagwell and Staiger [2] and is outlined below; see also the survey by Staiger [40] and Jackson's ([23], pp. 150-2) analysis from a lawyer's perspective.

For simplicity of exposition, consider a group of countries that are symmetrically related to each other, for example in the overall size of the economy and that of the export sectors of each, and ignore each country's internal politics. Let $U(T, t)$ denote each country's social welfare during one period, say a year, when its tariff rate is T and that of each of the other countries is t. A single-period non-cooperative Nash equilibrium t_0 is that rate which is the best for each country when all the others are using it, too. Formally, it is defined by the fixed-point problem:

$$T = t_0 \text{ maximizes } U(T, t_0)$$

Now consider the group in a repeated interaction, trying to sustain a cooperative common tariff rate t less than t_0. Each country has the temptation to cheat, and levy its own optimal higher tariff rate in response to the others' t. It can get away with this for only one period; thereafter cooperation will collapse and the situation will revert to repeated Nash play of t_0. Each country, in deciding whether to cheat, must balance the immediate gain against the future loss from so doing.

The benefit of cheating is given by:

$$B(t) = \max_T U(T, t) - U(t, t)$$

The cost of cheating is the capitalized value, at the appropriate interest rate r, of the drop in social welfare in going from the cooperative to the Nash outcome:

$$C(t) = [U(t, t) - U(t_0, t_0)]/r$$

These functions are shown in Graph 1. If the countries are not trying to sustain anything other than the non-cooperative Nash tariff level t_0, the benefit to one country from cheating is zero, as is the cost of cheating. Thus $B(t_0) = 0$ and $C(t_0) = 0$. Away from t_0, the benefit $B(t)$ rises on either side, and is a convex function of t because the farther away from the one-shot equilibrium the current situation, the more can one country gain by its deviation. $C(t)$ is a decreasing function, because the higher the current common level of the tariff, the less will one country be hurt by reversion to t_0. (If the current t is for some reason higher than t_0, then it will actually gain, so $C(t)$ is

GRAPH 1

COOPERATION IN REPEATED TARIFF GAME

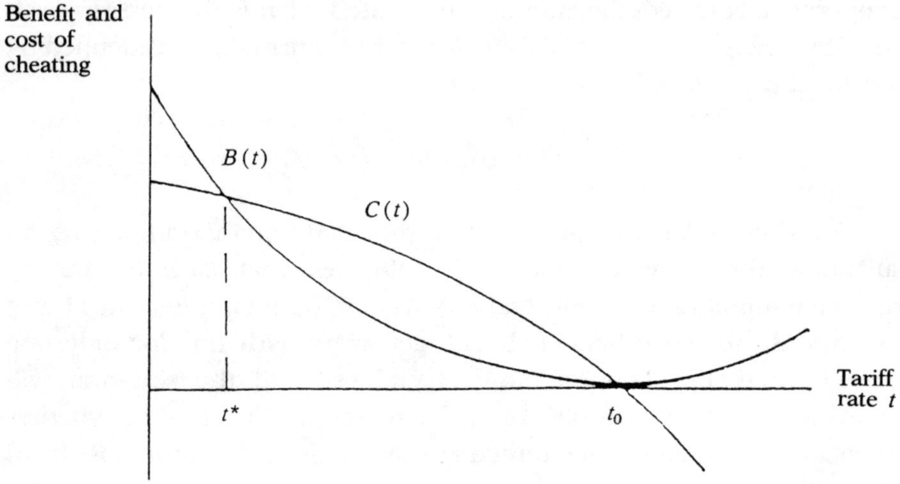

negative to the right of t_0, but that is not an economically relevant part of the picture). Since free trade is collectively optimal, $U\ (t, t)$ is maximized at $t = 0$; that is why the $C\ (t)$ curve is horizontal where it meets the vertical axis.

The $C\ (t)$ curve could stay above the $B\ (t_0)$ curve throughout the range $(0,\ t_0)$; then any cooperative arrangement to reduce tariffs would be self-sustaining, because for each member country the cost of cheating would be higher than the benefit. The graph shows a more interesting case where the two curves intersect at a positive t^* to the left of t_0. In the range $(t^*,\ t_0)$, the cost of deviation is greater than the benefit, so any tariff in this range is sustainable as a cooperative equilibrium of the repeated game. In particular, t^* is the lowest tariff (most cooperation) that can be so sustained.

The most important general idea conveyed by this analysis is just this limit on the feasibility of mutually beneficial cooperation. When no outside authority can enforce a cooperative agreement, attempting too much may give each member too great a temptation. In such a world, if we see the group of countries seeking more liberal trade but stopping short of complete free trade, we should not regard that as a political failure. Given the very real transaction costs – enforcement problems – they face, they may be doing the best they can. In Williamson's terminology, if the countries fail to achieve a cooperative tariff rate of less than t^*, this is not remediable. However, if they settle on a rate that exceeds t^*, then that is remediable because agreement on a tariff rate equal to t^* is feable.

The benefit and cost curves are determined by many things, including the rate at which the future is discounted, the accuracy and the delay with which deviations are observed, and by other possibly observable circumstances like economic booms or depressions. The above account leaves out all these details, but we can understand their effects by considering how they will shift the two curves. here are just a few of these considerations.

1) If the future is discounted more heavily, then $C(t)$, which is a discounted present value of future costs, is reduced in magnitude. Therefore the intersection t^* shifts to the right, less cooperation can be sustained. it is commonly believed that politicians have extremely short time horizons, and that the policy process operates with extremely high discount rates. Most governments, especially democratic ones, are under pressure from the media, the opposition, and the public, and are supposed to look for results demonstrable before the next election. Former British Prime Minister Harold Wilson's famous remark; "a week is a long time in politics", is an even more extreme statement of the same belief. Therefore repetition as a way of sustaining cooperation in policy games seems questionable. However, the political process can sometimes take a longer view, and major trade agreements seem to be such occasions. When ratification of various GATT rounds comes up, a concerted effort is usually made by diplomats, some media, and academics, to remind the public as well as politicians of the long term. Even then short-term arguments in favor of protection do arise, and they keep on arising with greater force in the interim years between these major economy-wide negotiationg rounds, as particular industries keep on confronting new trade-related problems.

2) If detecting cooperation becomes harder or slower, then $B(t)$ rises and again less cooperation can be sustained. Some observers of the GATT have claimed that its dispute settlement procedures, by

placing the onus to start them on the country that was hurt by another country's trade-restricting deviation, speeded up the detection of such deviations. However, the subsequent process, convening a panel, holding hearings, issuing a ruling, and subjecting it to a vote where the culpable country had an effective veto power – was slow and uncertain.

3) If countries can be made to fell some larger obligation to the international community, then a "psychic cost" adds to $C(t)$ and increases the range of possible cooperation. This may seem a slender thread to the economist, but some observers in trade law assert that this had some effect.

4) More subtly, the world is not stationary but is subject to various economic fluctuations. If one country is suffering from a depression, or is subjected to a sudden surge of imports that hurts some domestic groups particularly severely, this temporarily raises the benefit, economic or political, that it can gain from reneging on its trade agreements. This can lead to a collapse of the whole agreement. A wise system will anticipate this and allow for deviations in response to some clearly observed circumstances of this kind. Thus a country may be allowed to raise tariffs temporarily in response to some clearly defined circumstances without triggering a trade was. GATT's "Escape Clause" or "Safeguards" can be thought of as designed to serve exactly this purpose. Bagwell and Staiger [2] developed this idea.

3.4 *Rules versus Outcomes*

The GATT/WTO framework, like most policy constitutions, lays down rules. So long as these are being followed, the outcomes that result from the mixture of actions and chance are deemed acceptable. The United States has repeatedly expressed its dissatisfaction with the way this operates in the case of Japan. Japanese tariffs, and other formal barriers, are no higher than those of other major industrial countries. But many American companies find it very difficult to penetrate the Japanese market, and complain that the rules are not being observed in practice with the proper impartiality. The United

States government has been sympathetic; the Clinton administration most so. They want to use "objective measures", most commonly shares of United States exports in the Japanese market, as tests of whether Japan is actually complying with the broad rules of non-discrimination it claims to have[4].

The idea of using observable indicators when the magnitude that actually concerns us is not observable is, of course, well known in the economics of information. It forms the basis of the theory of incentive schemes to cope with moral hazard. The agent's output is a mixture of effort and chance. It is first-best to reward effort, but if that cannot be observed, using output is the best available substitute. If the Japanese cannot objectively demonstrate their compliance with the rules, and if the outcome is objectively measurable, then there is nothing wrong with using that. Of course the optimally designed scheme should recognize that a shortfall in the objective measure could be due to lack of compliance or to chance, and inflict a penalty that attempts to fit the former and not the latter. In other words, the power of the incentive scheme, in the sense that was explained in Section 2, should not be too high.

The more important objection to the United States position is that our firms' success also depends on their own efforts, which are equally difficult to verify objectively. If the United States wields its political stick on behalf of our firms, they may then relax their own efforts and expect to have export success delivered to them by political means. Coping with one side's moral hazard may aggravate the other side's, and the overal result may or may not be an improvement[5].

Incidentally, if Japan were to agree to apply "objective measures", say for autos or auto parts imports from the United States, these would be enforced by a Japanese government agency like the MITI. This would pose an inherent contradiction: it would strengthen

---

[4] There is a lively debate among economists about the facts of the situation; see a summary account in KRUGMAN P.R. ([25] pp. 116-9). I do not need to take part or sides in this; my only purpose here is to elucidate some transaction cost aspects of using rules and outcomes in this context.

[5] See BHAGWATI J.N. [6] for a strong, even impassioned, defense of the rules-based system.

the hand of exactly those bureaucrats whom the United States first accuses of controlling trade too much.

3.5 *Negotiating Rounds for Liberalization*

GATT's efforts at trade liberalization were conducted in several major negotiating rounds, culminating in the recent *Uruguay Round*. The idea was that bringing all relevant parties together to negotiate mutual removal of trade barriers in all sectors of the economy would make it easier to find and consummate mutually beneficial accords, by avoiding the need to find several "double coincidences of wants". In one respect the approach was very successful. Tariffs were negotiated downward, until they had effectively ceased to matter for imports into the advanced industrial countries. The most recent cuts in the *Uruguay Round*, in many cases down to zero, were relatively trivial.

Less developed countries (LDCs) retained higher tariffs and strict quotas on many manufactures. Formally, this was based on the GATT provision that temporary quotas could be used by countries with balance of payments problems, but the underlying rationale was usually some form of the "infant industry" argument for protection. After some four decades, it was only the poor experience with these measures, not any dynamics of GATT negotiations, that led may LDCs to recent moves toward unilateral trade liberalization (and more general economic liberalization).

More importantly, the tariff cuts did not eliminate the domestic political pressures for protection in any countries. These found their way into other protectionist measures, arguably with greater economic efficiency costs than the tariffs they replaced. More on this soon.

There are some features of these rounds that deserve special mention, because they bring out various aspects of transaction costs in negotiation. These include two important procedural devices: the "most favored nation" (MFN) principle, and "binding". The MFN principle says that any trade concession offered to one country must be automatically and equally available for all. This removes the fear in making preliminary deals that someone else will get a better deal in the future. The requirement of binding prevented countries from raising tariffs that had been lowered as a part of a previous round (except temporarily and under specified circumstances of domestic economic problems). This was to prevent countries jacking up tariffs as negotiating ploys in preparation for a coming round.

One other important point arises in the implementation of a GATT agreement in the member countries' domestic legislation. In parliamentary systems where the executive has de facto unchallenged powers during the lifetime of a government, this is not a problem; but in a system like the United States, the independent legislature may take the agreement as a mere starting point of a fresh set of negotiations, and attempt to extract further concessions to favor the interests it represents. Foreign countries, fearing this, would not make concessions to the executive in the original negotiations, and the whole process would stall. Therefore it is essential for the legislature to make a credible precommitment. In the United States this has taken the form of the "fast track" procedure: the legislation is subjected to a straight up-or-down vote, with limited debate and no amendments. Of course the legislature is reluctant to make such a commitment for any extended period, and the necessary frequent renewal becomes an item in the domestic political negotiations. I suspect that the new Europe will have similar separation of powers (in reality if not in theory), and will therefore have to devise a similar commitment mechanism if it is to participate credibly in trade negotiations of the future.

The new WTO is supposed to have a more continuous process of gradual measures of trade liberalization instead of the large fixed rounds of GATT. The merits of the two approaches are debatable, but the rounds have some distinct advantages. First, as we saw above, the explicit combination of issues and countries increases the possibility of formation of coalitions with mutually beneficial deals. Second, if industries or sectors are considered in isolation, the particular domestic import-competing interests in a country that is being asked to make concessions in this industry are concentrated with large per capita benefits from continued protection, whereas the beneficiaries of liberalization – consumers of the imported good who benefit from low prices, and all exporters who gain a little as the import-competing sector releases some resources – would be diffuse with small per capita stakes. The rounds bring together all these interests, making it more likely that the overall national interest is shared by most. Finally, the explicit reciprocity highlights the benefits to domestic exporting interests, and thereby marshals their support for liberalization (Moser [32], p. 22).

3.6 *Tariffs Versus Quantitative Restrictions*

The lowering and binding of tariffs caused various domestic import-competing interests to look for other means of protection. The GATT forbids quotas, except (oddly) on grounds of temporary balance-of-payments difficulties. Also, such attempts to circumvent the effects of the agreed tariff cuts could induce the exporting countries to make a complaint to GATT. At the minimum, this would bring the importing country some inconvenience and bad reputation.

The procedural answer was a variety of bilaterally agreed quantitative restrictions – "voluntary" export restraints (VER), "voluntary" restraint agreements (VRA), and orderly marketing arrangements (OMA). The idea was that the importing country would persuade the exporting country to take on the task of restricting trade. As compensation, and to induce it not to complain to the GATT, it would get to keep the economic rent associated with the restriction. The sums of these rents have been estimated for a number of such restraints, and are quite substantial.

Rents, at least, are merely transfers between countries. But such restraints also inflict aggregate costs – deadweight losses – since they increase consumer prices above marginal costs, either simply restricting supply or by facilitating monopoly or oligopoly pricing. For example, where the exporting country had some monopoly power, the reduction in exports might actually improve its terms of trade to an extent that it would actually benefit from the action, which it presumably could not have taken unilaterally for fear of disappointing some of its exporters. In others, where firms in the exporting and importing countries are in an oligopolistic relationship, the restriction can act as a collusion-facilitating device (Krishna [24]). In all these instances, consumers in the importing country are the losers, but they are not politically organized. There are also large dead-weight losses from the monopoly pricing, but these go unrecognized.

Here is an example where the system fails to cope with transaction costs at all efficiently. In part the problem is that tariffs, being an easily visible and controllable instrument of protection, were subjected to liberalization, and the countries had to have recourse to less efficient means of satisfying their domestic political interests. GATT might have done better to be less ambitious and allowed a larger cushion of tariffs to be used in specified circumstances. In other words, something similar to the safety valve of the Escape Clause would have served the system as a whole better.

In the WTO, such bilateral or small-group voluntary arrangements are formally forbidden, but how that organization is going to enforce this ban on consensual acts between sovereign countries is not clear.

3.7 *The Multi-Fiber Arrangement*

The most complex example of mutually agreed quantitative restrictions is the system of bilateral quotas in textiles and clothing. This is of special interest from the transaction cost politics perspective. It shows how a constitution has to make exceptions to respond to real forces, and how actions can have long-lasting effects[6].

The starting point was a "voluntary" agreement to restrict Japanese exports of cotton textiles to the United States. This was concluded in 1957, in response to pressures from United States textile producers, with the aim of giving them some breathing space to adjust and contract. It was supposed to last five years. It led to the growth of imports into the United States from other low-wage Asian countries. Then, under the threat that the United States would impose restrictions unilaterally, these countries were also brought into the agreement. The United States also pressured GATT to sanction this special

---

[6] The brief history below is based on YOFFIE D.B. - GOMES-CASSERES B. ([47] Chapter 18).

exception to its MFN principle and its prohibition of quotas. The results was called the Short Term Agreement. Within one year, it became the Long Term Agreement.

This led to a chain of substitution, both in private responses and in policy responses, that is easy to understand in the light of hindsight. Cotton textiles were defined as those with cotton content of 50% or more, so exporting countries shifted to blends including synthetic fibers. Asian exporters also expanded in European markets, and these countries wanted to impose their own restrictions. In the meantime Japan's economy had transformed to the point where it became an importer of textiles and clothing, and its producers wanted protection from the low-wage Asian countries' exports. Newer lower-wage exporters stepped in to replace the existing exporters subject to the quotas, and they were roped into the agreement whenever they became important enough to be perceived as a threat to the importing countries' domestic producers. Soon the agreement became a multi-country, multifiber, multi-garment maze of restrictions.

All the time, the preamble of the agreement paid lip service to the merits of trade: "to promote on a sound basis the development of production and expansion of trade in textile products". But Article 1 spoke of «special practical measures ... ensuring the orderly and equitable development of this trade and the avoidance of disruptive effects in individual markets». One does not need to ask what was the true purpose. Every renegotiation of the agreement spoke of allowing trade to expand, but in reality the restrictions were repeatedly tightened. The breathing space for the United States industry has lasted almost 40 years. New investment and employment has taken place under the protection of the agreement, and the domestic political forces for protection remain strong.

In the WTO, the quotas of the MFA are to be replaced by "equivalent" tariffs that initially restrict imports to the levels of the current quotas; this process is called "tariffication". The tariffs are then to be gradually phased out over a period of ten years. When we assess the likelihood of this becoming reality, we should remenber that the initial textile agreement itself was intended to last for only five years, but has lasted for more than thirty, and has if anything grown more restrictive and all-encompassing over this time. We should not be surprised to see the emergence of some loophole that justifies the perpetuation of the restrictions well into the next century.

3.8 *Agriculture*

Agriculture was treated differently from manufactures in the GATT[7].Most importantly, export subsidies (or price supports that had the effect of promoting exports) for manufactures were per se illegal, while those for agricultural products were treated much more leniently. First they merely had to be reported. Then they were made illegal if they caused the subsidizing country to get "more than an equitable share of world trade"; given the difficulty of defining equitable, this was a meaningless provision. Similarly, quantitative restrictions could be applied to imports of agricultural products for various reasons including "enforcement of domestic production or marketing restriction measures", to "remove a temporary surplus", etc. Again, judging these matters was effectively impossible. This special treatment was not the result of demands by the European Community (which did not then exist), nor by Japan (which was not then a member), but the United States. In fact the special treatment was tailored to the needs of the United States farm programs then in existence. Years later, the provisions were exploited by Europe for its Common Agricultural Policy, and Japan for its import bans on rice, beef etc., and the United States fought many fruitless battles to extend the standard GATT rules to agriculture[8].

The new GATT, or WTO, seeks only a partial reform. With a long transition period, export subsidies are to be cut by an average of 36%, and price supports by 20%. Non-tariff barriers are to be converted to their equivalent tariffs. In some cases such tariffs are very high, for

---

[7] The followng brief history is based on HATHAWAY D.E. (pp. 105-6, 108).

[8] A similar "biter bit" story comes from the auto industry. In the 1950s Japan and Italy concluded a bilateral agreement to restrict imports of autos from each other to a very small number. This move was initiated by Japan, which feared that its industry would not be able to compete with Italian imports. Two decades later, this agreement became the basis for serious market share restrictions on Japan's auto exports to all of the European Community.

example the tariff equivalent to Japan's import ban has been variously estimated at somewhere between 450% and 700%. over a longer period, it is hoped that these tariffs will be negotiated downward.

This is probably as much as could be hoped; Hathaway ([18], pp. 142, 144-5) counseled a similar compromise. But what are the prospects of even this much being realized? Again, I believe that the countries' commitments reflected in these agreements are not by themselves credible. If their internal political forces a year later call for a continuation of the existing supports or protection, a way will be found to do so. In the case of a powerful bloc like Europe or a powerful country like Japan, the WTO will be unable to prevent this, and will sanction a special arrangement just like the MFA. The hope must be that during the intervening period, the power of the agricultural groups in these countries will wane. Political economy offers some theoretical support to the idea that the power of special interests collapses when they get too small; see Cassing and Hillman [7], Hillman ([19] pp. 34-35) and Epstein and O'Halloran [15]. But food self-sufficiency has a powerful emotional or nationalistic ring, and agriculture has cultural or sentimental appeal in many countries, especially Japan and France. Therefore the outcome is difficult to predict.

Since GATT mixes elements of domestic and international politics, it is not surprising that its mechanisms to cope with transaction costs work less well than those in domestic politics alone. Shortfalls from an ideal standard of efficiency are easy to spot, but feasible changes – remediability – is much harder. The only general finding seems to be the merit of accepting the second- or third-best, for example allowing some limited and temporary escape clauses even when they depart from the ideal, so long as they are an important requirement to help preserve the larger system over the longer haul.

4. - General Lessons About the Policy Process

In this paper I have suggested the concept of "transaction cost politics" as an organizing framework for many issues that arise in the analysis of the political process of economic policy-making. A complete construction of such a framework will require a large and long research program, toward which the paper provides only a brief start. I hope it will arouse the interest of readers and generate more ideas, questions and criticisms. Any conclusions at this point must be very tentative. However, with this caveat, the theoretical analysis of Section 2 and the case study of Section 3 suggest a few things about the policy process and its analysis.

First, and as a precondition to everything else, we should recognize that the political process of economic policy-making is an ongoing game among several players. Each of these players has some information or action advantage, presenting problems of adverse selection, moral hazard, and opportunism, and making it harder to sustain mutually beneficial cooperation. Above all, political agencies must answer to many principals. We should understand the weakness or even the absence of conventional incentives in this light.

Such games can have multiple equilibria, and the rules or the objectives of players can change while the game is being played. This makes the outcomes path- or history-dependent. We should understand this, and recognize some observed features of reality as the products of accident, not consciously intended or put in place by anyone.

Where degrees of freedom are available for normative use, policy-makers should try to put in place, and facilitate the operation of, various "coping mechanisms". They should work to reduce informational asymmetries and improve mechanisms that can control opportunism. Conversely, they should try to avoid policies that create new transaction costs or increase existing ones. Policies like import quotas and price controls that create artificial rent, and then lead to political games to capture and perpetuate these rents, are particularly pernicious in this regard. Of course, many actors in the political process are trying to achieve exactly the opposite, namely create rents that they can then appropriate for their private ends regardless of the social costs. The economist's informative and persuasive role is very important in countering these forces.

Where political and economic specific investments are needed, policy should try to match the two sides' burdens and opportunities, and ensure sufficient longevity of their interaction, to enable them to avoid exploitation using mutual "hostage" or "reputation" mechanisms.

When we judge the performance of a policy-making system, we should admit the legitimacy of non-economic goals, and ask if a system that appears inefficient in its economic performance is in fact doing a reasonable job of serving a balance between the various interests, or multiple principals, given the transaction constraints.

Finally, we should not try impose, and perhaps not even think in terms of, too stringent or idealistic standards of some kind of "first-best" that ignore transaction costs. Repeated attempts to pursue goals such as completely free international trade, or fully balanced budgets, seem like Dr. Johnson's characterization of remarriage, "a triumph of hope over experience".

BIBLIOGRAPHY

[1] ARMSTRONG M. - COWAN S. - VICKERS J., *Regulatory Reform: Economic Analysis and British Experience*, Cambridge (MA), MIT Press, 1994.

[2] BAGWELL K. - STAIGER R.W., «A Theory of Managed Trade», *American Economic Review*, vol. 80, n. 4, September 1990, pp. 779-95.

[3] BALDWIN R.E., «The Economics of the GATT», in BALDWIN R.E. (ed.), *Trade Policy in a Changing World Economy*, Chicago (IL), University of Chicago Press, 1988, pp. 137-47.

[4] BANKS J.S., *Signaling Games in Political Science*, Reading (UK), Harwood Academic Publishers, 1991.

[5] BERNHEIM B.D. - WHINSTON M., «Common Agency», *Econometrica*, vol. 54, n. 4, July 1986, pp. 911-30.

[6] BHAGWATI J.N., *The World Trading System at Risk*, Princeton (NJ), Princeton University Press, 1992.

[7] CASSING J.H. - HILLMAN A.L., «Shifting Comparative Advantage and Senescent Industry Collapse», *American Economic Review*, vol. 76, n. 3, June 1986, pp. 516-23.

[8] COLLINS S.M. - BOSWORTH B.P. (eds.), *The New GATT: Implications for the United States*, Washington (DC), Brookings, 1994.

[9] DAM K.W., *The GATT: International Law and Economic Organization*, Chicago (IL), University of Chicago Press, 1970.

[10] DAVID P., «Clio and the Economics of Qwerty», *American Economic Review*, vol. 75, n. 2, *Papers and Proceedings*, May 1985, pp. 332-7.

[11] DESTLER I.M., *American Trade Politics*, Washington (DC), Institute for International Economics, 2ª ed., 1992.

[12] DIEBOLD W., «The End of the ITO», Princeton University, International Finance Section, *Essays in International Finance*, n. 16, October 1952.

[13] DIXIT A., *The Making of Economic Policy: A Transaction Cost Politics Perspective*, Cambridge (MA), MIT Press, forthcoming 1996.

[14] DIXIT A. - NALEBUFF B., *Thinking Strategically: The Competitive Edge in Business, Politics, and Everyday Life*, New York, Norton, 1991.

[15] EPSTEIN D. - O'HALLORAN S., «Common Agency and Representation», Columbia University, *Working Paper*, April 1994.

[16] EVANS P. - WALSH J., *The EIU Guide to the New GATT*, London, Economist Intelligence Unit, 1994.

[17] FUDENBERG D. - TIROLE J., *Game Theory*, Cambridge (MA), MIT Press, 1991.

[18] HATHAWAY D.E., *Agriculture and the GATT: Writing the Rules*, Washington (DC), Institute for International Economics, 1987.

[19] HILLMAN A.L., *The Political Economy of Protection*, Reading (UK), Harwood Academic Publishers, 1989.

[20] HOLMOSTRÖM B. - MILGROM P., «Multitask Principal-Agent Analysis: Incentive Contracts, Asset Ownership, and Job Design», *Journal of Law, Economics, and Organization*, vol. 7, Special Issue 1991, pp. 24-51.

[21] HUDEC R.E., *The GATT Legal System and World Trade Diplomacy*, 2 edn., Salem (NH), Butterworths, 1990.

[22] ——, *Enforcing International Trade Law: The Evolution of the Modern GATT Legal System*, Salem (NH), Butterworths, 1993.

[23] JACKSON J.H., *The World Trading System: Law and Policy of International Economic Relations*, Cambridge (MA), MIT Press, 1989.

[24] KRISHNA K., «Trade Restrictions as Facilitating Practices», *Journal of International Economics*, vol. 26, nn. 3-4, May 1989, pp. 251-70.

[25] KRUGMAN P.R., *The Age of Diminished Expectations*, Cambridge (MA), MIT Press, 1990.

[26] KYDLAND F.S. - PRESCOTT E.C., «Rules Rather Than Discretion: The Inconsistency of Optimal Plans», *Journal of Political Economy*, vol. 85, n. 3, June 1977, pp. 473-90.

[27] LAFFONT J.J. - TIROLE J., *A Theory of Incentives in Procurement and Regulation*, Cambridge (MA), MIT Press, 1993.

[28] LEVY B. - SPILLER P.T., «The Institutional Foundations of Regulatory Commitment», *Journal of Law, Economics, and Organization*, vol. 10, n. 2, 1994, pp. 201-246.

[29] MAGGI G., «The Role of Multilateral Institutions in International Trade Cooperation», Stanford University, *Working Paper*, November 1993.

[30] MCCUBBINS M.D. - NOLL R.G. - WEINGAST B.R., «Administrative Procedures as Instruments of Political Control», *Journal of Law, Economics, and Organization*, vol. 3, n. 2, Fall, 1987, pp. 242-77.

[31] MOE T.M., «The Politics of Structural Choice: Toward a Theory of Public Bureaucracy», in WILLIAMSON O.E., *Organization Theory*, New York, Oxford University Press, 1990, pp. 116-53.

[32] MOSER P., *The Political Economy of the GATT*, Grüsch (Switzerland), Verlag Rüegger, 1990.

[33] MUELLER D.C., *Public Choice II*, Cambridge (UK), Cambridge University Press, 1989.

[34] NOLL R.G., «Economic Perspectives on the Politics of Regulation», in SCHMALENSEE R. - WILLING R. (eds.), *Handbook of Industrial Organization*, vol. II, Amsterdam, North-Holland, 1989, pp. 1253-87.

[35] NORTH D.C., «A Transaction Cost Theory of politics», *Journal of Theoretical Politics*, vol. 2, n. 4, 1990, pp. 355-67.

[36] OLSON M., «Dictatorship, Democracy, and Development», *American Political Science Review*, vol. 87, n. 3, September 1993, pp. 567-76.

[37] PERSSON T. - TABELLINI G., «Monetary and Fiscal Policy», vol. I, *Credibility*, Cambridge (MA), MIT Press, 1994.

[38] SCHELLING T.C., *The Strategy of Conflict*, Cambridge (MA), Harvard University Press, 1960.

[39] SNAPE R.H. (ed.), *Issues in World Trade policy - GATT at the Crossroads*, Basingstoke (UK), MacMillan, 1986.

[40] STAIGER R.W., «International Rules and Institutions for Trade Policy», in GROSSMAN G.M. - ROGOFF K., in *Handbook of International Economics*, Amsterdam, North-Holland, 1995.

[41] STIGLITZ J.E., *Whither Socialism?*, Cambridge (MA), MIT Press, 1994.

[42] TIROLE J., «The Internal Organization of Government», *Oxford Economic Papers*, vol. 46, n. 1, January 1994, pp. 1-29.

[43] WILLIAMSON O.E., *The Economic Institutions of Capitalism*, New York, The Free Press, 1985.

[44] ——, «Transaction Cost Economics», in SCHMALENSEE R. - WILLIG R., *Handbook of Industrial Organization*, vol. I, Amsterdam, North-Holland, 1989, pp. 135-82.

[45] WILLIAMSON O.E., «The Politics and Economics of Redistribution and Efficiency» University of California, Berkeley, *Working Paper*, 1994.

[46] WILSON J.Q., *Bureaucracy: What Government Agencies Do and Why They Do It.* New York, Basic Books, 1989.

[47] YOFFIE D.B. - GOMES-CASSERES B., *International Trade and Competition*, New York, McGraw-Hill, 1994.

An Economic Analysis of Proposals for Constitutional Fiscal Constraints

Giovanni Somogyi *
Università «La Sapienza», Roma

The origins of the present plight of Italy's public finances lie far back in the past. In the 1960s, but above all in the 1970s, the growth rate of public spending was well above that of fiscal and social welfare revenues more or less everywhere in the western world. The result, with few exceptions, was the formation of high volumes of public debt.

This complex dynamic was to a large extent physiological: even in less statist countries, the public authorities took on more responsibilities (such as funding scientific and technological research, ensuring adequate health services, environmental protection, international cooperation and so forth). It is therefore not surprising that the revenues lagged behind spending; and only natural then that high levels of debt came into being. As usual, however, what was physiological abroad became pathological in Italy. Italy's public spending increased dramatically to satisfy not only the needs mentioned above but also and above all, unfortunately, other needs, such as patronage, welfare, and gaining votes, which were well known to all. To take only one example, Italy's millions of disability pensions make it seem as though Italians have the worst health in the world. But more generally, for decades Italy's political set-up survived thanks to the distribution of public funds to nearly all social groups.

---

* The author is Professor of Industrial Economy.

As for revenues, there was no serious consideration of the problem for a long time. The concept that states, albeit in a long term, are subject to the same rules which apply to companies and families would appear to be unknown in Italy. Companies and families can also borrow, and often they do well to do so, but companies are usually aware that excessive borrowing may court bankruptcy and all normal families follow the rule that spending (including that for servicing debts) should not exceed income. The Italian state has instead pursued another rule: one first spends and then decides how to pay.

This was the logic that, for a long time, led to deficit financing and hence continuing inflationary pressures. In 1979, Italy entered the EMS and in 1981, after its «divorce» from the Treasury, the Banca d'Italia progressively shed its role of lender of last resort to the state. It was thought that this would engender a discipline whose premise would be that the funds necessary to cover the difference between revenues and public spending would be procured by resorting solely to existing saving. But this was not to be, unlimited recourse to the savings market was believed possible and hence public debt continued to grow in the hands of families, companies and banks at the price of very high interest rate levels. If savers are offered government notes at conditions which cannot be matched by others bidding for the same savings, any discipline and constraint is annulled; the individual savers cannot realise that they are setting off on a path which is in the long term disastrous for society as a whole (this is the task of governments and Parliaments) and as a result the productive economy is progressively debilitated.

Lax spending policies have been the order of the day for far too long and beyond any reasonable limit. It is inappropriate to speak of spending cuts, which appear rather difficult (even though in 1994 there was a slight reduction in absolute terms). What would appear to be reasonable to propose, in a situation such as that which Italy now faces, is that the growth rate of public spending should not exceed that of GDP.

The usual objection to this proposal is that there is at least one spending component, debt interest, which is totally outside the control of the public authorities. But this objection does not hold. If we

TABLE 1

GDP, PUBLIC-SECTOR REVENUES AND SPENDING
(annual growth rates)

Year	GDP	Tax and soc. sec. revenues*	Total spending*	Spending net of interest*
1982	17.5	25.3	23.2	21.1
1983	16.2	20.8	19.7	19.3
1984	14.6	14	14.7	13.2
1984	11.7	12.5	14.6	15.1
1986	11	12	10.8	9.4
1987	9.3	11.9	8.2	9.3
1988	11	12.6	11.2	11
1989	9.3	14.5	11.7	10.1
1990	9.9	11.7	13.4	12.3
1991	8.9	11.5	9.8	8.4
1992	5.2	11.4	9	6.7
1993	3.1	6.6	6.3	5.7
1994	5.7	−0.5	−0.6	0.9
1995	8.1	8.6	4.3	2.2

* Net of imputed social security contributions.
Source, calculations from BANCA D'ITALIA data, *Governor's Report*, various years.

compare spending net of interest and GDP, we can see that in the last fifteen years, from 1981 to 1995, public spending net of debt interest increased by 10.2% per year, higher than the growth rate of GDP which was 10% per year.

Even in the latter years of this period, when there was a serious risk of a public finance crisis, the increase in spending net of interest was greater than that of GDP; this was the case for example in 1989, 1990, 1992 and 1993 (Table 1).

It is obvious that if public spending increased faster than GDP, it also increased faster than inflation. Therefore, public spending increased strongly in real terms, even though it was already very high in both absolute terms and with regard to the size of the Italian economy at the start of the 1980s.

When one speaks of the alleged insuperable difficulties of cutting or even merely braking public spending, one does not reflect on the circumstance that if, for example, public spending net of interest increased in the period 1986-1993 in line with inflation, at an average 5.5% per year, i.e., if it had remained unchanged in real terms for only eight years (and nobody could reasonably claim that in such circumstances mortality would have increased or that Italy would have risked remaining dangerously exposed to the threat of military attack or that essential public works would not have been realised or that public offices would have ceased to function) in 1993 Italy's net balance of public accounts would have totalled 5,835 billion lira and not 148,114 billion lira (furthermore, since in this case there would have been less debt service, in 1993, Italy's public accounts would have been in the black).

Another example: if in the decade 1984-1993, public spending net of interest had increased in line with GDP, i.e., had maintained its already high proportional weight vis-à-vis the size of the Italian economy, in 1993 Italy's public-sector net balance would have totalled 95,499 billion lira and not the aforementioned 148,114 billion lira (and again in this case it would have been considerably less, again as a result of the less onerous debt service). Such a deficit today seems like something out of science fiction.

As the vicissitudes of the Italian economy of the last decades have been somewhat akin to western films where the rescuers appear at the end, we can perhaps take consolation in the fact that in the last two years there have been signs of an inversion (or perhaps it is more appropriate to say the signs of a coming to one's senses). In 1994, GDP grew by 5.7% against an increase in spending net of interest of 0.9% (global public spending, if calculated net of imputed social security contributions, actually decreased by 0.6%). In 1995, GDP grew by 8.1% and spending net of interest by 2.2% (global spending by 4.3%).

In 1994, tax and social security contribution revenues also experienced a beneficial pause, thus enabling the fatigued national economy to enjoy a breathing space.

In previous years, to avoid an unremitting rise in interest rates, the spending dynamics had forced a dramatic increase in fiscal pressure. This pressure, defined as the ratio between taxes and real social security contributions on the one hand and GDP on the other, equalled 30.7% in 1981 while by 1993 it had reached the appalling

TABLE 2

PUBLIC-SECTOR REVENUES AND SPENDING
(as % of GDP)

Year	Tax and soc. sec. revenues[1]	Total spending[1]	Spending net of interest*
1981	30.7	44.9	38.8
1982	32.7	47.1	40
1983	34	48.5	41
1984	33.8	48.5	40.5
1985	34.1	49.8	41.8
1986	34.4	49.7	41.2
1987	35.2	49.2	41.2
1988	35.7	49.3	41.2
1989	37.4	50.4	41.5
1990	38	52	42.4
1991	38.9	52.4	42.2
1992	41.5	54.3	42.8
1993	42.9	56	43.9
1994	40.2	52.7	41.9
1995	40	50.9	39.7

* Net of imputed social security contributions.
Source, calculations from BANCA D'ITALIA data, *Governor's Report*, various years.

level of 42.9%. The growth rate of revenues had even surpassed the strong increase in spending (which averaged 13.6% per year in the period 1981-1993) (Table 2).

It should be recalled here that 1992 and 1993 in particular were characterised by a full-blown «fiscal panic» engendered by the threat of a crisis of confidence on the part of savers which would have led to deficit-financing and hence to high inflation and a worrying stop to the process of European integration. Fiscal folly or madness are the proper terms here when talking of measures such as the tax on bank and post-office accounts (which was one of the determinant causes of the lira crisis), the tax on family doctors (which was not paid by millions of tax-payers and was thus the first case of mass tax evasion, crowned by complete success for the tax-evaders, in the history of the Italian Republic. Significantly the entire affair is now shrouded in silence), the «lunatic» income tax return forms distributed in May 1993, the tax on balconies which was blocked by Minister Tremonti.

These are only some of the more sensational examples of such folly.

As has just been observed, in 1994, concurrent to the pause in spending, fiscal and social security contribution revenues also fell slightly in absolute terms and there was a significant decrease in fiscal pressure (to 40.2% of GDP). In 1995, however, not only did spending increase, but there was a further increase in revenues which lifted fiscal pressure to 40.4% of GDP. Therefore, despite the lull of 1994, the problem of fiscal pressure is still there.

If the remedies were to be concentrated solely on the spending side, scepticism would, I believe, be justified. Italy is perhaps the sole country in the world where the increases in spending are always real while the decreases in spending are always virtual; in other words, it is the only country in the world where it can be stated in complete seriousness that, if spending had been left to its own momentum, it would increase, for example, by 100,000 billion, but thanks to the government's «vigilance», it will increase by only 50,000 billion and hence the government can claim the credit for having «cut» spending by 50,000 billion lira. Everyone, for example, recalls the famous minibudget of 90,000 billion lira (later reduced to 75,000 billion) announced by the Amato government in September 1992. In 1993, fiscal and social security revenues actually increased by 60,000 billion lira; for the Italian language to have any meaning, a budget designed to correct the public accounts by 75,000 billion lira should have ended with a reduction in spending of 15,000 billion lira. Instead, public-sector spending increased by 50,000 billion lira.

In the past, as noted above, it was thought that spending could be braked as a result of the so-called divorce between the Treasury and Banca d'Italia, the idea being that closing the channel of deficit financing and leaving open only that of recourse to savers would place a serious constraint on public spending. This was a mere illusion. Public spending has continued to increase, even though interest rates have reached levels which seriously endanger the possibility of production growth and the creation of jobs by the Italian economy.

The time has now come to impose stricter constraints. In particular, I believe that it is necessary to block fiscal revenues at their present level, even resorting to constitutional constraints, which should be more effective than Article 81 of the Constitution which has to date served little purpose. The reasons for this proposal are that the high level of fiscal pressure risks further amplifying the pernicious reactionary effects of high interest rates and also because stable or diminishing fiscal pressure would gradually lead to a rationing of spending, i.e., to the identification and elimination of spending which was useless and in any case superfluous to our possibilities. For example, we could «constitutionalise» a limit for fiscal and social security contribution pressure, equal to 40% of GDP, certified by the national statistics institute, ISTAT: if the pressure exceeds this ceiling, the President of the Republic should dissolve Parliament.

From this viewpoint, it would be best not to place too much reliance on the fight against tax evasion. How can one realistically expect to raise significant amounts from uncovering tax evasion when the distinguishing characteristics of the present tax system are the number, frequency, oppressiveness and often uselessness of the duties of tax-payers, who are not even able to find the forms needed to pay the taxes?

Reducing the level of tax evasion requires a radical modification of the spirit informing Italy's tax legislation, with a significant shift towards indirect taxation (nobody can evade paying tax on petrol), a massive resort to automatic mechanisms of determining taxable income, a drastic reduction in the number of taxes and also tax brackets.

In the present situation, however, caution is the order of the day when talking about the inequality of tax pressure. It is not sufficient to take the data for personal income tax (IRPEF) as a reference. This data indicates that there is strong evasion on income other than that from subordinate employment. Subordinate employment accounts for just over 50% of GDP net of factor costs, but almost 70% of IRPEF revenues. It would be more correct, I believe, to refer to all direct taxes. In 1993, revenues from subordinated employment generated only 42% of the total yield, other forms of revenues 58%. The Italian tax system is therefore so perverse that, if evasion did not exist, it would be a lethal weapon for income from non-subordinate employment and business income.

BIBLIOGRAPHY

[1] BRENNAN, G. - BUCHANAN, J.M., *The Reason of Rules. Constitutional Political Economy*. Cambridge, Cambridge University Press, 1985.

[2] BUCHANAN, J.M., *Limits of Liberty: Between Anarchy and Leviathan*, Chicago, University of Chicago Press, 1975.

[3] BUCHANAN J.M. - TULLOCK G., *The Calculus of Consent: Logical Foundations of Constitutional Democracy*, Ann Arbor, University of Michigan Press, 1962.

[4] CONIGLIANI C.A., *Saggi di economia politica e scienza delle finanze*, Torino, Bocca, 1903.

[5] D'ANTONIO M. (ed.), *La Costituzione economica*, Milano, Il Sole 24 Ore, 1985.

[6] FUÀ G. - ROSINI E., *Troppe tasse sui redditi*, Bari, Laterza, 1985.

[7] MARTINO A., *Noi e il fisco. La crescita della fiscalità arbitraria: cause, conseguenze, rimedi*, Pordenone, Studio Tesi, 1987.

[8] ONIDA V., *Le leggi di spesa nella Costituzione*, Milano, Giuffrè, 1969.

[9] TABELLINI G. - ALESINA A., «Voting on the Budget Deficit», *American Economic Review*, March 1990.

[10] TREMONTI G. - VITALETTI G., *Le cento tasse degli italiani*, Bologna, il Mulino, 1986.

The Governance of a Globalising World Economy

Salvatore Zecchini *
OECD, Paris

1. - Going Beyond Market Liberalisation

Of the few phenomena that since the late 1980s are ushering in a new defining trend in the world economy, none is more challenging for governments, enterprises and people than the globalisation of national economies, particularly in the OECD advanced economic area. A few data suffice to give a measure, albeit approximate, of this phenomenon. it is estimated that in 1991, world-wide sales of foreign affiliates have exceeded the volume of world exports of goods and non-factor services, (Aranda *et* Al. [1]). In 1989, sales of US affiliates in the UK were 5 times US manufacture exports to the same country, while US affiliates' sales in Germany were 3 times greater than exports, (Dunning [5]). At the same time, about one third of US and Japanese exports were represented by intra-firm sales within multinational enterprises.

A growing number of manufacturing enterprises have gone "global" to the extent that they have segmented and decentralised their production, sourcing, financing and marketing in various locations in the globe. In pursuing this approach, firms aim basically at exploiting at the source the comparative advantages of different economies in terms of access to material, labour, technology and capital inputs, or at widening the scale of their market, or at gaining more efficient access to protected market areas, (Dunning [5], Markusen [12]). The driving force of the globalisation process is the firm and its new

---

* The author is Deputy Secretary General of the OECD and Director of the CCET.

strategic approach to business, but one of the necessary conditions for this to take place is the opening of economies. Globalisation is not, however, tantamount to a mere return to the free movement of goods and capital across borders, free movement that characterised the world economy in the late decades of the 19th century and the first decade of this century, i.e. the period of the "gold standard" at its hey-day. It is rather a geographically wider and economically deeper process of cross-border interconnection among national markets, enterprises and authorities, leading ultimately to interlinkages between the value added of different economies. Going beyond that historical experience of market liberalisation, globalisation's distinctive trait lies in the functional links that are established by enterprises among national economies on a worldwide scale.

Three main factors have triggered this process: *a*) the increasing liberalisation of national markets for goods, services and capital; *b*) the technological advances in telecommunication and transport facilities; and *c*) the revolution in information processing as a result of the availability of powerful electronic instruments. Under these conditions it has become feasible for firms to spread inputs and outputs among countries throughout a geographically dispersed area, while establishing backward and forward linkages with cross-border firms, investors and markets all along the functional chain of their activities. Thus, a radical transformation in business organisation has resulted, leading the world economy to a new techno-economic paradigm, (Hart [6]), that is affecting production, finance and trade.

As regards foreign trade, since the late 1970s a fundamental shift has been occurring in the pattern of international exchanges. In the period between 1950 and the 1970s, the expansion of international trade mostly concerned firms and national economies that generally aimed at expoliting their comparative advantages and consequently maintained a degree of separation from their trading partners even within custom unions or free-trade areas. In this approach to trade, foreign direct investment (FDI) in the manufacturing sector [1] was seen

[1] The main exception to such approach is in the raw material and energy sectors, in which FDI is motivated by the need to gain direct access to the sources of these inputs. On the expansion of FDI, see OECD [17].

N.B.: the numbers in square brackets refer to the Bibliography at the end of the paper.

as an alternative to exports and was mainly directed to serve the market of the country where investment was located. In the last fifteen years, instead, a rising share of foreign trade reflects exchanges within the network of multinational enterprises or between related firms, i.e. firms which have entered into some sort of networking arrangement. Increasingly, exports and foreign investment have been seen by firms as complementary instruments rather than as substitutes for each other. Market presence as a result of FDI has also become instrumental to developing access for exports to the local market. Furthermore, in a strategy of global allocation of production and service facilities, FDI has not been oriented to serve just the local market (i.e. import substitution) but to export from there to the rest of the world as well, (Lawrence [9]).

2. - Globalisation Issues and Governance

The "shallow" type of market integration, (Zampetti - Sauvé [25]), that has marked trade liberalisation outside the European Community since the post-war period, has been giving way since the 1980s to the deep integration that globalisation entails, with the attendant impulses to expand the international exchanges of products of the same category (intra-industry trade) and to move capital, technology and know-how abroad.

Nowadays, the trend towards the globalisation of the world economy is well established but it is not all encompassing. It concerns particularly sectors with a large potential for economies of scale, firms that are fully engaged in process and product innovation or differentiation, and R&D intensive products. Hence, it is still a limited phenomenon. In their search for economies of scale and a large sales volume to recoup high R&D investment costs, some firms are pushing for increasing globalisation. At the same time, other firms press governments for resisting the globalisation of national markets through a variety of instruments that reduce domestic market contestability. The globalisation trend is, therefore, far from being irreversible or irresistible and it will remain so until the main problems of managing the implications of a globalised economy find satisfactory solutions.

Three orders of implications pose a serious challenge to governments. First, as a result of integration into a global market, a significant portion of a country's economic activity is subject to the extranational influences stemming from the economic policies and business decisions of foreign countries. Second, in the presence of highly-interconnected national markets, free movement of goods and competition among countries in attracting foreign capital and technology can lead to a race to the bottom of the standards that act as a frame for economic activities, including social standards. Third, as the sharing of benefits and costs of globalisation can be uneven among countries and within each country at least in the initial stages of this process, globalisation can give rise to international trade frictions or to governmental actions aimed at preserving the distinction of the national model of market economy from the foreign models, a phenomenon that has been called "system friction", (Ostry [20]). Let us consider each of these problems.

In a globalising economy, the nation-state dimension loses relevance, (Hart [6]), for the purpose of organising economic activity at both government and enterprise levels. This forces governments to search for new ways and means to pursue their policy goals. In modem societies, governments are entrusted by voters with the tasks of promoting the well-being of the population and of regulating the impact of market competition outcomes on the society, particularly when these outcomes jeopardise certain socio-economic aspects that are proper to the nation. To this effect, countries make use of the economic power they exercise over their territory, and in particular the power to influence trans-border flows of resources. With the liberalisation of economic borders and as a result of the increasingly global orientation of business stragegies in the past two decades, governments have been confronted with a reduction in their policy autonomy to influence market behaviour. In other words, they have lost a portion of their economic sovereignty and surrendered it *de facto* to the market itself and, indirectly, to the dominant foreign economy or group of economies. Such a silent power transfer has altered established balances between democratic control over the management of the national economy and the market's power, and it has given rise to fears that globalised market outcomes might jeopardise the attainment of the democratically determined objectives of a country.

One of such fears is related to market outcomes in terms of unemployment and wages. Strategies of globally-oriented firms aim, in principle, at taking advantage of the best conditions that are offered internationally in the supply of production factors and inputs as well as of infrastructures. Economic theory suggests that free trade tends to equalise wages and profits globally and, in particular, would reduce, under certain conditions, the income for the production factor which is used more intensively in import, (Lawrence [10], Stolper - Samuelson [23]). On both grounds, it is to be expected that the competition of imports from countries with low wages and low social standards would eventually crowd out products of the same category from higher-wage, higher-standard countries.

This can lend support to the view held in some quarters of OECD countries that globalisation can be responsible, together with other factors, for the higher unemployment that they have been experiencing in the past decade or so, especially among the low-skill or unskilled workers. But there is not enough statistical evidence to confirm such a contention. Low-wage countries' exports to the OECD area so far represent a tiny proportion (about 1.5%) of total expenditure for goods and services in OECD countries, although the range of markets which they contest is expanding, (OECD [14] and [15]). Their negative impact on the demand for unskilled labour is analytically estimated to be modest and largely offset by job gains in other sectors through trade. There is instead no clear analytical evidence as regards a claimed negative relationship between imports from those countries and wage earnings. Likewise, conclusive, theoretical and empirical evidence on the impact of trade and FDI liberalisation on labour standards is still lacking, (OECD [16], Schoepfle - Swinnerton [22]).

In the face of these analyses, there remain fears that unchecked competition in a global market would lead to the erosion of national standards. In contrast, others argue in favour of such erosion since this is seen as an instrument to achieve efficiency in resource allocation. In fact, many regulations are an impediment for enterprises to sustain competition worldwide since they add to their operating costs. The two contrasting views are another manifestation of the classical conflict between allocation efficiency and distributive equity which usually emerges at the national level. The new elements, that globalisation brings in, are that this conflict is due to factors originating outside the country, and that globalisation may involve for some time an excess of costs over benefits for some countries. Over the long term, all countries are going to benefit from market integration, and these benefits will go beyond the initial efficiency gains as increased market size and competition will generate dynamic gains in terms of higher investment and accelerated technological innovation and productivity growth, (World Bank [24]). However, over the short- and possibly medium-term, the cost involved in resource reallocation, particularly for low-skill labour and industries, might outweigh the benefits in some industrial countries. In this context, domestic measures are not suitable for the redistribution of these costs on a transnational basis. A viable solution has to be found at international level or, even better, at global level.

As trade barriers fall and competition becomes global, remaining differences among countries in their market economy models and in the trade-off by which they solve the allocative-distributive conflict, acquire more relevance in orienting trade and investment flows. The more integrated national markets are, the more likely it is that market competition will evolve into system competition among countries, a broad domain of which competition in trade is just one segment. System competition focuses on the cross-country disparities that exist even within the OECD area, for instance between European countries, USA and Japan, as regards approaches to public policies, extent of government intervention in the economy, legal structures, social structures, competition and subsidy policies, and other structural policies. If system competition is not accommodated by or sustainable for a country, it can lead to system friction with the consequence that new impediments might be introduced to delay or to reverse market integration.

3. - A Global Governance Approach

The three orders of problems, that have been outlined, are symptoms of a wider problem, namely what governance model is appropriate for a globalising economic system. Of course, a country can resort to unilateral measures to safeguard domestic policy independence in pursuing domestic policy objectives. However, these measures tend to be in the nature of instruments to prevent the national economy from interacting with the others, and consequently they tend to reduce efficiency in resource allocation, factor productivity and economic growth. Furthermore, in an interdependent world economy not all domestic policy goals can be met, or met in an effective way, by governments acting alone. This is the case, for instance, for the protection of intellectual property rights, environment conservation, new technologies' development, the stability of the financial system.

Resorting to international agreements on a bilateral basis is already an improvement but is not sufficient to deal coherently with the multiplicity of spillover effects flowing from a large number of countries. A regional approach to governance can constitute a major step towards multilateral solutions, provided that it is an "open" regionalism which does not aim at erecting barriers vis-à-vis the rest of the world. Regionalism helps to build trust and mutual confidence among countries in dealing with their international economic interactions.

The most appropriate solution to the governance problem seems, nevertheless, to lie in reaching multilateral agreements on global governance mechanisms or approaches. These offer an opportunity to each participating country to regain part of the lost sovereignty over its market by sharing with other countries the responsibility of ruling the global system. Through such mechanisms countries, particularly those with a small economy, can exert more influence over the policies of larger countries. Global governance does not, instead, require or mean global government or world federalism, (Commission on Global Governance [3]), since national governments can jointly reach and apply common solutions to global problems with the help of international institutions and without renouncing their powers. World government still remains in the realm of utopia.

In addressing the implications of a globalising economy, the objective of global governance is not just to regulate international trade relations but to rule over or manage a broad range of economic interactions among countries in areas such as production, trade, competition, investment, finance, and to do so in a way that is compatible with the economic and social interests of all participating countries, (Hart [7]). A piecemeal approach of sectoral trade agreements with a scope limited to groups of countries or to a regional area would not suffice to solve globalisation problems and eliminate system friction unless these groups either isolate their economies from the rest of the world or accept external spillover effects stemming from other countries' policies.

In a governance system there are in principle four main components: rules, institutions, accountability and enforcement mechanisms, (Zecchini [26]). In the framework of these four components a number of issues need to be addressed for the purpose of establishing a global governance approach.

What balance has to be struck between global rules and global institutions? Rules, better than the international institutions' discretion, can offer a guarantee that extraterritorial effects of unilateral actions or rules by individual countries (in particular those with major economic weight, not to mention the hegemonic ones) can be contained and made compatible with the general interest. By agreeing on global rules, it is possible to draw clearly the limit up to which a participating country is willing to lose policy autonomy within its market. In the field of international trade, for instance, global rules represent the most effective way to define the boundaries of national autonomy in trade policy and to provide a clear basis to assess and to sanction inadmissible trade intervention by the individual country. The business community also values a global rule-based approach to the extent that it serves to dispel uncertainty over the scope of government intervention in the economy.

In dealing with a global market, rule-making cannot actually reach a global scope if it follows the route of a series of intergovernmental agreements involving bilateral concessions within a limited group of countries. To tackle global problems are necessary global rules that have much in common with those applied domestically, as if they are directed to a unified world economy. Unfortunately, not all economic areas lend themselves to effective management through rules. For example, to reach an actual contestability of a market involves issues so complex as to defy any rule definition, however detailed it may be.

Institutions are, therefore, a necessary complement to rules. But what institutions: national or supranational, or a combination of the two? National authorities do not necessarily have sufficient awareness of the external spillover effects of their policies or the willingness to deal with them in an international framework. The optimal solution would then be that applied in the European Union, since its institutions manage or enforce directly policies aimed at the unified, internal market in the context of a coherent set of rules agreed upon by member countries that have several policy objectives in common. But it cannot be expected that this approach is extensible to a global scale encompassing most sectors because not all countries wish to integrate their policies so closely with those of other States, especially when other policy goals outside the economic realm differ. Hence, it appears more realistic to expect a compromise solution, with supranational institutions having a limited scope for action and relying on the support of national authorities for actual governance in line with the multilaterally agreed principles.

The accountability of these institutions is, however, crucial to achieve both effectiveness and democracy in the governance of the global system. While in a democratic state, economic authorities are accountable to parliament and the judiciary, in a global governance system it is not clear how to make supranational institutions accountable to people or their elected representatives. Once important policy decisions are shifted from democratically accountable domestic institutions to international bodies, a deficit in democracy could appear to the extent that the activities of these bodies do not meet criteria of transparency, responsiveness and accountability to the same degree as their domestic counterparts. A major challenge in global governance is, therefore, to build multilateral institutions that are fair and effective in carrying out their mandate and open to democratic scrutiny.

Such a difficulty could be eased by establishing a minimum set of rules for the global market and leaving to national authorities the task of monitoring their enforcement in the market place. Obviously, even enforcement among equally sovereign states is not easy to obtain because of shortage of effective tools. Trade policy instruments are often ill-suited to this task as they involve other costs for the economy at large and the risk of retaliation. Other instruments based on bilateral agreements or reciprocal concessions on a sectoral basis have the drawback of segmenting rather than globalising the market. As these could be considered at best instruments of last resort, enforcement has basically to hinge upon co-operation mechanisms, co-operative compliance among countries, and effective dispute settlement procedures. These three conditions can best be achieved through supranational or multilateral organisations.

Is there the political will to establish a global governance system? Among the countries with the largest and most developed economies there is reluctance to share economic sovereignty on a multilateral basis through such a system unless its advantages are evident on many grounds. This has been possible in the European Community, in which a number of countries share the same economic and social goals and accept supranational enforcement of common rules. In other international co-operation frameworks, global governance has not been feasible, not even in the *NAFTA Agreement*, since the latter leaves limited scope for supranational ruling. Few exceptions can be cited. The major one is represented by the IMF, but the results appear quite mixed because its rules are somewhat loose and the enforcement procedures not effective enough. On the basis of this experience, one can expect that as economies continue globalising, instead of quantum leaps there will be incremental progress towards global governance. Rules and institutions that cover the global economy in its main building blocks could gradually emerge from the multiplication and extension of intergovernmental agreements that are initially negotiated within limited groups of countries and deal with narrow sectors.

4. - International Trade Governance

The trade area is the one in which in the past two decades more advances have been made towards the establishment of a governance system for the global economy than in any other. Many of the problems raised by globalisation have been tackled on the grounds of the impact that they have on the international contestability of markets, and they are treated as trade-related issues. In this respect, 1994 has represented a turning point in trade governance since the *Uruguay Round* negotiations have produced a body of basic rules that are applied to the majority of countries, an institution, the WTO, with the task of completing them and monitoring compliance, and intergovernmental dispute settlement procedures.

This approach is a major step forward as compared to the GATT but still needs further improvements. In contrast to the GATT system, that included different obligations for different States and relied on diplomatic solutions to trade conflicts, the new system established both a common legal base for the overall trading system and less ineffective mechanisms for ensuring compliance with the rules. However, the strength of this legal basis is uneven. For instance, in the realm of intellectual property rights, it provides a code of rules that ensures their protection in foreign trade, while in the foreign investment sector the rules, which were agreed, are of marginal relevance since they cover few negative practices. The new enforcement procedures are better defined than those under the GATT but they have still limited scope. More importantly, the institutional and legal dimensions of the new trade regime are not yet geared to cope with the full array of interferences with global competition, especially with those that are not taking place at the national borders.

Contrary to expectations, the reduction of tariffs to the modest levels envisaged in the new trade regime has not automatically opened national markets to worldwide competition. There remain trade barriers that are located deep inside the structure of the economy, (OECD [18]). It could even be the case that, while tariffs were lowered, trade barriers were transferred from the national borders to the inner working of the economy. But in general, these structural aspects are related to domestic policy choices and business practices that have been adopted over many years; consequently, they should be dealt with in an internal context, knowing the trade-offs that are involved over the entire range of economic and non-economic policy goals. Similarly, once these aspects acquire the relevance of obstacles in the framework of global market competition, to remove them it is appropriate to use a supranational or global approach as if they pertain to a unified, international economy.

This approach implies a major departure from the traditional approach consisting of limited inter-governmental agreements involving reciprocal obligations not to impede competition. Rather it requires the definition of a set of general principles together with detailed rules, whenever possible, and institutions that address in a comprehensive way the different issues of market access and market presence in a global perspective. Ultimately, the aim is to establish and enforce a code of minimum requirements for both business conduct and government intervention in the market place, similar to the governance mode employed at the national level. The geographical scope of these rules should cover both developed and developing economies with no difference in treatment among them, in contrast with the GATT regime. Although these principles and rules have to be negotiated among governments, they should be aimed directly at the enterprise level. In order to ensure even enforcement across countries, the primary responsibility of rule enforcement should be entrusted with the global institutions while national authorities would have a complementary role in ensuring compliance. In sectors in which it is difficult to devise rules for a level playing field, then it is the task of supranational institutions to examine and rule on individual cases in accordance with the general principles. More generally, firms should have direct access to the multilateral institutions that preside over the application of these rules without having to resort to the intermediation of their governments, as is the case at present.

5. - Governance for Fair Competition

It is evident that there is still a wide gap between this global approach and the one that resulted from the conclusions of the *Uruguay Round*. To appreciate the importance of moving towards global governance, it is necessary to consider the variety and complexity of the factors that can keep foreign competition out of the domestic market even in a country with no customs. Three broad categories of factors can be identified: those hindering market access for foreign products, those discouraging market presence of foreign firms and those distorting competition, (May [8]). Among these impediments or trade distortions, some are caused by government policies, others by the particular structures of the economy and still others by business practices.

Among the obstacles due to government action, of particular relevance are public procurement policies, subsidies and taxation, product or process standards, sectoral regulations, and subsidies to private R&D programs. The extent of their impact on foreign competition varies widely and it is not easy to identify and quantify it in several instances. Some of these measures, such as technical standards, tax disparities, support to high-tech projects are mainly, but not exclusively, motivated by reasons other than to ward-off foreign suppliers. As they also reflect concerns over quality, safety, technological progress of the country or preservation of traditional product standards, it is not a simple choice for governments to place the global market interest above national concerns by eliminating these trade distortions. In fact, it is difficult for governments to accept the erosion of national standards or regulations unless they are convinced of offsetting benefits on different grounds, such as the improvement of standards or of the working of the economy. The same applies to international disparities in taxation of certain products or firms or sources of income. As a result of tax competition with countries that apply a lighter tax burden, a country would lose tax revenue that could not be compensated by other benefits. This could result, for instance, from enterprises' transfer pricing policies in intra-firm trade, policies that can have an increasing and differentiated impact on countries' tax revenues due to the expanding globalisation of production.

Within the borders of a country there are political mechanisms for making trade-offs between benefits and costs across a wide range of economic and social sectors for the purpose of raising national welfare, but in a global economy context such mechanisms are not available and the scope for cross-sectoral compensation is limited to the concessions that countries may agree bilaterally with respect to different sectors. Under these conditions, it is not clear whether merely removing these trade distortions will always bring about higher economic welfare and therefore there is still ground for countries demanding reciprocity clauses in market liberalisation, (Arndt [2], Rothschild [21], OECD [13]). The approach of the EU for its member countries has been to make all national standards mutually acceptable and to push towards tax harmonisation. Such a global approach might not, however, be politically acceptable to all countries in a global economy, (Dixit [4]). Furthermore, a rule-based approach, such as through the OECD [19] code on transfer pricing, does not appear to be adequate enough to deal with the problem of the unevenness of globalisation's impact on fiscal revenue. As the optimal solution of tax harmonisation is a goal too difficult to achieve, limited inter-governmental agreements might still be the only available option for some time to come. In this context, the use of reciprocity clauses might be justified in order to make markets truly contestable.

Specific market structures could turn to the advantage of domestic firms in competing in internal or foreign markets. Price controls or price regulations, local-content rules, lax enforcement of competition laws or even government's support of monopolies and oligopolies can reduce the contestability of the domestic market. Albeit the opening of the domestic market would erode monopoly power, such government policies could make it unprofitable for foreign firms to enter the market or could help domestic firms to generate the resources that are needed to face their competitors in foreign markets.

These distortions are generally less difficult to identify than those originating from business behaviour. Groups of firms or individual dominant firms can follow strategies directed to inhibit market entry to competitors or to drive them out of their markets. To this effect, firms can use aggressive or predatory price policies, or vertical integration with other firms, or vertical restraint agreements that end up shifting transactions from the marketplace to within the network of inter-related enterprises. In these cases it is problematic to draw the dividing line between predatory or exclusionary behaviour, on one side, and commercial practice that is compatible with market competition on a global scale, on the other side. Furthermore, vertical arrangements are also a source of benefits for the economy, since they can lower transaction costs among related firms and can raise their supply efficiency. The negative effects in terms of reduction in market competition or market "foreclosure" resulting from exclusive contracts have to be weighted against those benefits. An independent and accountable institution at supranational level seems better suited for ruling on these cases than resorting to either a code of rules or *ad-hoc* intergovernmental negotiations.

A rule-based approach, instead, seems appropriate and feasible for dealing with the impediments that foreign enterprises can face in a country when they aim at setting up an affiliate or acquiring a firm that is already established in that market. This approach offers clear advantages in terms of preventing backtracking on FDI liberalisation or discriminating in FDI liberalisation on a country or regional basis, (Low [11]). In the OECD, member countries are already following this approach through the negotiation of a multilateral agreement on investment. The goal is to reach an agreement by mid-1997 and to open it to the adhesion of other countries. Recent progress towards a rule-based approach does not imply that all the countries are ready to change their company law or equity market regulations in order to globalise presence in their market. If a multilateral agreement is not reachable among a significant number of countries, then countries have no option but to negotiate bilateral concessions and reciprocity agreements with other countries. From the proliferation of these agreements, a set of global rules on FDI and corporate governance could eventually emerge.

More challenging seems the problem of introducing on a global scale some standards for the purpose of ensuring that all countries contribute to the attainment of globally relevant goals, such as environmental protection and the safeguard of labour rights. In an economy open to global competition, the high standards applied in some countries could be undermined by the imports from low-standard economies. This issue can best be addressed by setting a code of minimum requirements that have to be met by any country regardless of their economic implications. Unfortunately, in their fear of losing some trade advantages, some countries do not attach great importance to these global values, and consequently incentives or international pressure are needed to achieve global rules and compliance.

6. - Governance Areas

A general problem concerns ways and means by which it is possible to establish and apply global governance. Countries tend to focus on the trade dimension, besides the financial one, as a tool to press countries to accept common rules and to sanction non-compliance. This is a rather unbalanced approach which can lead to two equally unsatisfactory outcomes: either an overestimation of the effectiveness of trade sanctions without due regard to their limits and their negative consequences for the economy as a whole, or the assignment of the task of designing or applying global rules to institutions or authorities operating in fields which are not within their range of expertise. For instance, trade instruments such as national treatment and MFN clause are not always suitable to deal with rule-making for non-trade issues. The application of national treatment, for example, in the case of countries in which a given sector is under monopoly or subject to restrictions on competition would not help globalise the national market.

In this light, the WTO does not seem to be the ideal place to find a solution to the problems of global governance that are not related to foreign trade even if trade sanctions are used by countries in order to deal with these problems. Several other institutions should share the responsibility for making rules for the global economy and some, such as the BIS, the ILO, the OECD, have already been engaged in this function in their sectors of competence.

Global rules can be made in different international institutions but also through different paths other than explicit rule-making for this purpose. Harmonisation of national rules or standards is a feasible option when differences among countries in their legislation and policy goals are not too wide. Another approach is to launch negotiations on rules and institutions among a group of countries with similar objectives and to let other countries join the agreement later. Still another avenue is to agree on general principles and to let individual countries translate them into detailed domestic rules.

Inconsistencies can emerge the rules and activities that are directed to address different aspects of the governance of a globalising world economy, for instance, among the exchange rate regime, foreign payments system, financial system, trade liberalisation, market contestability, and other sectors. The ideal solution would be to create a "directoire" of all the multilateral institutions having the responsibility of global governance over different economic sectors[2]. As the time may not yet be ripe for this solution, it seems necessary at least to establish co-ordination mechanisms among these institutions for the purpose of examining the interactions among their global governance activities and eliminating inconsistencies. Such co-ordination is not yet in place except on an ad-hoc basis, while a systematic approach would constitute major progress towards effective governance.

In this respect, it should be considered, in particular, whether a fully integrated market across countries, i.e. a globalised market, can be achieved or sustained in the face of inadequate governance, on a global scale, over the exchange rate system, or the international financial and payments system. At present, very few rules govern the exchange rate movements of the three main currencies of the world, while most other currencies are pegged according to different patterns. As exchange rate stability is currently the exception rather than the rule, a system of multilateral governance of the international monetary system (IMS) is required in order to prevent exchange rate distortions or a monetary anarchy similar to those that crippled free international trade and economic growth in the interwar period.

At present, monetary global governance is provided by the IMF with the support, on a regional basis, of institutions such as the European Community Council. In spite of this governance system, the period of currency floating since 1973 to date has been characterised by pronounced nominal exchange rate volatility and prolonged misalignments in real exchange rates. If there is no evidence that volatility has been a significant impediment to trade expansion, the same cannot be said for currency misalignments. The latter have complicated countries' task of adjusting imbalances in their external current accounts and might have contributed to encourage major

---

[2] Such a "directoire" could also include a few national institutions of countries that have a major influence over the global economy.

trading countries to introduce forms of managed trade, such as voluntary export restraints, or other obstacles to free trade.

Problems of IMS governance have spilled over into the trade area, hindering the market globalisation process. Furthermore, a tendency to regionalise trade, by erecting hindrances vis-à-vis outside competitors, has been gaining ground among countries that are willing to take a commitment to stabilise their intra-regional exchange rates. Hence, it can hardly be envisaged that the present trend towards a globalising world economy would continue unless new advances are made towards a more effective global governance of the IMS. This does not necessarily imply setting exchange rate rules in order to limit the range of currency fluctuations. A degree of currency stability can be reached through an effective multilateral surveillance over macroeconomic policies together with more binding than at present commitments by countries to co-operate among themselves in the management of their macroeconomic policies, (Zecchini [27]).

With the globalisation of capital markets, new impulse has been given to "real" globalisation (i.e. globalisation of production and trade), but at the same time weaknesses have appeared in the national and international structures to govern financial markets. The regulatory framework and supervision over national financial institutions have shown gaps, with the result that several major countries have experienced important crises in their financial systems since the 1980s. Without a well-functioning financial and payments system on a global scale, it would be difficult to advance towards globalisation, namely to promote both the intensification of trade and production relationships among countries and an efficient allocation of savings that favours the countries with the best investment opportunities. In fact, following the integration of national capital markets, crises in a country's financial system have shown their potential of spreading rapidly across the global system and jeopardising trade and output growth on a wide scale. In the face of disparities in national approaches and a lack of well-established co-ordination mechanisms on a worldwide scale, crisis prevention requires new progress towards a global approach to financial governance. This does not have to be based necessarily on multilateral institutions since national authorities are in principle capable of carrying out these activities. However, these activities must be framed within a set of rules or standards that are agreed internationally for the purpose of regulating and supervising financial institutions on a global scale, (Zecchini [26]). These rules and standards should represent minimum requirements for the global financial system.

7. - Conclusions

In conclusion, the following question remains, i.e. whether, in the light of the current trends towards cross-border production, trade and finance, it is to be expected that the process of globalisation of economic activities can be sustained in the future and expanded across sectors and across countries. A positive outcome appears to depend crucially on the ability to govern at the transnational level the implications of globalisation, namely it depends on the success in developing a global governance approach. There are already signs that failure to deal with the negative spillover effects falling on national economies and failure to reach an even sharing among countries of the initial benefits and costs of globalisation can delay or even derail this process.

Managing a globalising economy requires developing a new functional relationship between national sovereignty and supranational governance. The objectives are to reach multilateral agreements on core rules or policies that have to be applied globally and to make countries accept that supranational institutions monitor their application. In the latter respect, national authorities still retain a crucial role in co-operating with other countries and the multilateral institutions for the enforcement of these principles and rules. Core rules can emerge from the harmonisation of national rules, or from a piecemeal process of agreeing on narrow commitments with respect to particular activities and sectors, on the expectation that this might eventually lead to a comprehensive code with a global scope. As these approaches seem rather gradual and-out-of-pace with the speed of globalisation, it is preferable to address squarely the issue of creating a framework to govern the various sections of the globalised economic system.

While multilateral negotiations and interventions have traditionally been focused on trade barriers at the border, global governance has instead to adopt a horizontal approach to influencing policy-making and rule-making, since border barriers have already been drastically reduced and have less relevance than ever in determining the degree of contestability of domestic markets. In contrast, a host of domestic policies in both the public and private domains, in areas such as regulations, competition, investment and labour market, can lead to market failures in a global perspective as they can constitute obstacles to market access and sources of distortions for competition.

A final question should be answered: "Who would take the lead in pushing towards a global governance system?" Markets cannot produce such a system by themselves, particularly in a trans-national context. The initiative to this end must be taken at the national political level or by international bodies. As history teaches us, such initiatives usually originate in the face of a serious crisis, since governments are traditionally reluctant to relinquish portions of their sovereignty in normal times. It is, however, to be hoped that the world economy should not wait for a major crisis to develop in order to receive the governance that is appropriate to its increasingly global dimension.

BIBLIOGRAPHY

[1] ARANDA V. - ECONOMOU P. - SAUVANT K., «Trends and Policies in Market Presence», in OECD, *New Dimensions of Market Access in a Globalising World Economy*, Paris, 1995.

[2] ARNDT H.W., «The Political Economy of Reciprocity», Banca Nazionale del Lavoro, *Quarterly Review*, vol. 48, n. 190, 1994.

[3] COMMISSION ON GLOBAL GOVERNANCE, «Our Global Neighbourhood», *The Report of the Commission on Global Governance*, New York, Oxford University Press, 1995.

[4] DIXIT A., «Transaction Cost Politics and Economic Policy: A Framework and a Case Study», Roma, SIPI, *Rivista di Politica Economica*, June 1996.

[5] DUNNING J.H., «The Role of Foreign Direct Investment in Globalizing Economy», Banca Nazionale del Lavoro, «*Quarterly Review*», vol. 48, n. 193, June 1995.

[6] HART M., «Globalization and Governance», *Policy Options*, Special policy issue, Summer 1995.

[7] ——, «What's Next: Negotiating Rules for a Global Economy», in OECD, *New Dimensions of Market Access in a Globalising World Economy*, Paris, 1995.

[8] HAY D.A., *Anticompetitive Practices, Market Access and Competition Policy in a Global Economy*, mimeo, Paris, OECD, June 1995.

[9] LAWRENCE R.Z., *Toward Globally Contestable Markets*, mimeo, Paris, OECD, February 1995.

[10] ——, *Single World, Divided Nations? Globalisation and OECD Labour Markets*, Mimeo, Paris, OECD Development Centre, June 1995.

[11] LOW P., «Market Access Through Market Presence: a Look at the Issues», in OECD, *New Dimensions of Market Access in a Globalising World Economy*, Paris, 1995.

[12] MARKUSEN J.R., «The Boundaries of Multinational Enterprises and the Theory of International Trade», Nashville (TN), American Economic Assoociation, *The Journal of Economic Perspectives*, Spring 1995.

[13] OECD, *OECD Reviews of Foreign Direct Investment, United States*, Paris, 1995.

[14] — —, *The OECD Jobs Study, Facts, Analysis, Strategies*, Paris, 1994.

[15] ——, *The OECD Jobs Study, Evidence and Explanations*, Part I and II, Paris, 1994.

[16] ——, *Trade and Labour Standards*, mimeo, Paris, OECD, January 1995.

[17] ——, *International Direct Investment Statistics Yearbook 1995*, Paris, 1995.

[18] ——, «After the Uruguay Round: The Way Ahead», *Report to the OECD Council at Ministerial Level*, Paris, 1995.

[19] ——, *Transfer Pricing Guidelines for Multinational Enterprises and Tax Administrations*, Paris, 1995.

[20] OSTRY, S., «New Dimensions of Market Access», Washington (DC), Group of Thirty, *Occasional Papers*, n. 49, 1995.

[21] ROTHSCHILD K., «The Political Economy of Reciprocity: A Comment», Banca Nazionale del Lavoro, *Quarterly Review*, vol. 48, n. 192, 1995.

[22] SCHOEPFLE G. - SWINNERTON K. (ed.), *International Labour Standards and Global Integration: Proceedings of a Symposium*, US Department of Labour, Washington (DC), 1994.

[23] STOLPER W. - SAMUELSON P.A., «Protection and Real Wages», *Review of Economic Studies*, November 1941.

[24] WORLD BANK, *Global Economic Prospects and the Developing Countries*, Washington (DC), 1995.

[25] ZAMPETTI A.B. - SAUVÉ P., «New Dimensions of Market Access: an Overview», in OECD, *New Dimensions of Market Access in a Globalising World Economy*, Paris, 1995.

[26] ZECCHINI S., «Globalisation and International Institutions», *Rivista di Politica Economica*, Roma, SIPI, June 1995.

[27] ZECCHINI S., «Rifondare o no il sistema di Bretton Woods?», *Incontri con l'economia, raccolta delle lezioni Beneduce*, Napoli, Il Denaro, December 1995.

Two Approaches to Economic Governance

Bruno Jossa *
Università di Napoli

1. - Introduction

Despite the proliferation of formalisations in economic studies and hence notwithstanding the increasing accuracy of economic analysis, there is still considerable disagreement, even among the most qualified economists, on a large number of issues, including those regarding pure theory. Furthermore, there is still a clear division into schools of economists of different background. This division into schools is, moreover, clearly attributable to the different «value judgements» which continue and will continue to be important in suggesting solutions for the various problems because economic science, as is known, is a «difficult» science by virtue of the fact that the number of variables in play in the economy rarely allows the theorist to reach definitive conclusions as regards the interpretation of events [1]. In other words, as the complexity of economic reality almost never allows the theorist to reach definitive conclusions, economic

---

* The author is Professor of Political Economy at the Faculty of Law.

N.B.: the numbers in square brackets refer to the Bibliography at the end of the paper.

[1] That economic science is «difficult» is well argued above all by Hayek, who in many of his writings distinguished between natural and social sciences on the basis of the consideration that, while the former can isolate the single problems (and thus study the interrelations of a few variables at a time), the social sciences *a*) deal with complex phenomena, where there is a high number of variables in play which cannot be limited by the researcher and *b*) they cannot avail themselves of experiments (HAYEK F.A. [31], [36] and [41]). The same opinion is expressed by, for example, Baumol who states that the natural sciences with all their successes are still heavily reliant on experiments

science leaves, in a manner of speaking, a vacuum which the different manner of feeling or the different visions of the world of those who produce this science can fill (Beckerman [6]).

However, the crisis of statism has made it difficult to properly classify the various schools, distinguishing between them, for example, still, as was always the case in the past, into right and left. Hence there arises the problem of whether the various schools of economic thought should not now be defined and distinguished from one another solely on the basis of purely intellectual or «scientific» criteria, without any further reference to the differences between value judgements[2]. On this matter, it is interesting to note that Hayek himself (who, as he considered economic science «difficult», should have emphasised the importance of value judgements in it) maintained that one of his most important theoretical contributions was the demonstration that the differences between socialism and non-socialism are founded on purely intellectual questions which can be resolved on the basis of science and not of different value judgements (Hayek [42], pp. 295-6 and 304-5).

These are the issues to which this paper is dedicated. The paper, however, will dwell solely on the main divisions in schools of economic governance. At the foundation of our considerations, we should state at the outset, lies the consideration that the collapse of the Soviet system and the crisis of statism (which was further fuelled by the collapse of centrally-planned socialism) have made it impossible to continue to classify the various orientations existing on the basis of the familiar state-market or plan-market contraposition because today hardly anybody is prepared to admit that the opposite of non-intervention is centralised planning (or, to be even clearer, because

---

which are controlled, and focus their attention on the influence of one or a few variables at a time, rather than attempting to account for the complex phenomena of reality in their entirety (BAUMOL W.J. [5], p. 1714).

As regards Hayek, however, it should be noted that he gradually toned down the contrast between the two types of science, particularly after he had acknowledged that natural sciences also generally deal with complex phenomena (HAYEK F.A. [34], [38], Preface, BARRY N.P. [3], pp. 27 onwards and GRAY J.N. [25], pp. 19-20).

[2] On the inevitable importance of value judgements, particularly as regards state intervention in the economy, see, for example, BECKERMAN W. [6] and RYAN [79].

almost nobody is prepared to assert today that planned socialism is the ideology to counter laissez-faire).

Another consideration on which we shall base our discussion is that, precisely as a result of the loss of the old role of the plan-market pair (a dialectic pair, for some), a new guiding star on which the classification of economists' different visions should be based is the contraposition between capital and labour (another possible dialectic pair). The contraposition between capital and labour has been at the heart of economists' theoretical writings for some two centuries now, but the proliferation of studies on self-management has made it increasingly clear that the only feasible and efficient system to set against capitalism (a market economy managed by the owners of capital or their representatives) is self-managed socialism, which is a market economy managed by workers or their representatives. But if, in outlining the various possible visions of economic governance, we discard the contraposition between plan and market and substitute it with that between capital and labour, one possible solution to the search for a guiding criteria for tracing the main distinctions is to state that the distinction between the different economic policy approaches is that which sets the democratic control of the economy (i.e., a system where the man-worker controls nature and capital) against laissez-faire or non-intervention (i.e., capitalism, where the law of capital alone is king).

2. - Types of Economic Policy

An OECD classification lays down four categories of public activities which can give rise to public spending: 1) public goods, such as public order and defence; 2) the so-called merit goods, such as education and health; 3) income support, such as pensions and unemployment benefits; and 4) others, such as interest on the public debt (OECD [74], Table 9).

For public goods, for which there is no market, there can, as a rule, be only one type of public intervention in the economy, namely public spending whose efficiency cannot be easily measured using commercial criteria either because one cannot or does not wish to do so[3]. Similarly, for merit goods, such as education and health, many rightly consider that the public spending sustained to produce them should not be evaluated with strictly economic criteria. But the problem of the type of public intervention to be chosen does arise for the remaining part of the public intervention in the economy, whether it gives rise to public spending or concerns, instead, the public control of private activities; and the types of possible intervention can be classified as follows: *a*) non-intervention; *b*) an economic policy which intervenes via laws or, in any case, general and abstract rules; *c*) an economic policy of control via the public administration, in other words, discretionary control; and *d*) an anticyclical macro-economic policy.

In this classification, the first two types of economic government clearly respect the spontaneous nature of the market order. As has been rightly pointed out, spontaneous orders can be conceived in two manners. They can describe first and foremost a series of regularities in a social system which is self-organised in some manner within the framework of a series of social rules; in this interpretation the constraints of the system can derive from man's designs. But spontaneous orders can also be conceived as evolutive orders, where the same rules are the unintentional result of man's actions (Vaughn [93], p. 171). The second type of order is a spontaneous order in which things are left as they are; the first is a spontaneous order in which man consciously dictates the rules of the game.

The third type of economic government, on the other hand, is that of the state's conscious and direct intervention in the market, that of control of the spontaneous order of the market via the discretionary action of the government and public administration.

Finally, the fourth type of public intervention is that to which economists, from Keynes onwards, have dedicated by far the most attention. It may be discretionary or non-discretionary; but in any case it is a technical discretion, entrusted to bodies or persons with considerable responsibility who should be very competent and whose actions are open to the scrutiny of all (and subject to evaluation by the mass media and public opinion). We shall not discuss this fourth type

---

[3] For possible exceptions BECKERMAN [6], pp. 76-7.

of intervention in this paper for three reasons — in order not to further extend the field of investigation, because economists have discussed it *ad abundatiam*, and finally because the opinions concerning it should not be excessively influenced by political opinions[4].

Confining our considerations to the first three types of economic government or economic policy, it would be erroneous to think that the order in which they are listed is justified by the fact that the third is more interventionist than the second as the second is more interventionist than the first. The second and third types of economic policy differ by virtue not of their degree of intervention, but by the different type of control of the economy that they propose. They are therefore three different types of economic policy and hence the idea that the fundamental criterion which distinguishes the different manners of governing the economy is that of the level of intervention each proposes would appear to be unfounded. This is so true that liberalists, as a rule, tend to defend the first type of economic policy but then often propend for type *b*, while socialists, or more generally, interventionists often do not accept the third type of economic policy and also defend type *b*. Adam Smith, to take one example, did not clearly indicate whether he favoured type *a* or type *b* (Vaughn [93], pp. 171-2) and neither did Keynes, to name another convinced interventionist, indicate a clear propensity for either type *b* and type *c*, as we shall see. It is therefore not true that the «right» is in favour of type *a* and the «left» of type *c*; and there are grounds for stating that the majority of economists is today in favour of an economic policy of type *b*. What then is the criterion which distinguishes the opposing visions?

3. - The Public Choice Theory's Criticism of Discretionary Interventions

Before replying to this question, and to clarify why interventionists do not nowadays generally accept economic policy of type *c*, it should be noted that the progress of economic science has highlighted

[4] An interesting, general discussion of this issue is to be found in Alsopp C. [1].

in various ways and in thousands of contributions the full extent of the weakness of an economic policy based on discretion on the part of the public administration.

The public choice theory is enlightening on this issue. As is known, this strand of thought often refers to Hume's affirmation that in constructing any system of government, one should assume that each man is a rogue and has no purpose in all his actions other than private interest (Hume [48], pp. 117-8). One of the central ideas of Buchanan and of his school is that in the public choice theory one should also apply the *homo economicus* model (under which each individual acts, as a rule, solely in his own interest), hence one should consider that even in public offices those who have a discretionary power will make use of said power more often than not for their own personal objectives[5]. In other words, the initial premise of the public choice theory is that the individual's decision-making behaviour is subject to the application of the same type of analysis whatever the choice environment (Buchanan [13], p. 6)[6]. As a result the public choice theory criticises the formulation of public finance theory, which still prevails to this day, under which the government is perceived as a «benevolent despot» (which exercises political power in the public interest) and the classical preconception that people enter politics to do public good[7]. Buchanan and his school are therefore unwaiving supporters of the principle that, if the discretionary rights of political players to distribute income are increased, individuals eager to obtain one will invest more resources in attempts to influence the player's decision (Buchanan [13], p. 6)[8]. The same holds for the activities of public administrators.

---

[5] In Buchanan's opinion, the main difference between markets and politics lies not in the type of values and interests which individuals pursue, but in the conditions under which they pursue their numerous interests. (Rowley C.K. [78], p. 177).

[6] Hobbes and Mandeville, who are sources of liberalist thought both old and new, were the first to maintain the idea that virtue does not exist because personal interest is the ultimate motive for all of man's actions.

[7] North maintains that the state should be likened to the mafia rather than endow it with the image of an organisation dedicated to the «public good» (North D.C. [70], p. 128).

[8] In an important paper, Brennan and Buchanan argued that criticism that the public choice theory did not take into account that in public activity individuals are very often led by moral considerations is mostly ill-conceived, as there are strong arguments for saying that, if the purpose of the discussion is to choose the best organisational form, the *homo economicus* model produces the best results as regards measuring the

The public choice theory, it should be noted, criticises not only the basic tenet of modern public finance science, but criticises en bloc «Keynesians», «monetarists», «new classical macroeconomics», «neo-Keynesians», etc., because they all pose the problem of what the government should do when a scientific study, by its very nature, is charged with clarifying first and foremost what the government does (see, for example, Kirchgassner [61], pp. 11-12). Nonetheless, the idea, so strongly upheld by public choice theorists, that man is essentially interested in his own personal problems would appear to be so widespread among men of science and those of common sense nowadays that there is certainly no need to be a liberalist (or politically conservative or a follower of Buchanan) to consider it a possible key for interpreting what is happening in the public sector[9].

The same ideas are reaffirmed if we note that present-day economic theory holds that the only behaviours those who study society should take into consideration are rational behaviours; and economic rationality, as is well-known, is Max Weber's purposeful rationality, i.e., which realises personal interest according to the principle of the least means. But if the basic assumption of economic science is that man normally tends to realise his own personal interest, it is clear that an economic policy based on the public administration's discretion is not advisable because it is held that the bureaucrat endowed with discretionary powers would not generally act for the public good and hence would not allow the public administration to pursue those objectives it should pursue in the public interest[10].

We can thus conclude that there are two types of long-term economic policy on which contemporary theory should concentrate its attention, namely: *a)* laissez faire; *b)* non-discretionary public intervention.

---

losses of welfare than a more genuinely «realistic» model of the positive science of forecasting (Brennan G. - Buchanan J.M. [11], pp. 90 and 103).

[9] The issue of pressure groups is different, albeit related. Olson believes that the more active and powerful pressure groups are, the more they diminish efficiency and economic growth because they act as «free riders» against society (for example, Olson M. [73] and Naert F. [69]).

[10] As he is sometimes accused of ignoring the strand of the public choice theory (Gray J.N. ([25]), it is interesting to recall that Hayek rejects the hypothesis of *homo economicus* as part of that rationalist tradition against which he has always polemicised (Hayek F.A. [35], p. 61).

4. - Legislative Control of the Economy in Liberal Thought

Even the most convinced liberalists find it difficult to criticise policies for controlling the economy via general and abstract rules with rational arguments[11]. The distinction between rules and discretion is, in fact, central to Hayek's thought. The rules furnish the legal framework which reduces uncertainty and favours the development of production activities to the point that Hayek even talked about rules as «tools of production» (Hayek [32], p. 73). And on this issue it has been rightly pointed out that the defence of rules is one of the few points where Hayek's thought parallels that of Buchanan and of the public choice theorists (Boettke, [9], p. 10).

Nonetheless, Hayek believed that «to control a spontaneous order is a contradiction in terms» (Hayek [45], p. 74); and at the start of his *opus magnum*, after having recalled the fundamental distinction between spontaneous order and organisation, the Austrian economist wrote that «what today is generally regarded as 'social' or distributive justice has meaning only within the second of these kinds of order, the organisation; but < ... > it is meaningless in, and wholly incompatible with, that spontaneous order which Adam Smith called 'the Great Society' and Sir Karl Popper called 'the Open Society'» (Hayek [39], p. 2) But is this so?

Hayek claims that in every spontaneous order man «will therefore have to use what knowledge he can achieve, not to shape the results as the craftsman shapes his handiwork, but rather to cultivate growth, by providing the appropriate environment, in the manner in which the gardener does this for his plants». (Hayek ([41], p. 34). But this is not an obvious affirmation, because in a garden man intervenes in a thousand ways — he irrigates the land, prunes and fertilises, he moves the plants from one place to another and grafts, creates protection and support for trees which need such, etc., etc.; and it is therefore by no means obvious why man, so propense to intervene to favour a better trend for natural phenomena, should not do so to modify and change the market order which is not even a natural order[12].

---

[11] This and the subsequent section revise issues already published in Jossa B. [54].

[12] More than one author has remarked that Hayek's central idea on the control of the economy is that it is unjustified and counterproductive, particularly if realised by a

A distinction in line with the most strict liberal thought is that between interventions in institutions (or in the rules of the game; see Pejovich [75], p. 1), which are always allowed, and interventions in the rules of behaviour, which should not be consciously modified. This distinction was proposed by Menger, who undoubtedly influenced Hayek (Hayek [37], p. 84 and Shearmur [85]). Menger emphasised the importance of rules which come into being spontaneously and institutions which are not consciously created[13] but he criticised the jurists of the Historical School, followers of Savigny,

---

planner, because it produces unforeseen effects which are generally harmful; in view of the extreme complexity of the economy, in fact, planners and social scientists can only have a limited understanding of it and, given this limited understanding, control of the economy inevitably has unforeseen and harmful consequences. Hayek is also charged with claiming that the idea that there are some unforeseen results of man's actions can provide a profound insight into an economy's workings (SEN A.K. [84], pp. 1-3 and HELM D. [46], pp. 20-1, who attribute this idea also to Popper).

This is however rather a travesty of Hayek's thought. Hayek never claimed that his opposition to state control of the economy derived from the (extremely banal) observation that it produces undesired effects (GRAY J.N. [25], pp. 131-32). Each action produces a host of effects, some desired, others undesired, as Sen does not fail to point out. Hayek's opposition to state control in the economy instead derived *a*) from the fact that in the market, while everyone tends to pursue his own personal interest, the result of the actions of everyone is also the achievement of a social objective, of the ordered and prosperous working of the economy as a whole, and *b*) from the fact that for Hayek this result, which is so important socially, is due to the action of individuals which is based on a myriad of knowledge which the state is unable to collect; and it is the fact that the state cannot collect the knowledge of individuals (not, we repeat, the fact that individuals' actions have unforeseen effects) which induces Hayek to say that the state cannot consciously seek to improve the results achieved by the market «spontaneously» or unconsciously.

Sen, in criticising Hayek, recalls that he lamented the «uncomprehending ridicule» to which Smith's principle of the «invisible hand» was sometimes subject (SEN A.K. [84], p. 1); but then himself misrepresents this principle when he writes that the observation that many consequences of our actions do not reflect our design is, in itself, very commonplace, and hence he finds it difficult to uphold «the Hayekian claim regarding the profundity of the insight provided by the perspective of the results of human action but not of human design» (SEN A.K. [84], p. 3). For a detailed criticism of Sen, see BARRY N.P. [4].

Furthermore, it is erroneous to argue that Hayek claims that the unforeseen consequences of state action are more damaging than advantageous without justifying this hypothesis (HELM D. [46], p. 20). Hayek did not advance a *hypothesis*, but a deduction that the inevitable consequences of the fact the state can never acquire all the knowledge dispersed among individuals are that the results consciously pursued by the state will be worse than the results achieved, in part unconsciously, by individuals.

[13] For Barry, the principal merit of Menger's *Untersuchungen* lay not in its contribution to the debate on the method, as is usually claimed, but in its reaffirmation of the theory that institutions develop as the spontaneous and unforeseen consequence of human actions (BARRY N.P. [3], pp. 81-9; see also HAYEK F.A. [33], pp. 146-9).

who maintained that rules and institutions which spontaneously come into being are always better than those consciously designed. Menger also criticised the supporters of rationalist liberalism, whom he (wrongly) identified with Adam Smith and his followers, who maintained that social institutions would always be a product desired by the legislator and that a good government should design the best institutions possible. And some have observed that this vision of Menger is similar (albeit with some small differences in emphasis) to that of Hayek, who, it is claimed, «includes a recognition of the importance of 'undesigned' institutions, but also a recognition of the importance of their being scrutinised critically» Shearmur [85], p. 215); an important difference between the opinions of Menger and Hayek on this matter is noted, on the other hand, in Hutchinson 1974 [14]. Those who, like Shearmur, maintain that Hayek also thought it right to consciously intervene to design the best institutions can havever cite on this issue only a paper from 1933, where Hayek explicitly wrote that the economist's appreciation of the spontaneous order of the market «does not by any means imply that the economist will arrive at a purely negative attitude towards any kind of deliberate interference with the working of the system» (Hayek [30], p. 133). Other liberals, even the most radical, on the contrary, have no doubts that intervention in the institutions is admissible. Buchanan, for example, interpreted Hayek's aversion to intervention on institutions as a manifestation of faith in social evolution which supposedly ensures the survival of efficient institutional forms and criticised Hayek's opposition to institutional reform because, in his (Buchanan's) opinion the institutions which survive and prosper are not necessarily those which maximise man's potential (Buchanan ([12], pp. 13-24). In other words, contrary to what Hayek appears to believe, Buchanan believed that cultural evolution does not ensure the survival of the best institutions [15].

---

[14] It should be noted that in the paper Hayek wrote for the express purpose of highlighting Menger's role in the history of economic thought there is no hint of the influence that Menger's thought had on his (Hayek's) on the issue in question (HAYEK F.A. [40]).

[15] North's theory of institutions, with its idea that institutions are subject to increasing efficiency, is a strong argument in favour of this thesis (NORTH D.C. [70], pp. 94 ff.).

5. - Law and Legislation According to Hayek

We cannot enter into a detailed discussion of Hayek's view of the distinction between laws and legislation in this paper because it would take us too far from our topic. Hayek, as is known, was against leaving Parliamentarians free to legislate on any question. But let us take the extreme case of a Parliament which lays down the structure of wages in law. Our general consideration on this issue is that it is unclear how Hayek, who obviously approves a government which imposes taxes and duties and which determines the salaries for its officials, could find logic arguments to argue that a parliament or government should never approve a wage structure which the free decision of the representatives of the majority of citizens consider better than that which spontaneously comes about in the market[16]. And this, we repeat, is an extreme case of state intervention in the economy via law.

In discussing these issues, we should also bear in mind that Hayek not only wrote that «the law serves, or is the necessary condition for, the formation of a spontaneous order of actions» (Hayek [39], p. 112), but also wrote that the spontaneous evolutive process of law «for a variety of reasons ... may lead into an impasse from which it cannot extricate itself by its own forces or which it will at least not correct quickly enough» and that «that fact that law that has evolved in this way has certain desirable properties does not prove that it will always be good law or even that some of its rules may not be very bad», and this means that we cannot altogether dispense with legislation (Hayek ([39], p. 88)[17].

Hayek sees many reasons why the spontaneous evolution of law gives rise to unsatisfactory results. The spontaneous evolution of law is often very slow and, above all, the evolution which is born from

---

[16] Kukathas observed that, given his system of thought, Hayek should resort to *ad hoc* arguments also to justify taxation (KUKATHAS C. [62], p. 162).

[17] In defending the universal and abstract character of laws, Hayek adds that they should not tend to achieve specific concrete purposes (HAYEK F.A. [39], p. 109). But it has been rightly pointed out that this request of Hayek is impossible as «all statute law is enacted to achieve certain concrete purposes, whether it be as broad as prohibiting theft or as narrow as proscribing entry into a specific defense installation without authorization» (HAMOWY R. [29], p. 382).

case-law decisions is as a rule unable to invert a consolidated trend, even if this has bad consequences. Very often, moreover, the development of law is the result of the influence of a specific class or social groups and in this case it will reflect the specific interests of these groups which may not be general interests[18]. In this case, therefore, what may be needed is «the revision not only of single rules but of whole sections of the established system of case law» (Hayek [39], p. 89)[19].

Hence for Hayek the system of rules «is the outcome of a process of evolution in the course of which spontaneous growth of customs and deliberate improvements of the particulars of an existing system have constantly interacted» (Hayek [39], p. 100); and it cannot be otherwise.

As regards laws and legislation, therefore, as Hayek believed that «the former is good» and «the latter bad, or at least dubious and quite possibly and probably at variance with the law of liberty», we can conclude that «Hayek praises legislation while he condemns it» (Dietze [21], pp. 136 and 138).

On this issue, we should note, a central point of Hayek's argument is that there is a close link between economic freedom and political freedom because control of economic activities is not merely control of a sector of human life, which can be separated from the rest of our activities; it is instead control of the means for attaining our goals and hence it is also control of our goals, because, in Hayek's opinion, anyone who has sole control of the means should also determine what goals are to be achieved, what values should be judged more important and therefore in what men should believe and to what they should aspire (Hayek [32], p. 92).

---

[18] With regard to the frequency of those cases in which the spontaneous evolution of law should be criticised and opposed, Barry rightly points out that «it is surely quite common for a legal system to develop spontaneously in undesired directions» (BARRY N.P. [3], p. 88).

[19] Elsewhere, Hayek wrote that the reason why one should modify the rules in certain situations «will not be that their application in the particular case would cause hardship, or that any other consequence in the particular instance would be undesirable, but that the rules have proved particularly insufficient to prevent conflicts» (HAYEK F.A. [39], p. 116).

But this is the point at which the paths diverge on the basis not of logical arguments, but on that of value judgements; because there is no doubt that, while some wish to leave all choice of the goals to be pursued to the individual, others prefer that the political will of the community, expressed freely by Parliament, should prevail for some important choices.

If it is true therefore that not even Hayek can find convincing logical arguments which induce one to state that «to control a spontaneous order is a contradiction in terms», if, in other words, not even so radical a liberal as Hayek can find strong arguments for maintaining that control of the economy via law (or in any case via non-discretionary interventions) is contrary to the principles of laissez-faire, it would appear we can only conclude that non-discretionary control of the economy is in line with those principles. As noted above, Buchanan, another champion of liberalism, was explicitly in favour of institutional intervention.

How then are we to distinguish between the two types of economic policy? Before replying to this question, it is opportune to better clarify what is, or how one may implement, non-discretionary control of the economy.

6. - Control of the Economy Via General Rules: Some Examples

Control of the economy via general and abstract rules, which leave little room to discretion, may be the rule for economic policy and may be quantitatively massive. Take, for example, the extreme case, mentioned above, of a state which has nationalised the tools of production and which wishes to regulate distribution on the basis of social criteria. To this end, Parliament could approve the wage structure, assigning an income to each category and the public administration could organise a well-ordered system of examinations to create, on the basis of merit, a classification of those who wish to carry out a certain type of work. An examination regulated by merit consists of non-discretionary rules which realise a non-mercantile distribution but which can be achieved in a market economy without destroying its spontaneous character (Jossa [54], pp. 87-94).

Another case of state intervention in the economy which may also be massive and which is achieved via non-discretionary intervention is that of state-controlled enterprises which behave according to the so-called «Saraceno's» model. Saraceno, who was the leading theorist of state-controlled enterprises in Italy, was convinced that said enterprises were the best tool for what he defined as «balanced» growth, i.e., for a type of growth which the country's social conscience judges convenient to rebalance the north-south gap (Saraceno [83], p. 37). With the purpose of maintaining public enterprises efficient and untainted from corruption, while endowing them with a political task, Saraceno proposed some general principles for regulating these enterprises' activities. In state-controlled enterprises, Saraceno noted, there co-exist two autonomous and differently motivated decision-making centres, the managerial and the political, which give different impulses to the enterprise's action. The management is charged with achieving economic efficiency[20], while the public action consists in directives from the public owner; but the management is also charged with ensuring that the two impulses are reconciled, and making sure that the enterprises attain the maximum return within the limits of the conditioning laid down by the public side (Saraceno [81], pp. 20 and 28-9; the same idea is argued in Guarino [28], pp. 82-3). But how can this reconciliation be guaranteed? In Saraceno's opinion, if state-controlled enterprises are all charged with a single political purpose (that of developing the Mezzogiorno), «the improper burden» imposed on them by the conditionings of the public hand should be covered by an endowment fund, established by Parliament with appropriate criteria, which leaves the enterprises a completely free hand to pursue the maximum return (Saraceno [82], pp. 59-60). As Stiglitz writes, in the public sector there are a number of objectives both economic and extra-economic; as a consequence, public managers can always claim that their enterprises are in the red not as a result of incompetence or

---

[20] Article 3 of the law of 22 December 1956 which established the Ministry of State Holdings in Italy lays down that state-controlled enterprises should operate «in accordance with criteria of economic efficiency».

For the different interpretations of the principle of economic efficiency laid down by the law of 1956, see, for example, SARACENO P. [81], pp. 20-1; DI CHIO G. [20]; and CAFFERATA S. [15], Chapter 3.

inefficiency but rather as a result of their striving for objectives other than profit (Stiglitz [88], p. 37 ff.). To this end, Saraceno's model proposes organising things so that the managers of state-controlled enterprises are engaged in pursuing only the maximum return.

This is not a suitable place for a detailed discussion of Saraceno's proposal, which has moreover already been comprehensively discussed elsewhere (Coda [17]; Grassini [23]; Martinoli [66]; Momigliano [68]; Vacca [91]; Leccisotti [63]; Macrí [65]; Bottiglieri [10]; Jossa [51]). The remarks above, however, should make it clear that «Saraceno's model» represents another important case of state intervention in the economy which does not contrast with the «spontaneous» market order theorised by Hayek[21], neither is it open to the abuses on which the public choice focuses its attention[22].

But the above are only two particularly important cases of state intervention in the economy which, while being so extensive as to embrace the whole economy, do not have the vices of statism, as they do not give the public administration any discretion. Other examples of the type of economic policy which we are discussing spring readily to mind: fiscal policy, monetary policy, labour legislation, regulations for public services, ensuring male-female equality, regulation of the ownership rights, rules for shop licences drawn up on the basis of very general parameters, etc., etc. To generalise, the type of policy to which we are referring is therefore that of a state intervention in the economy which takes place via general and abstract rules, equal for all. These rules do not necessarily have to be laws passed by Parliament, because provisions and regulations equal for all which leave no

---

[21] On the public enterprise Hayek wrote: «There is great difficulty in ensuring that such enterprise shall be conducted on the same terms as private enterprise; and it is only if this condition is satisfied that it is not objectionable in principle» (HAYEK F.A. ([35], p. 224).

[22] It has been pointed out that the economic justification for nationalisations is complex, but is basically based on a macro- and a micro-economic argument. The macroeconomic argument sees public enterprises as a tool for controlling the economy, the microeconomic argument is based on the supposed superiority of the planned allocation of resources vis-à-vis allocation entrusted to the market alone (HELM D. [44], pp. 29-31). If planned allocation of resources means an allocation which tends not only to correct but also to substitute allocation of resources via the market, the distinction between the two arguments can be used to state that the Saraceno's model justifies nationalisation with the macro- but not with the microeconomic argument.

discretionary margin to the public administration can also be issued by the government and the executive in general. Henceforth, we shall therefore refer to this type of state intervention in the economy as «non-discretionary».

7. - Control of the Economy According to Keynes

On this issue, let us consider the thought of Keynes[23], who is usually considered as the main point of reference for those who propose systematic intervention of the state in the economy. Keynes, we recall, had sympathy for the «socialisation» of economic life and wrote, in passages which are perhaps little known, that big enterprises tend to socialise, because in them the control increasingly separates from the ownership to the point that it becomes irrelevant whether the company is publicly or privately owned (Keynes [55], p. 290). But the statement that big companies tend to socialise did certainly not lead Keynes to claim that in the long term the market should be increasingly replaced by state intervention in the economy.

Keynes believed that «progress lies in the growth and the recognition of semi-autonomous bodies within the State — bodies whose criterion of action within their own field is solely the public good as they understand it, and from whose deliberations motives of private advantage are excluded» (Keynes [55], p. 288). In other words, Keynes saw «a natural line of evolution» which led companies to socialise and he approved this tendency and wrote, without mincing his words, that «we must take full advantage of the natural tendencies of the day» (Keynes [55], p. 290) and foster the socialisation of enterprise. Nonetheless, it should be noted that Keynes's sympathy for the «socialisation» of economic life meant that he regarded the transition from private enterprise to public enterprise without concern, not that he looked favourably on the extension of the public administration's sphere. In *The End of Laissez-Faire* he noted that «the ineptitude of public administrators strongly prejudiced the practical man in favour of laissez-faire» (Keynes [55], p. 275) and added

[23] I dwelt on Keynes and the public enterprise in Jossa B. [50].

that «we must probably prefer semi-autonomous corporations to organs of the Central Government for which Ministers of State are directly responsible» (Keynes [55], p. 290).

It is true that, in his *General Theory,* Keynes made it clear that the central controls needed to ensure full employment will naturally require a vast extension of government's traditional functions, (Keynes [58], p. 379), especially because socialisation of a certain size of investment will prove the sole means for allowing an economy to approach full employment (Keynes [58], p. 378). But Keynes was also explicit that the function of control of the public hand, the fundamental function of the state in economic activity, which alone can ensure that the market system achieves the general interest, should be carried out by semi-automous corporations. He wrote: «I believe that in many cases the ideal size for the unit of control and organization lies somewhere between the individual and the modern State» (Keynes [55], p. 288).

It may seem, therefore, that Keynes thought that a system such as that of state-controlled enterprises, which other countries have often envied in Italy, was particularly suited to carrying out the state's fundamental role in the economy (Keynes [56] and Jossa [53], pp. 208-11). But others are not of the same opinion. Keynes not only had little faith in, but also had a bad opinion of politicians (Skidelsky [86], pp. 260 and 345, and [87], p. 148); and that led him to believe that the task of stimulating or making public investments to maintain aggregate demand should be entrusted to monetary policy or to semi-autonomous bodies, public or private, which gave guarantees that they would act for the public good (Skidelsky [87], p. 148-52).

As Skidelsky pointed out, Keynes's conception of the state was very different from that which is common today; and he did not trace the economic limits of the state in the manner in which we do so today. He made a crucial distinction between the government, the public administration and politicians, on the one hand, and the state, on the other. The characteristic of the type of administration that Keynes called state is not that it is a publicly-owned body, but that it acts for the public good; by state Keynes understood the group of institutions, public or private, which, like the central bank, pursue public purposes (Skidelsky [87]).

Whatever interpretation we wish to give to Keynes's thought on this matter it is clear that the type of economic policy Keynes suggested was certainty not that of direct state intervention in the economy but rather that which was entrusted to competent, efficient bodies dedicated to the public good which use the levers available to the public hand to achieve goals of general interest. Furthermore, Keynes did not suggest, in a vague manner, more state intervention in the economy, neither did he in any way suggest a state intervention which endowed politicians and public administration with wide-ranging discretion but rather suggested a state intervention which, while controlling the market, guided it to do what the market by itself could not (Keynes [55], p. 291).

8. - Control of the Economy Via Laws and the So-called «Negative Liberty»

It was noted above that a very interventionist economic policy which is implemented via general rules cannot be easily criticised by the more radical liberalists, for example by those who accept Hayek's thought. This should be no surprise, because such an economic policy conforms to the principle of «negative liberty» which for Hayek and many others coincides with the idea of liberty itself. Negative liberty is a concept which dates back to Hegel and has been used, more recently, by Berlin and Nozick (see Berlin [7] and Nozick [72] among others). Negative liberty is defined as the liberty which is born from the absence of voluntary interference on the part of somebody aimed at reducing the spheres of action of somebody else, i.e., the absence of coercion on the part of other humans. In the vision of Hayek and others, the idea of negative liberty is linked to the distinction between liberty and liberties; and Hayek has made clear here that «the difference between liberty and liberties is that which exists between a condition in which all is permitted that is not prohibited by general rules and one in which all is prohibited that is not explicitly permitted» (Hayek [35], p. 19); and in Hayek it is this vision of liberty as negative liberty which makes all those who wish to impose a conscious design on society enemies of liberty (Tomlinson [90], pp. 20-1).

According to Nozick, each individual has rights or historical claims to appropriate goods and resources which the state cannot infringe because those rights and claims come before any other right and are inalienable and unexpropriable. For Nozick, these rights give life to what he calls «the minimum state», i.e., a state which intervenes only to protect persons against violence and deceit on the part of others and ensure the observance of contracts. But the fact is that an economic policy implemented by general and abstract rules, however massive it is, respects negative liberty. An economic policy without discretion, in fact, entails precisely that lack of voluntary interference of anyone in the spheres of activity of others which may in some way limit human liberty. When economic policy is regulated by general and abstract rules, it is the will of the law, to which we are all subject, which limits the liberty of the individuals, not the will of this or that individual. And this suffices to save the principle of negative liberty, even if the state often intervenes to control and regulate economic activity.

However, in the vision of negative liberty which Tomlinson attributes to Hayek, the attempt to impose a conscious design on society, even if realised by general and abstract rules, violates negative liberty (Tomlinson [90]). But here Tomlinson confuses two different questions. That Hayek criticises any government which attempts to impose a conscious design on society is a well-known fact; but this does not mean that a government which seeks to realise a distributive policy by general and abstract rules or a government which seeks to develop those regions which lag vis-à-vis the rest of the country in accordance with Saraceno's model violate the principle of negative liberty. Hayek, it is true, after having himself defined liberty as that situation in which nobody is subject to coercion from the arbitrary will of another person or persons (Hayek ([35], p. 11), cites, in the notes, Bentham's affirmation that «liberty then is of two or even more sorts, according to the number of quarters from whence coercion, which is the absence of, may come». But Hayek states literally, as we noted above, that liberty «is a condition in which all is permitted that is not prohibited *by general rules*» (our italics) and this clearly means that (at least for Hayek in 1960) negative liberty is not infringed by limits to its exercise which are placed by general rules. In fact, Hayek is explicit in stating that «the range of variety of government action that in, at least in principle, reconcilable with a free system is thus considerable. There is ample scope for experimentation and improvement within that permanent legal framework which makes it possible for a free society to operate most efficiently» (Hayek [35], p. 231)[24].

9. - The Two Approaches to Economic Policy

If, therefore, economists of the very different monetarist and Keynesian schools often concur that the best economic policy is non-discretionary control of the economy via law, how are we to distinguish between the various orientations of economic policy which even today divide economists into schools which are very different from one another? Or, more specifically, is it still possible today to identify two economic policy lines which superimpose (one of the right and one of the left, if we use the language of politics), two economic policy lines whose nature is such that the more one follows one of the approaches the less one necessarily follows the other?

A preliminary response to this issue is as follows. The crisis of statism, the acceptance by all of the market economy and also the acceptance by many, qualified economists of different schools of the idea that the optimum economic policy is that of non discretionary control does not make the division of economists into two schools, that which defends the market and that which criticises it, outdated because, the more one criticises the market, the more one should seek to correct its outcomes (even via non-discretionary intervention measures). For those who accept this opinion, the two lines of economic policy which clash are those of the «minimum state» and that of massive state intervention in the economy via general and abstract rules.

A second response to the question posed is that of those who maintain, with Hayek, that the basic contrast between the two lines of

[24] In Gray's judgement, «by contrast with all doctrines of minimum government, Hayek's contention is that government may supply any good or service desired by a democratic electorate, provided that its doing so involves no coercion beyond that entailed in its being funded from taxation» (GRAY J.N. [25], p. 137).

economic policy is between those defend the spontaneous nature of the market economy and those who maintain the need for control. But, for those who have accepted the observations made to this point, it should be said to clarify this contrast that: *a*) the control in question is control via the levers of the market and not the discretionary control of public officials; *b*) control via general and abstract rules does not destroy the impersonal nature of the market order, as well described by Hayek, neither does it transform that order into organisation.

In justification of this second response it should be pointed out that, as we have already noted, discretionary control lays itself open to abuse, to use for personal aims; hence control in the public interest, which seeks to correct the disfunctions of the market, can only be control via non-discretionary rules valid for all.

Even for those who accept this second opinion, naturally, the two lines of economic policy which are set against one another are those of minimum state intervention in the economy and that of massive (but non-discretionary) intervention.

The second manner of tracing the two opposing lines of economic policy becomes, we believe, more convincing if, to follow marxist ideas, we observe that the spontaneous nature of the capitalist market is, on close investigation, the control of capital over human activity. As Marx observed, indeed, free competition liberates not individuals but capital; and «as long as production resting on capital is the necessary hence the fittest form for the development of the force of social production, the movement of individuals within the pure conditions of capital appears as their freedom», but is, on closer examination, their subjection (Marx [67], p. 650). To the spontaneousness of the capitalist market one can therefore oppose man's control of his production activities (which achieves its highest form in self-management).

The above observations may appear open to criticism. In a recent book, in fact, Stiglitz states that criticism of the market does not automatically entail the acceptance of planning or control. As is known, Stiglitz considered that the attention paid by economists to the problems of uncertainty and information in the past ten or twenty years had given birth to a new paradigm of economic science, the so-called «informational paradigm». This new paradigm shows that the «market failures» are rules and pervade the entire economy: in all transactions between private players deficiences of information or market imperfections give rise to inefficiencies which, although small in each single case, are cumulatively of significant importance. Furthermore, the market failures highlighted by the new paradgm are not those dealt with by the standard welfare theory (for example, air pollution) for which the remedy is a specific economic policy. The character and diffusion of these market failures, therefore, not only destroy trust in the efficiency of the market mechanisms, but also destroy the conviction that the state can correct the market's deficiencies.

In other words, the main conclusion of the informational paradigm, namely that the markets are not, as a rule, in equilibrium and that «externalities» are to be found everywhere, would appear to furnish a formidable argument in support of planning: if the market does not function (this is the old argument of the socialists) it has to be substituted with centralised choices. But, according to Stiglitz's analysis, each central authority has only a limited capacity for acquiring, processing and diffusing information; and the state's capacity to correct the market's deficiencies is also limited. The upshot is that there is no reason to believe that centralisation is better than decentralisation (Stiglitz [89], Chap. 9; and also Helm [46]).

Stiglitz's arguments are undoubtedly of great interest. However, we believe that, despite his observations, the classification we propose, which is of a very general nature, is not invalidated by them. Criticism of the market implies corrective interventions; as Stiglitz himself observed (Stiglitz [88], pp. 42-4), if corrective interventions are not possible, they will obviously not take place. But this does not diminish the fact that each new criticism of the market, if founded, suggests the need, in general, for more state control.

10. - Conclusions

We have sought above to demonstrate that, given the state of the debate, with the crisis of statism, the two lines of economic policy to be set against one another are, as Hayek argued throughout the second phase of his extensive research activities, that which seeks to leave the economy to the spontaneousness of the market and that of man's conscious control of economic activity. But the control which economic policy should realise wherever such is possible, we have argued, is not the bureaucratic control of which Hayek spoke when he associated socialism to «constructivism», it is not the discretionary control which substitutes another regulatory mechanism for the market, but it is control via rules which can and should be a control which leaves the public administration no space for discretion. Control via rules can be very pervasive, because economic activity does not take place in a vacuum, without regulations, in a space which is unchanging, which history and institutions have not changed in the past and cannot modify in any way in the future.

We should continue to accept the distinctions between the «economic» and the «political» spheres, between «private» and «public», between individual decisions and collective decisions; but the two spheres interweave in a myriad of ways and thus it is far from easy to hypothesize a pure economic sphere, free from any legal constraint, or a pure political or legal sphere which is not conditioned by the economic structure (Samuels [80], Chap. 5); and this makes it clear that control of the economy by law can be even more pervasive that running the economy in accordance with a planner's orders.

An excellent, recent paper notes that today «the separation of the economic and political object of analysis turns out to be ambiguous, and undesirable, leading to a blurring of the borders which were traditionally drawn in social sciences, between market and non-market contexts, between individual and collective decisions» (Grillo [27], p. 76). But others continue to think otherwise and believe that other steps (in addition to those made by the authors discussed by Grillo) have to be made before politics can be reduced solely to the language of buyer and seller, of trade and contract, thus removing all «logic foundation» to the separation between economics and politics (Reale [77], p. 103); and we also share the opinion that economics and politics should be kept apart because the logic of individual decisions is different from that of collective decisions, the economy is a spontaneous order and the political system is the set of rules, commands and institutions which control that spontaneous order. But if we accept this distinction, it is clear that the truly collective decisions are those taken by a democratic procedure, they are, above all, the rules established in conformity with a democratic process, not the bureaucratic and discretionary choices of the public administration[25].

The above observations may tempt us to conclude that the division of economic thought into schools should no longer be based on the contraposition between market and state or between liberalism and socialism, or between state intervention or non-intervention in the economy, as has been the case for some two centuries now, but rather on the contraposition, in a market economy, of non-intervention and intervention via general and abstract laws. But this would perhaps entail giving too much weight to the arguments of this paper, which deals with only one aspect of a much broader series of problems for which it is not easy to draw definitive conclusions[26].

---

[25] Hayek's distinction between order and organisation would appear to lie at the base of the distinction between the two types of planning identified by Cairncross and Helm who claim there is a socialist or egalitarian planning, which tends to be a non-mercantile organisation activity (and which therefore overlooks the role of the price mechanism in the allocation of resources), and a liberal or Keynesian planning, which tends to correct the results of the market (CAIRNCROSS A. [16], p. 308 and HELM D. [47], pp. 25-36).

[26] On the extent of the problems raised when discussing the economic role of the state see, for example, the papers in HELM D. [46], which have been cited several times above, STIGLITZ J.E. [88] and SAMUELS W.J. [80].

BIBLIOGRAPHY

[1] ALSOPP C., *The Macro-Economic Role of the State*, 1989, in HELM D. [46].

[2] BALDASSARRI M. - PAGANETTO L. - PHELPS E.S. (eds.), *Privatization Processes in Eastern Europe*, London, MacMillan, 1993.

[3] BARRY N.P., *Hayek's Social and Economic Philosophy*, London, McMillan, 1979.

[4] ——, «In Defence of the Invisible Hand», *The Cato Journal*, Spring-Summer, 1985.

[5] BAUMOL W.J., «Sir John Versus the Hicksian, or Theorist Malgré Lui», *Journal of Economic Literature*, vol. 28, n. 4, 1990.

[6] BECKERMAN W., *How Large a Public Sector?*, 1989 in HELM D. [46].

[7] BERLIN I., *Four Essays on Liberty*, Oxford, Oxford University Press, 1969.

[8] BOETTKE P.J., «Hayek's *The Road to Serfdom* Revisited: Government Failure in the Arguments Against Socialism», *Eastern Economic Journal*, vol. 21, n. 1, 1995.

[9] BOITANI A. - RODANO G. (eds.), *Relazioni pericolose*, Bari, Laterza, 1995.

[10] BOTTIGLIERI B., «Linee interpretative del dibattito sulle partecipazioni statali nel dopoguerra», *Economia Pubblica*, vol. XIV, n. 4-5, 1984.

[11] BRENNAN G. - BUCHANAN J.M., «Predictive Power and the Choice among Regimes», *Economic Journal*, vol. 93, March 1983.

[12] BUCHANAN J.M., «Law and the Invisible Hand», reprinted in *Freedom in Constitutional Contract*, Texas, College Station, 1979.

[13] ——, «Costituzione e politica», *Economia delle Scelte Pubbliche*, vol. 5, n. 1, 1987.

[14] BUNGE A.M., *The Critical Approach to Science and Philosophy*, New York, McGraw Hill, 1964.

[15] CAFFERATA S., *Pubblico e privato nel sistema delle imprese*, Milano, F. Angeli, 1983.

[16] CAIRNCROSS A., *Years of Recovery: British Economic Policy, 1945-51*, London, Methuen, 1986.

[17] CODA V., «Come rendere operante un corretto modello decisionale per le Partecipazioni Statali?», *Economia e Politica Industriale*, vol. III, n. 10, 1975.

[18] COLONNA M. - HAGEMANN H. - HAMOUDA O., *Capitalism, Socialism and Knowledge; The Economics of F.A. Hayek*, vol. II, Aldershot, Edward Elgar, 1994.

[19] COTTINO G. (ed.), *Ricerca sulle partecipazioni statali; studi sulla vicenda italiana*, Torino, Einaudi, 1978.

[20] DI CHIO G., «L'impresa a partecipazione statale: profili storici e giuridici» 1978, in COTTINO G. (ed.), [19].

[21] DIETZE G., *Hayek on the Rule of Law*, 1977 in MACHLUP F. [64].

[22] EATWELL J. - MILGATE M. - NEWMAN P. (eds.), *The New Palgrave*, London, MacMillan.

[23] GRASSINI F., «Il ruolo del fondo di dotazione degli enti pubblici di gestione», *Economia e Politica Industriale*, vol. III, n. 10, 1975.

[24] GRASSL W. - SMITH B. (eds.), *Austrian Economics*, Sidney, Croom Helm, 1986.

[25] GRAY J.N., *Hayek on Liberty*, Oxford, Basil Blackwell, 1984.

[26] ——, *Hayek on the Market Economy and the Limits of State Action*, 1989, in HELM D. [46].

[27] Grillo M., *Economia e politica*, 1995, in Boitani A. - Rodano G. [9].

[28] Guarino G., *Le Partecipazioni Statali: crisi del sistema o della collettività?*, 1976, in Various Authors [92].

[29] Hamowy R., *The Hayekian Model of Government in an Open Society*, 1991, reprinted in Wood J.C. - Woods R.N. [94].

[30] Hayek F.A., «The Trend of Economic Thinkings», *Economica*, vol. 40, n. 3, 1993.

[31] ——, *Scientism and the Study of Science*, 1979, in Hayek F.A. [44].

[32] ——, *The Road to Serfdom*, London, Routledge, 1944.

[33] ——, *The Counterrevolution of Science. Studies on the Abuse of Reason*, 2nd edn., Indianapolis, Liberty Press, 1979.

[34] ——, *Degrees of Explanation*, 1967, in Hayek F.A. [38].

[35] ——, *The Constitution of Liberty*, Chicago, University of Chicago Press, 1960.

[36] ——, *The Theory of Complex Phenomena*, 1967, in Hayek F.A. [38].

[37] ——, *Kinds of Rationalism*, 1967, in Hayek F.A. [38].

[38] ——, *Studies in Philosophy, Politics and Economics*, London, Routledge and Kegan, 1967.

[39] ——, *Law Legislation and Liberty*, Vol. I, *Rules and Order*, Chicago, University of Chicago Press, 1973.

[40] ——, *The Place of Menger's Grundsätze in the History of Economic Thought*, 1978, in Hayek F.A. [43].

[41] ——, *The Pretence of Knowledge*, 1978, in Hayek F.A. [43].

[42] ——, *Socialism and Science*, 1978, in Hayek F.A. [43].

[43] ——, *New Studies in Philosophy, Politics and the History of Ideas*, London, Routledge and Kegan, 1978.

[44] ——, *Law, Legislation and Liberty*, Vol. 3, *The Political Order of a Free People*, Chicago, University of Chicago Press, 1979.

[45] ——, *The Fatal Conceit; the Errors of Socialism*, London, Routledge and Kegan, 1988.

[46] Helm D. (ed), *The Economic Borders of the State*, Oxford University Press, 1989.

[47] ——, *The Economic Borders of the State*, 1989, in Helm D. [46].

[48] Hume D., *Essays; Moral, Political and Literary*, in Hume D., *Philosophical Works*, Vols III and IV, London, 1886.

[49] ——, *Philosophical Works*, Vols III and IV, London, MacMillan, 1886.

[50] Jossa B., «Keynes and Lange on the Public Enterprise», *Contributions to Political Economy*, n. 10, 1991.

[51] ——, *Mezzogiorno, partecipazioni statali e ruolo dell'impresa pubblica*, 1991, in Jossa B. [52].

[52] —— (ed.), *Il Mezzogiorno alle soglie del 1992*, Napoli, Guida Editori, 1991.

[53] ——, *Is there an Option to the Denationalization of Eastern European Enterprises?*, 1993, in Baldassarri M. - Paganetto L. - Phelps E.S. [3].

[54] ——, *Hayek and Market Socialism*, 1994, in Colonna M. - Hagemann H. - Hamouda O. [18].

[55] Keynes J.M., *The End of Laissez-faire*, 1981, in Keynes J.M. [59].

[56] ——, *The Public and the Private Concern*, 1981, in Keynes J.M. [60].

[57] ——, *Essays in Persuasion*, 1981, in Keynes J.M. [59].

[58] ——, *The General Theory of Employment, Interest and Money*, London, MacMillan, 1936.

[59] KEYNES J.M., *The Collected Writings of John Maynard Keynes*, vol. IX, London, MacMillan, 1981.

[60] ——, *The Collected Writings of John Maynard Keynes*, vol. XIX, London, MacMillan, 1981.

[61] KIRCHGASSNER G., «On the Political Economy of Economic Policy», *Economia delle Scelte Pubbliche*, vol. 7, nos. 1-2, 1989.

[62] KUKATHAS C., *Hayek and Modern Liberalism*, Oxford, Clarendon Press, 1989.

[63] LECCISOTTI M., «Obiettivi sociali delle partecipazioni statali e fondo di dotazione», *Economia Pubblica*, vol. VII, June 1978.

[64] MACHLUP F. (ed.), *Essays on Hayek*, London, Routledge & Kegan, 1977.

[65] MACRÌ R., *Il fondo di dotazione e il ruolo di programmazione degli enti di gestione*, 1980, in PENNACCHI L. [76].

[66] MARTINOLI G., «Meditato pessimismo sulle imprese a partecipazione statale», *Economia e Politica Industriale*, vol. III, n. 10, 1975.

[67] MARX K., *Grundrisse*, Harmondsworth, Penguin Books, 1973.

[68] MOMIGLIANO F., "Astrattezza e irrealtà di un processo decisionale", *Economia e Politica Industriale*, vol. III, n. 10, 1975.

[69] NAERT F., «The Political Economy of Pressure Groups», *Economia delle Scelte Pubbliche*, vol. 3, n. 1, 1985.

[70] NORTH D.C., *Comment*, 1989, in STIGLITZ J.E. [88].

[71] ——, *Institutions, Institutional Change and Economic Performance*, Cambridge, Cambridge University Press, 1990.

[72] NOZICK R., *Anarchy, State and Utopia*, Oxford, Basil Blackwell, 1974.

[73] OLSON M., *The Rise and Decline of Nations*, New Haven, Yale University Press, 1982.

[74] OECD, *The Role of the Public Sector*, Paris, OECD, 1985.

[75] PEIOVICH S., *A Property Right Analysis of Alternative Methods of Organising Production*, mimeo, 1993.

[76] PENNACCHI L. (ed.), *Il sistema delle partecipazioni statali*, Bari, De Donato, 1980.

[77] REALE M., *Commento*, 1995, in BOITANI A. - RODANO G. [9].

[78] ROWLEY C.K., «The Economic Philosophy of James Buchanan», *Economia delle Scelte Pubbliche*, vol. V, n. 3, 1987.

[79] RYAN, *Value-Judgements and Welfare*, 1989, in HELM D. [46].

[80] SAMUELS W.J., *Essays on the Economic Role of Government*, London, MacMillan, 1992.

[81] SARACENO P., *Il sistema delle imprese a partecipazione statale nell'esperienza italiana*, Milano, Giuffrè, 1975.

[82] ——, «Il processo decisionale nel sistema delle imprese a partecipazione statale», *Economia e Politica Industriale*, vol. III, n. 9, 1975.

[83] ——, «Il sistema delle partecipazioni statali», *Economia e Politica Industriale*, n. 29, 1981.

[84] SEN A.K., «The Profit Motive», *Lloyds Bank Review*, n. 147, January 1983.

[85] SHEARMUR J., *The Austrian Connection: Hayek's Liberalism and the Thought of Carl Menger*, 1986, in GRASSL W. - SMITH B. [24].

[86] SKIDELSKY R., *John Maynard Keynes: Hopes Betrayed, 1883-1920*, London, MacMillan, 1983.

[87] ——, *Keynes and the State*, 1989, in HELM D. [46].

[88] STIGLITZ J.E., *On the Economic Role of the State*, Oxford, Basil Blackwell, 1989.

[89] ——, *Whither Socialism?*, Cambridge (MA), MIT Press, 1994.

[90] TOMLINSON J., *Hayek and the Market*, London, Pluto Press, 1990.

[91] VACCÀ S., «Potere politico e tecnostrutture delle imprese a partecipazione statale», *Economia e Politica Industriale*, vol. III, n. 10, 1975.

[92] VARIOUS AUTHORS, *L'impresa nell'economia italiana*, Milano, F. Angeli, 1976.

[93] VAUGHN K.I., *Invisible Hand*, 1987, in EATWELL J. - MILGATE M. - NEWMAN P. [22].

[94] WOOD J.C. - WOODS R.N. (eds.), *Friedrich A. Hayek; Critical Assessments*, vols I-IV, London, Routledge and Kegan, 1991.

Wage Control and Economic Performance

Carlo Dell'Aringa *
Università del Sacro Cuore, Milano

Recent experience in Italy appears to indicate that the choice of a particular industrial relations model can have important effects on the level of economic performance.

The 1980s saw a growing interest in the economic effects of the various systems of collective bargaining. These systems differ considerably from country to country. One important conclusion reached was that centralised collective bargaining systems fostered wage moderation and greater employment.

Subsequent literature on this issue shows that not only centralised collective bargaining systems but also very decentralised ones can produce good macroeconomic results. The only systems at a disadvantage from this viewpoint are those 'intermediary' ones whose wage control systems are based on collective bargaining at sector level.

The purpose of this note is to summarise the theoretical and empirical contents of this literature, and bring it up to date with the results of the latest contributions.

The theoretical models which have dominated wage determination literature in recent years are the monopoly union, efficiency-wage and bargaining models. To a greater or lesser extent, each of these models has highlighted the system of incentives which influences the behaviour of each contracting party. In this context, the level of bargaining centralisation can be considered as the level of

---

* The author is Professor of Political Economics.

cooperation between trade unions on the one side and employers on the other in the wage determination process.

The fundamental tenet of the aforementioned literature is that an increase in wages of one group of workers can have negative externalities for other groups. These externalities can be internalised via a process of cooperation between trade unions on the one hand and employers on the other.

The literature identifies several negative externalities. These include: *a*) the effect on consumer prices; *b*) the effect on the production costs of other companies; *c*) fiscal effect deriving from the increased spending on the unemployment engendered; *d*) an effect on unemployment and on job search duration of other unemployed; *e*) an "envy" effect in other workers; *f*) an inverse "wage-efficiency" effect (workers of other sectors or companies are demotivated).

Given these externalities, cooperation internalises the negative effects and makes the wage increase of each group of workers more expensive (or less attractive). The upshot is wage moderation which increases employment.

The arguments above would appear to indicate that there is a monotonic relation between the degree of centralisation and employment. But this is not so. Other authors have shown that very decentralised systems can also achieve excellent results. Calmfors-Driffil, among others, have shown the «hump» relation between economic performance and the degree of bargaining centralisation. The worst situation is to be found when bargaining is at the intermediate, sectoral, level in a closed economy context. Under these conditions, workers and companies have little inhibitions as regards requesting and granting wage increases. Companies can increase the prices of their products so that the increase in the «consumer wage» does not imply an increase in the «product wage». In a wholly decentralised (competitive) system, companies cannot increase prices as the product wage would increase in line with the consumer wage. In a wholly centralised system there is no difference, by definition, between the trend of product and consumer wages. In a wholly centralised system neither relative wages nor relative prices can change. Under these conditions, in both centralised and decentralised systems, workers and companies are inhibited in requesting and granting wage increases.

The strength and persuasion of the arguments above diminish in the case of an open economy. If the product of a production sector can be replaced by an imported product, even sectoral bargaining may be constrained (and hence moderated) by international competition. This is obviously less true for sectors protected from international competition.

Similarly, the advantages of the decentralised model (at company level) are much fewer if monopolistic rather than perfect competition is the prevailing market form.

Finally, the degree of centralisation can influence the bargaining power of the parties. A strong, centralised trade union is likely to have the upper hand in wage talks if the employers are not similarly organised.

Two other aspects of the problem, in addition to those found in existing literature, should be considered. These two additional aspects concern the central level of collective bargaining.

Firstly, the central level of bargaining is accompanied by a further, decentralised level of bargaining. I.e., a high level of centralisation often coincides with bargaining at several levels. This is the case in, among others, Italy. Secondly, the centralisation of bargaining does little to harmonise the wage differentials to the need for a properly functioning labour market.

We shall examine these two aspects separately.

A level of centralised bargaining which overlaps with a decentralised one engenders the problem of the summation of the wage increases requested. If a problem of summation exists *de facto*, there is a problem of nominal wage rigidity and it is necessary, all other conditions being equal, to at least tolerate a higher level of inflation. The success of some countries (Japan, Germany and Austria) can be attributed to the fact that there has only ever been one (centralised) level of bargaining.

The difficulties in keeping wage differentials flexible enough under a centralised bargaining system give rise to a similar problem. At the central level «solidaristic» logics may prevail, but these logics may contrast with the good functioning of the local labour markets. Here again, as in the previous case, it is by no means certain that this gives rise to real rigidities (for example rigid wage differentials). It may be that the real values of the variables achieve their equilibrium values at higher (and increasing) nominal wage levels. In other words, the system may function well only with a higher level of inflation.

Italy's recent experience would appear to suggest that these last two aspects examined are of considerable importance and should be carefully analysed before concluding, once and for all, that the wage bargaining policy adopted to date and that consists of a strong central level of bargaining accompanied by a further decentralized level is always and at any event the best for the creation of additional employment.

Origins of Bad Policies: Control, Corruption and Confusion

Andrei Shleifer
Harvard University Cambridge (MA)*

1. - Introduction [1]

Many, if not most, economic policies pursued by governments around the world reduce public welfare. Governments routinely start, and fail to end, inflations, introduce regulations whose costs vastly exceed their benefits, fail to provide protection to private property, and get involved in an ever-increasing set of activities they cannot properly run. The question is why? What are the origins of bad economic policies?

Economic theory has offered some persuasive answers to this question. Buchanan and Tullock [6], following in the footsteps of Federalist Papers, have argued that democratic majority rule can lead to inefficient policies that redistribute resources from the minorities to the majorities. Stigler [19] argued in contrast that organized minorities often gain control of economic policies, and convince the government to pursue highly inefficient policies that redistribute resources from the public as a whole (majority) to themselves. Still other economists attribute bad economic policies to government mistakes.

This paper does not have much new to contribute theoretically to this work. Rather, it tries to develop some of the standard ideas in a

* The author is Professor of Economics.

N.B.: the numbers in square brackets refer to the Bibliography at the end of the paper.

[1] This paper draws on many of the conclusions obtained in joint research with Maxim Boycko and Robert W. Vishny.

bit more detail using the examples of policies toward property rights that have been discussed and pursued in Russia in the early 1990s. Few of these policies have reflected the will of the majority, since Russia's youthful democracy is not yet especially responsive to public concerns. Excessive pensions, minimum wages, and other middle class benefits are yet to hit Russia in the same way as they have hit developed countries or even Eastern Europe. As a result, the federalist concerns about populism and majority rule are not of much relevance in the analysis that follows. However, many of the policies considered and pursued in Russia reflect the power of lobbies, so the Stiglerian analysis is highly relevant. In addition, the so-called policy mistakes are highly relevant, and I devote most of the paper to the analysis of such mistakes.

For my purposes, it is useful to distinguish three sources of bad policies. The first is the politicians' desire to control property so as to use it to gain political support. For example, politicians often prefer political control over firms in order to force these firms to hire extra people who would then support these politicians with votes or political services (Boycko, Shleifer and Vishny [3], [4] and [5] and Shleifer and Vishny [17]. The second source of bad policies is politicians' interest in personal income, namely bribes (Shleifer and Vishny [15], [16]). Both control and corruption are best understood in a Stiglerian framework, where politicians pursue bad policies to appeal to particular concentrated interests. Finally, the third critical reason for bad policies is the confusion of politicians – their using wrong models of the economy, and even more important of the government, in making policy proposals. Confusion of policy makers is universal, yet I will argue that it has presented absolutely devastating problems for transition economies. My goal is to illustrate the role of these three sources of bad economic policies in the case of Russian policies toward property in the last few years, and to suggest strategies to improve the quality of economic policy making during transition.

The next two sections deal with control and corruption relatively briefly, since these issues have been discussed extensively elsewhere. Section IV focuses on the role of confusion. In addition to a few straightforward examples, I will discuss in some detail economic policies proposed by one of Russia's leading reform politicians (Yavlinsky and Braguinsky [22]). This example dramatically illustrates the policy predicament of many transition economies. Section V concludes. Although the examples in this paper come predominantly from Russia, I believe that the analysis is highly relevant to many developing, as well as developed, economies.

2. - Control

Politicians throughout history have tried to control productive assets through public ownership or regulation. Historically, such control brought sovereigns income which would have been difficult to obtain through taxation alone (Ekelund and Tollison [8]; Tilly [20]). Sovereigns established quasi-public monopolies to collect rents from consumers, regulated trade to charge fees and claimed ownership of natural resources to raise funds for the state. These funds were then used to support the sovereigns' lifestyles, as well as to wage wars, which took up the vast majority of public budgets. The sovereign was typically too weak, and his vassals too strong, to raise all the desired revenues through taxation of income or wealth (De Long and Shleifer [7]).

With the growth of democratic government throughout the world, the need to control property to raise revenue has diminished, since the state has generally become powerful enough to satisfy its needs through taxation. Instead, control over property has become a way for politicians to direct its use to win elections. For example, many countries in the world nationalized bankrupt industries, such as coal and steel, to prevent significant unemployment and win votes. More generally, politicians often control firms to force them to hire extra people and pay higher wages, with the idea that the beneficiaries will vote for the politicians, work on their campaigns or even terrorize their opponents. Grossly overstaffed European state airlines and steelmakers, third world parastatals in all sectors, and municipal government enterprises in the United States all illustrate how control over firms brings politicians support from their employees as well as from the trade unions. Without direct control, politicians could not get such inefficient employment and wage levels out of private firms, except by making politically unacceptable transfers from the public to the private sector.

While employment and extra wages paid to political supporters are the most common political benefits accruing to politicians controlling firms, there are many other benefits as well. For example, politicians controlling banks can direct these banks to lend money to political allies (witness Credit Lyonnais' loans to the friends of the socialist party). Control over food distribution has enabled African politicians to extract resources from farmers, and to transfer them to political allies, including city dwellers (Bates [2]). Control of the railroads allows politicians in many countries to provide free transport to specific population groups whose support they seek. More generally, control over all productive assets in the economy has been the principal mechanism of controlling population pursued by communist regimes around the world: it enabled them to ignore the consumers, build up the armies, and deprive their opponents of any means of subsistence.

The behavior of Russian politicians following the collapse of communism illustrates how bad economic policies — some proposed and some actually pursued — are governed by politicians' preference for maintaining control over productive assets. The collapse of the communist party deprived politicians of their control over firms, since the communist party served as the traditional enforcer of that control through central planning and the power to fire and hire managers. This control reverted to managers and employees of former state firms, as well as to outsiders who received shares in privatization. Not surprisingly, politicians have fought this loss of control tooth and nail, by both opposing privatization and promoting policies reestablishing political control.

One unfortunate illustration of this phenomenon is the failure of land privatization in Russia, where the agricultural interests have successfully prevented the breakup and privatization of collective farms. The effect is that agriculture remains highly inefficient and dependent on government subsidies, which in turn allows the directors of collective farms to maintain their control over the farm workers and to deliver farmers' votes for the agrarian party that lobbies for and gets the subsidies. In cities as well, the local governments have maintained control over registration and transactions in land, which has enabled them to keep control over much of small business that has no choice but to cater to the local politicians (as well as bribe them, see below). Control over land and real estate has been a critical source of political power of both national and local politicians.

With respect to industrial assets, a dramatic attempt by the traditional politicians to maintain control has been the repeated introduction of proposals to form financial-industrial groups. When defending these proposals, the industrial ministers usually referred to the Japanese keretsu and Korean chaebol. In practice, they wanted to maintain control over firms by putting together whole industries into organizations that would be controlled by the former ministries, with powers to coordinate major production and investment decisions. The ministries offered firms a key service — lobbying for cheap state credits — in exchange for the political support for the preservation of these ministries. If adopted, this policy would have frozen the former state firms in the position of gross inefficiency and dependence on the government for survival. Fortunately, unlike in the case of land, these mechanisms of political control of firms have not succeeded in Russia, largely because of the popular appeal of the privatization program and the desire of enterprise managers to free themselves from the ministries.

The inefficiency of communism, and of state production more generally, vividly illustrates the enormous costs of political control of business. The fundamental question, then, is how can these costs be reduced. One commonly advocated approach is to rely on bureaucratic reform, which would replace the existing political control by that of publicly spirited, efficient bureaucracies that are free of political influence. There are a small number of such allegedly efficient and publicly-spirited bureaucracies in the West (e.g., Electricite de France, perhaps BBC), as well as in rapidly growing East Asian economies, such as Japan, Korea, Taiwan and Singapore, although even in those countries public interference in business has been extensively criticized. Unfortunately, in countries with weak and corrupt governments, and traditionally parasitic rather than public-spirited bureaucracies, the inefficiencies of public control cannot be eliminated unless bureaucracy is radically reformed. Without a dictatorship or a foreign occupation, there are no good ideas for how to reform bureaucracy. Good public control, therefore, is usually not a viable option.

In these circumstances, political control needs to be reduced rather than upgraded. The principal policy for reducing political control of assets is privatization. Privatization deprives politicians of their control over firms, and also makes it more difficult for the politicians to persuade firms through subsidies to serve political goals. In Russia, privatization went a long way toward freeing firms from political influence by turning firms over to their managers, employees, and outside investors. As a result, most of the industrial ministries have either disappeared or lost much of their power. In other countries of the world as well, including those in Western Europe, privatization helped to weaken or destroy much of the political influence on firms, as well as some of the institutions through which this political influence is maintained, such as the labor unions. The result is that bad policies — such as the maintenance of extra employment or the provision of politically desirable product mix — have receded and efficiency of the economy has begun to improve. The accumulating evidence from Russia as well as Western Europe indeed shows that the efficiency benefits of privatization have been substantial, largely because of the decline of political influence over firms (see Megginson *et* Al. [13], Lopez-de-Silanes [11] and Boycko, Shleifer and Vishny [5] for some of the evidence on the benefits of privatization).

3. - Corruption

Political benefits are not all that politicians derive from controlling productive assets. The other important benefit is bribes. When politicians have the power to control the decisions of firms, to regulate them, or to issue them permits to pursue new activities, they can collect bribes in exchange for less intrusive control, regulatory relief, or fast issuance of permits. Politicians readily take advantage of these opportunities. Many of the laws and regulations that politicians put in place have little social benefit, but facilitate the collection of bribes in exchange for relief from these very laws and regulations. The bad policies are put in place because they enhance politicians' personal income when private agents pay bribes to escape these policies. (I should note that in some countries, some corruption is legalized, and hence the word "bribes" is not used. For example, in the United States, politicians receive campaign contributions in exchange for favors that in other countries bring bribes).

Again, examples abound throughout the world. Many countries have customs regulations that are sufficiently complex and inconsistent as to make imports and exports that do not violate these regulations impossible. Trading companies then simply pay bribes to customs officials to get on with their business. Even if a shipment does not violate any of the regulations, the customs officials have the authority to take long enough to ascertain this fact that it is easier to pay a bribe to let the goods move. Many of the shortages of goods in communist Russia were created through underpricing explicitly to provide bribe income to the officials allocating these goods.

Economic transition, and the resulting need for a new legal and regulatory structure, presents politicians with a broad range of new opportunities for bribe-seeking policies. Three examples will suffice, but they can be multiplied. When Russia created a new national anti-monopoly committee to deal with the problems of market power, the first act of this committee was to create a list of firms it classified as monopolies. Once the list was put in place, the committee could claim jurisdiction over pricing and other policies of these firms. Some major national enterprises appeared on this list, but many small local businesses, from bakeries to bathhouses, also appeared as local monopolies. Firms immediately began to pay bribes to the local anti-monopoly officials just to get themselves off the list.

The federal bureaucracy charged with the creation of a private land market began its activities by claiming monopoly over the registration of all land plots and land transactions. Very few rules were put in place by the bureaucracy obligating the officials to actually do anything. Not surprisingly, the local employees of this bureaucracy were often bribed by private parties that had no ability to do anything except with a registration. It is not clear that the registration system that was put in place had any purpose other than to provide income for the officials.

Another famous example of a bad policy designed to enrich the officials is oil export quotas that are allocated by government fiat rather than auction. These quotas give the government officials in charge of allocating them enormous power to favor one oil company over another, and to charge for the favors. Not surprisingly, the relevant officials strongly oppose not only the elimination of the quotas but even attempts to auction them off.

Dealing with corruption is often difficult. One approach — similar to privatization — is to reduce the role of government in the economy by eliminating regulations and perhaps even whole agencies that have the power to write them. But this approach goes only so far, since in many instances transition economies need laws and regulations for markets to function. No government at all is not an answer to this need. Another approach is bureaucratic reform. Again, the problem is that only a few political leaders without dictatorial power have enough authority to reform the bureaucracy. In effect, a major revamping of government — including both the people and the rules by which it functions — is needed (Klitgaard [10]). In a country like Russia, no leader has such authority at the moment, and therefore top down bureaucratic reform is not imminent.

The best available strategy for controlling corruption in the short run is probably the democratic process, since voters do not like corruption. Elections can work in two ways. First, corrupt officials often, though not always, lose them. Second, at some point in time elections can bring in leadership that is prepared to undertake government reform. In this way, the structure of government, and not just the people, will change through the electoral process. Democratization is thus an essential element of eliminating corruption, but it is not a fast process.

The importance of substantial turnover of existing politicians through the democratic process should not be underestimated. Many of the politicans in power in Russia and other transition economies have taken bribes, and are beholden to the people who paid them. This is the reason these politicians are so afraid to lose office: they become useless to those who paid them, and hence vulnerable to exposure. A new cadre of politicians, who have not yet been compromised by corruption and who might clean up the government, is needed to control corruption.

4. - Confusion

Politicians sometimes pursue bad policies simply because they are confused, in the sense of having a bad model of the economy or of the government. Confusion is fundamentally different from control and corruption, in the sense that the latter both serve politicians' self-interest whereas confusion often does not. Confused politicians maximize their welfare given their beliefs about the world, but end up worse off than they would have been if they used a more accurate, and publicly available, set of beliefs. Confusion thus refers to failure to use available knowledge.

The prevalence of confusion is not surprising, especially in transition economies. Economic models are quite difficult, and economists themselves often disagree on the right model of the economy. In fact, many distinguished Western economists have revealed the same confusion as some of the Russian politicians about the process of transition. Moreover, many of the politicians in transition economies have developed their world views under communism. Like most other people, they have developed their models of the world based largely on their personal experiences, which in most cases did not include much exposure to markets. Even if these politicians were free thinkers under communism, they often have trouble understanding the market economy. Last but not least, the Western economists, to whom the transition politicians sometimes listen, tend to be the professional outcasts who have failed to find an audience in the West, and who therefore try to establish a reputation in transition economies. Because they have trouble figuring out which experts to listen to, politicians end up exposed to the wrong ideas, which only reinforce their confusion.

Confusion pervades economic policy making even in advanced market economies: witness President Reagan's expectation that tax cuts in the United States would increase revenue, or President Clinton's notion that government control of healthcare would make its provision more efficient. Nonetheless, several factors ameliorate the confusion of politicians in market economies. First, by definition, these politicians have personally observed market economies in action, and hence have formed their beliefs based on some observation of reality, in contrast to the politicians in post-communist economies. Second, the marketplace of ideas is more open in market economies, and hence these politicians had more, though not necessarily enough, opportunities to disabuse themselves of their most egregious misconceptions. Of course, politicians in market as well as transition economies often make confused arguments because they lie to appeal to voters, even if they are not confused themselves. Still, as I show below, at least some of the confusions appear to be genuine.

Some of the examples from Russia are straightforward enough to require little comment. Gorbachev has argued that the communist party — the essence of whose governance has been complete control over all aspects of life — would lead Russia toward some sort of a social market economy. He appeared to have little notion of the limits that market economies place on politicians, and of how fundamental these limits are for market economies to function. In privatization, many people in Russia have argued for turning firms into an equivalent of collective farms as a means of privatization, with worker control and no traded shares. The fact that such firms have failed in most countries because they could not make decisions, raise capital, or change management did not stop the argument. In the legal arena, Russia's Civil Code — written by the best legal minds of the communist era — holds shareholders in some cases liable for the debts of their companies. Despite explanations from French, German, Italian and American experts that limited liability is essential for the ability of corporations to raise funds, the Russian lawyers refused to accept it, virtually destroying the hopes for foreign (or any other outside) investment in Russian firms. It is difficult to attribute this feature of the Civil Code to anything but confusion[2].

Last (but not least), Russia is not unique in the world in having suffered from the theory — advanced by the governor of its central

[2] Thanks to Jonathan Hay for this example.

bank among others — that inflation is a consequence of monopoly pricing and not money creation, and that regulation of monopolies and price controls can stop inflation even if money supply continues to expand. There are few theories in economics as well documented and widely professionally accepted as monetarism, particularly in the case of rapid inflation. Still, the alternative theory managed to get a lot of air. This and the previous arguments, of course, have been made by intelligent people, and many have lead to disastrous economic policies.

There is another, much more subtle, class of ideas about transition economies, that deal with the role of government in the transition. These ideas tend to be based on the economic model of a benevolent and effective government, and to ignore the reality of actual governments in Russia and elsewhere. To illustrate this extremely common type of confusion about economic policy, I will rely on an article by Yavlinsky and Braguinsky [22]. This article has three advantages. First, the authors' vision of the proper nature of transition in Russia is very clearly described and so can be analyzed in some detail. Second, this article represents the case of a major Russian politician of reformist orientation clearly putting his views on paper, so that they can be discussed. Third, Mr. Yavlinsky is surely one of the most sophisticated and westernized politicians in Russia, who until his recent conversion to the ideas of Lance Taylor has been influenced by the best Western thought about economic transition. He is both a leader of a reform faction, and a co-author of the *500 day plan,* a highly orthodox reform program proposed, but not accepted, in Russia in 1991.

One could argue that, as a politician, Mr. Yavlinsky might be misrepresenting his true beliefs to create a politically appealing platform. This is surely true. However, the fact that Mr. Yavlinsky took the trouble to publish his views in a professional journal likely to be read by at most a few dozen people suggests that he is not just campaigning. There are no political benefits to the publication of this article. It is much more likely that the article was published because Mr. Yavlinsky is anxious to convey to the academic world, and to record for posterity, his conception of economic transition.

The general theme of the YB article ([22], p. 89) is to contrast two fundamentally different approaches to economic reform. The shock therapy approach they reject specifies that «the transition to a market economy should be accomplished by freeing the activity of economic agents to the utmost possible degree and at the highest possible speed». Instead, (YB [22], p. 111) they advocate «an entirely new strategy of transition, one that would emphasize active government intervention in privatizing, developing national industry and providing financial backing for savings, investment and growth, which is the only way to ultimate financial stabilization». Indeed, YB propose a transition strategy with extensive control of the economy. Below I describe their argument in some detail, both because of its intrinsic interest, and because it reveals clearly how bad policies can come about.

YB ([22], p. 93), begin with a perceptive, if not always accurate, analysis of the Russian transition, and in particular of the laissez-faire policies which were part of that transition. First, they criticize privatization on two grounds: the lack of a mechanism in the privatization program for replacing ineffective managers, and the related slowness of post-privatization restructuring. Second, they claim that price liberalization in Russia was not complete and that therefore «policy design chosen in Russia in 1992 was a further increase in relative price distortions and conservation of an inefficient industrial structure» (YB [22], p. 96). Third, they argue that stabilization policies have been ineffective because «it is impossible to attain macroeconomic stabilization prior to institutional, structural and other real adjustment». In particular, absent such adjustment, government subsidies to firms have to continue. Finally, they complain that free trade policies are deindustrializing Russia (YB [22], pp. 102-103).

Although all these complaints have some plausibility, they are all basically false. While privatization has not lead to as fast a management turnover and restructuring as one would wish, the process of change has begun in hundreds of firms, and has surely been much faster than would have occurred under state ownership (see Boycko, Shleifer and Vishny [5] for an overview of the evidence). While some price distortions in Russia remain, an enormous rationalization of prices has actually followed price liberalization, with consumer prices actually clearing markets and energy prices reflecting more accurately its value in alternative uses. Far from increasing distortions, price liberalization has been the clear and unambiguous success of reforms. Nor is it accurate to argue that stabilization should come only after structural reforms. As Sachs [14] has shown on numerous occasions, most reforming economies have begun by achieving macroeconomic stability, and implemented deeper reforms only after the government gained solvency and effectiveness. Finally, Russia and other transition economies desperately needed a rapid transformation of their productive activities from heavy manufacturing to consumer goods and services. To the extent that free trade accelerated this transformation, it surely helped Russia to move to markets faster.

But the inaccuracy of YB criticisms is not really that important: it is common in Russia, as well as in politics more generally, to criticize what others have done regardless of merit. The real trouble comes from their alternative view of transition, "the policy-led transformation design". Here again they touch on several aspects of policy, each of which illuminates a widely-shared confusion.

With respect to privatization (YB [22], p. 106) they argue that «the government should exercise its rights as the owner of state property for one last time, and it should satisfy that it is transferring property into the right hands». In particular, «establishing a system of specially designed long-term investment banks with technical and perhaps financial assistance from the West and especially Japan, would go a long way toward solving the problem» [of deciding what to do with firms]. In short, YB want the government to continue controlling firms, and to restructure them with the assistance of government-controlled investment banks. To be fair to YB, this sentiment is not unique to them: it is shared by a variety of Western economists (see, for example, McKinnon [12], Tirole [21]).

This strategy reveals a profound confusion about the effects of government control. As we argued above, politicians throughout the world have used their control over firms (either direct or through government banks) to keep defunct firms afloat, delay restructuring, maintain excessive employment, and otherwise promote politically undesirable inefficiencies. The idea of enhancing government control before privatization to promote restructuring simply flies in the face of all the evidence of the effects of such control. Moreover, the YB approach overlooks the basic fact that, by 1992, the government in Russia had lost much of its control over firms, which have reverted to their managers. The reason that the privatization program showed much accommodation of managers is precisely because they controlled firms already. In reality, the government in Russia owned very little, and to the extent that it tried to exercise its control, it was strictly detrimental to efficiency.

Secondly YB ([22], p. 108) advocate a policy of government investment. «Instead of just relying on market forces, the government should design a serious program of developing manufacturing industries on a new basis, and one of the priorities from the government side should be the basic infrastructure, roads, railways, communications facilities and housing». The issue of efficiency of government investment has been quite controversial even in some of the best-governed economies, such as those of East Asia (Young [23]). In economies with weak and corrupt governments, such as Russia, investment projects inevitably support the least efficient industries, precisely the "prestige and military projects" that YB want to get away from. Even today, the government of Russia's effectively dead textile region (Ivanovo) is putting its last funds into building new textile factories, while the old ones are standing idle. The governor of Amur region (on the border with China in Southern Siberia, where hardly anyone lives) speaks of his plans to bring an automobile factory to the regions. The history of the last 20 years of communism has revealed a great deal about the grotesque waste coming from investment projects pursued by the Russian government.

On the question of monetary policy, YB ([22], p. 110) are inconsistent. They first denounce premature macroeconomic stabilization, they suggest the urgent need for «a system of government and private long term investment banks» to make long term loans (to whom?). They (YB [22], p. 110), also advocate «special savings deposits that are repaid in kind, for instance, in automobiles», a gimmick that they acknowledge has been already tried and failed. Finally, having aired these creative proposals for fighting inflation, they advocate the introduction of a new currency, which would be stable internationally and fully convertible, to be issued by «a specially created bank under the supervision of an international currency board». That is, in the end, YB want to turn to a hard core monetarist stabilization, whereby the government gives up control of its money supply.

With respect to trade policy, (YB [22], p. 113) they go back to the traditional «strategy of strengthening the competitiveness of national industry, including export and import subsidies where necessary». In practice, as world experience has shown, this means retention of the existing, grossly inefficient and uncompetitive industrial structure. Such policies have been discredited around the world, for solid empirical and theoretical reasons.

YB ([22], p. 105), conclude their paper with a memorable paragraph, worth quoting in full: «As we have shown time and again in this paper, in advising on Russian reforms, mistakes were made that even the most mainstream theorists could not have made if they had only cared to think. In the old days, engineers who constructed a railway bridge in Russia had to stand under it when the first train crossed. One should either stake one's life in this transformation or better do something else. Hence, in concluding this paper we risk going outside the usual academic style and ask all those advisers who care so little about the countries they try to help that they are unable even to theorize properly to stay at home». In other words, leave us to our own confusion.

The YB paper is depressing for a variety of reasons. It shows the extremely poor quality of understanding by even the best liberal Russian economists. Importantly, the errors that YB make have to do with failures to understand not basic economics but rather the nature of government in transition economies (Goldman [9]). The analysis raises serious questions about the likely quality of the Russian economic policy in the decades ahead. After all, YB are not far from the best policy analysts who exist in Russia. Their paper shows how lucky Russia has been to have decent leadership in the first years of its transition.

Yet the real question, as always in Russia, is what's to be done? How can the quality of economic thinking and policy making be improved? Part of the answer is surely the continuation of the attempts to persuade Russian policy makers about the wisdom of laissez-faire policies. Although they often have inaccurate models of the economy, many policy makers in transition economies are extremely intelligent. Some of them can be persuaded by logic and by pointing at the obvious successes of economic freedom in Western Europe, Latin America, and the Far East. The success of Jeff Sachs as a world-wide policy adviser is an eloquent testimony to the effectiveness of persuasion in many circumstances.

The trouble with persuasion is that its effects are fickle. A politician persuaded by Jeff Sachs one year can turn to Lance Taylor the next, as we have seen from the YB paper. Russian President Yeltsin shows considerable volatility in his beliefs as well. The results can be highly unfortunate. Even if a politician is permanently persuaded, in a democracy he can be easily replaced by another politician, with very different views and with an explicit agenda to change policies.

A bigger problem with the effectiveness of persuading politicians of the wisdom of laissez-faire policies is that such policies are broadly incompatible with their interest in control and corruption. Interventionist policies of the sort YB advocate typically go hand in hand with extraordinary discretionary power of the politicians, which gives them both the ability to generate political benefits through their control and access to bribes. The Lance Taylor approach to economic reform is a sure-proof recipe for political control and corruption. One needs to go no further than to recall the emphasis on controlling trade and increasing government investment. To persuade a Russian politician of the wisdom of laissez-faire policies is to convince him to give up the benefits to which his predecessors have been accustomed since time immemorial.

All this suggests that persuasion is not enough. A much more fundamental set of changes is needed to reduce the level of confusion in public decision making. These changes are of two broad categories: democratization and the replacement of human capital. Neither will do enough on its own, but together, if they go far enough, they can spell a fundamental change in the quality of economic decision making — with respect to property rights as well as other issues — in both Russia and many other countries in the world.

The principal benefit of democratization is that it shifts political power — and hence the attention of the politicians — from the established lobbies to new political groups and to voters. In particular, democratization usually reduces the benefits to politicians of allocating the society's wealth to the traditional political constituencies, such as defunct state firms and the military. Instead, politicians begin to pay more attention to voters (which is not always good, since it can lead to destructive populist policies — witness macroeconomic populism in Latin America or the growth of social spending in Eastern Europe) as well as to the new propertied classes, who often have a strong interest in macroeconomic stability and property rights reform. In addition, democratization is probably the single most effective strategy for combatting corruption, since voters' anti-corruption sentiment is strong and fairly universal. Thus, while this is not always true, democratization generally makes laissez-faire economics a more likely outcome.

But democratization is probably not enough. Many traditional policians are too closely tied to their traditional constituencies, as well as too deeply involved in corruption schemes to move to laissez-faire policies. This, combined with exceptionally poor training, makes it unlikely that they can be persuaded of the wisdom of markets. For economic policies in Russia to change, politicians need to change. In this respect, unfortunately, the prospects for Russia are considerably gloomier than they are for Eastern Europe, since Russia experienced much less turnover of its political elite when communism fell than did the East European countries. Even many of the so-called liberal economists and politicians in Russia are tied to the Gorbachev regime, which after all was only an enlightened communist regime. To make genuine progress with economic policy, Russia needs new and younger faces in its politics.

There is a striking parallel here between economic and political restructuring. A clear lesson of the Russian privatization is that new people rather than new incentives for the old people, are responsible for enterprise restructuring. Firms that change are firms run by new people (for some statistical evidence, see the evidence on Russian shops in Barberis, Boycko, Shleifer and Tsukanova [1]). But there is casual evidence pointing in the same direction from industrial firms as well. New policies for the economy in this respect are similar to new policies for firms: they require new human capital, embedded in new people, to be successfully carried out.

But youth and novelty alone are not sufficient for enlightened views of the economy. Russia provides numerous examples of young politicians who begin with some interest in laissez-faire but then slide into policies more compatible with the existing political powers. Yavlinsky of course is one example, but there are even members of Yeltsin's initial reform team who turned to communist or pseudo-communist view. One of the most difficult problems is how to keep young, intelligent politicians from getting confused, or from switching their ideologies away from liberalism?

The only real answer is transfer of knowledge through education and training. Some education occurs by osmosis, as politicians and business people become exposed to more and more Western ideas. Other education, such as Ph.D.'s in economics or less time consuming degrees, is obviously more expensive. Still, there are no real alternatives. The Latin American investment in the training of its political elites in economics has proved a remarkable success — despite the recent setbacks in Mexico. (Imagine what would have happened in Mexico if the elites were not trained in economics). The same approach in the long run is probably the best strategy for Eastern Europe and Russia as well. Unfortunately, this implies that, in the short run, these countries will be stuck with extraordinary policy volatility, and with a great deal of confusion as to what the best strategies for transition really are. Unless these countries are lucky to get very good politicians from the start — as the Czech Republic was with Vaclav Klaus — their transition is going to be slow.

5. - Conclusion

This paper has tried to describe the three fundamental origins of bad economic policies: control, corruption, and confusion. It emphasized Russia, but with the hope that the reasoning elaborated here can be applied elsewhere as well. The fundamental conclusion of this paper is that the battle against poor policies has to take place on all feasible fronts. The role of government in economic life has to be reduced; hence policies such as privatization are essential for reducing the damage from poor economic policies. Political institutions, and politicians themselves, need to be revamped and upgraded; hence the democratic process plays a crucial role in steadily removing bad politicians as well as improving the institutions. Finally, the knowledge and beliefs of the political elites need to be upgraded; hence the critical role of training and Western exposure more generally in the process of improving policy formation.

These are all slow, evolutionary steps. One could hope instead that the political process in Russia (and other countries) leads to the election of top leadership that really shakes up the political system, revamps institutions, brings new, more knowledgeable people into politics, and thus radically improves the quality of economic policy making. While this can happen, it makes no sense to do nothing and just wait for the messiah. Given the enormously poor quality of economic policy making, the returns to even slow, evolutionary methods of improving policy formation can be very high. And it is equally important to remember that the charismatic leaders who win on the platforms of radical political reform can change things radically for the worse, as well as for the better.

BIBLIOGRAPHY

[1] BARBERIS N. - BOYCKO M. - SHLEIFER A. - TSUKANOVA N., «How Does Privatization Work: Evidence from the Russian Shops», *Journal of Political Economy*, 1996.

[2] BATES R., *Markets and States in Tropical Africa: the Political Basis of Agricultural Policies*, Berkeley, University of California Press, 1981.

[3] BOYCKO M. - SHLEIFER A. - VISHNY R.W., «Privatizing Russia», *Brookings Papers on Economic Activity*, n. 2, 1993, pp. 139-9.

[4] ——- ———-——, «A Theory of Privatization», *Economic Journal*, March 1996.

[5] ——- ———-——, *Privatizing Russia*, Cambridge (Mass)., Massachusetts, Institute of Technology Press, 1995.

[6] BUCHANAN J.M. - TULLOCK G., *The Calculus of Consent*, Ann Arbor, University of Michigan Press, 1962.

[7] DE LONG J.B. - SHLEIFER A., «Princes and Merchants: European City Growth Before the Industrial Revolution», *Journal of Law and Economics*, n. 36, 1993, pp. 671-702.

[8] EKELUND R.B. - TOLLISON R.D., *Mechantilism as a Rent Seeking Society*, College Station (TX), Texas A&M University Press, 1981.

[9] GOLDMAN M.I., *Lost Opportunity: Why Economic Reforms in Russia Have Not Worked*, New York, Norton, 1994.

[10] KLITGAARD R., *National and International Strategies for Reducing Corruption*, Durban (South Africa), University of Natal, manuscript, 1995.

[11] LOPEZ-DE-SILANES F., *Determinants of Privatization Prices*, Cambridge (MA), Harvard University, manuscript, 1994.

[12] MCKINNON R.I., *The Order of Economic Liberalization: Financial Control in the Transition to a Market Economy*, Baltimore, Johns Hopkins University Press, 1991.

[13] MEGGINSON W.L. - NASH R.C. - VAN RANDENBORGH M., «The Financial and Operating Performance of Newly Privatized Firms: an International Empirical Analysis», *Journal of Finance*, 1994.

[14] SACHS J.D., *Proceedings of the World Bank Annual Conference on Development Economics 1994*, 1995, pp. 57-80.

[15] SHLEIFER A. - VISHNY R.W., «Pervasive Shortages under Socialism», *Rand Journal of Economics*, n. XXIII, 1992, pp. 237-46.

[16] ———-———, «Corruption», *Quarterly Journal of Economics*, n. CVIII, 1993, pp. 599-618.

[17] ———-———, «Privatization in Russia: First Steps», in BLANCHARD O. - FROOT K. - SACHS J. (eds.), *The Transition in Eastern Europe*, vol. 2, Restructuring, Chicago, University of Chicago Press, 1994.

[18] ———-———, «Politicians and Firms», *Quarterly Journal of Economics*, n. 109, November 1994.

[19] STIGLER G.J., «The Theory of Economic Regulation», *Bell Journal of Economics*, n. II, 1971, pp. 3-21.

[20] TILLY, C., *Coercion, Capital, and European States, AD 990-1990*, Berkeley and Los Angeles, University of California Press, 1990.

[21] TIROLE J., «Privatization in Eastern Europe: Incentives and the Economics of Transition», *NBER Macroeconomic Annual*, 1991, pp. 221-59.

[22] YAVLINSKY G. - BRAGUINSKY S., «The Inefficiency of Laissez-Faire in Russia: Hysteresis Effects and the Need for Policy-Led Transformation», *Journal of Comparative Economics* n. 19, 1994, pp. 88-116.

[23] YOUNG A., *The Tyranny of Numbers: Confronting the Statistical Realities of the East Asian Growth Experience,* Cambridge (Mass.). Massachusetts Institute of Technology, manuscript, 1995.

Economic Theory and Institutions: An Introductory Note

Giovanni Caravale *
Università «La Sapienza», Roma

1. - Introduction

The purpose of my paper is threefold. First, it emphasizes that reference to the institutional framework represents an integral part of economic theory if this latter is to be conceived as a tool mainly directed to the comprehension of the functioning of actual economic systems. Thus conceived economic theory emerges as basically evolutionary in nature.

Second, it underscores that the integration of the institutional framework in the theoretical construct cannot be achieved with reference to the neoclassical scheme of analysis, either in its traditional, or in its more recent versions. An alternative theoretical approach, of Classical and Keynesian flavour, seems to offer – it is maintained – a far better chance.

Third, the paper supplies a critique of Pasinetti's recent position on the relationship between economic theory and institutions: though placed in the correct "alternative" (i.e. non-neoclassical) perspective, Pasinetti's distinction between two phases in the construction of economic theory (the "pre-institutional" one of "pure" theory; and that in which institutions are introduced in the argument) should give

---

* The author is Professor of Economics at the University of Rome "La Sapienza".

N.B.: the numbers in square brackets refer to the Bibliograpy at the end of the paper.

way – it is concluded – to the direct consideration of the institutional framework in the theoretical context.

2. - Istitutions and Economic Theory

It has been recently maintained, by Langlois ([4], p. 5) and Coase ([3], p. 230) respectively, that «neoclassical theory is a theory without institutions», while «[early] American institutionalists... had nothing to pass on, except a mass of descriptive material waiting for a theory, or fire».

I shall comment later in a little more detail on the former statement. I feel however it is important to emphasize at once that the substance of the point emerging from the compound sentence can be shared with no reservation whatsoever. Neither a theoretical scheme without appropriate institutional foundation nor an institutional framework without a theory can be of any use from an economic viewpoint; and that therefore the two aspects, or the two "sides" as Pasinetti ([7], p. 2) calls them, must be put together in the construction of an adequate interpretative tool.

The problem is connected with the very conception of our discipline, Economics, or – to use the old and perhaps more appropriate term – Political Economy. As I emphasized elsewhere (Caravale [2]), this is to be thought of as the social science whose principal aim is that of spelling out the regularities that characterize the phenomena of value, production and distribution in given social and institutional contexts, with a view to supplying points of reference for those responsible for the policy choices to be made.

The central logical moment of the process of theorizing is the identification of the model, i.e. a simplified representation of the world (or that portion of it which is the object of the analysis) capable of capturing the essential features, the fundamental traits of the reality that surrounds the political economist, like the drawing of a landscape or of a portrait where the artist makes no attempt at a faithful reproduction of every single aspect of the real world, but tries only to fix on paper what appear to him the most important elements of what he is looking at. In order to be relevant, the representation of economic reality must show a series of essential, and strictly interconnected, properties:

(*i*) the description should be *significant* in that it should capture the essential features of the world; in other words it should depict, on the one hand, the dominant, or systematic forces at work in the economic system (as the classics put it), and, on the other hand, the context – *the institutional context* – in which these forces operate;

(*ii*) the decription should also be *significant* in another sense: in that the position so described should represent a (potential) point of attraction for actual values[1]. Should this attraction not exist, or not be proved, the desciption – however accurate – would in a way remain *separate* from the actual working of the economic system, and would thus be meaningless for the comprehension of this latter;

(*iii*) the position described by theory should represent the "outcome" of the rational choices made by economic agents in the institutional framework which has been assumed.

It is clear that this way of conceiving Political Economy implies an essentially evolutionary vision of its nature. Differences in the institutional framework of different economic systems in the same period; or changes in the institutional context of one country through time, imply – in this perspective – different behaviour patterns on the part of the agents, or different outcomes of their decisions; therefore a different theoretical explanation of the functioning of the economy, and a different position of equilibrium for the system. In turn this implies the need for a much more *humble* approach to economic theorizing: the Lucifer-like ambition to identify "eternal" economic laws can no longer be cultivated, thus giving way to the more down-to-earth attempt to identify specific "regularities", or "uniformity rules" in specific institutional frameworks.

---

[1] This expression should be taken to mean a situation which would be reached if the basic conditions contributing to identify the equilibrium position were to remain unchanged through time (at least until the adjustment process is completed). The fact that this condition is never met, since there is a continuous change in the above mentioned conditions, implies that the point of attraction for the actual system moves through time (and may in fact never be actually reached), but does not deprive the "description" of its significance. The process of gravitation can in fact be thought of as the movement of the actual system in the direction of the relevant equilibrium position; a direction which is bound to change continually as a consequence of the change in the "basic conditions".

3. - Neoclassical Analysis and the "Alternative" Approach

The recognition of the need to integrate economic theory and institutions does not in itself solve the question concerning the choice of the theoretical approach upon which the integration should be based.

The first candidate is of course the theory which has been dominant for over a century: what is generally termed neoclassical economics. The point allows me to go back to the statement by Langlois cited above, according to which "neoclassical theory is a theory without institutions". Is that true? Is neoclassical economics a theory without institutions? According to Pasinetti ([7], pp. 4-6) the question calls for a negative answer. «Neoclassical theory, both in its traditional and in its more recent formulation, presupposes – he writes – the set of institutions of a perfectly functioning free market economy» Pasinetti ([7], p. 6); that is a social framework characterized by private ownership of the resources and by the assumption that utility maximizing individuals freely exchange their resources in perfectly competitive markets. "[S] tripped down to its essentials – writes Pasinetti ([7], p. 5) – the basic features of neoclassical economics are reducible to a ... model that is known as the Walrasian pure exchange model. In it, there are; a set of resources, that are taken as given and are supposed to be scarce; a set of individuals, with very well defined and perfectly known set of logically consistent preferences; and the postulate is made that they maximize their utilities, subject to their budget constraints». The same is true also of the more recent, and highly sophisticated version of the theory supplied by Arrow and Debreu ([1]), the basic problem posed being the optimum allocation of scarce resources.

Contrary to what is maintained by Pasinetti, Langlois's thesis that neoclassical economic theory is a theory "without institutions" appears substantially correct, in the sense that it refers to an institutional framework which has no counterpart in historically experienced economic systems. The delicate issue is made no easier by the fact that neoclassical economists, while denying that their theoretical edifice plays an apologetic role with regard to existing "market" systems, claim that the theory only intends to show how a fully decentralized economic system is capable of reaching an equilibrium which is optimal both from the viewpoint of the utilization of available resources and from that of social equity. This contention raises in effect a number of problems:

a) first of all, in order to attain its objective – whatever this may be (the abstract representation of an allegedly decentralized system, or the representation of the "core" of the functioning of actual market economies), the theory should be free from ambiguities and logical inconsistencies. As the long and intense debate of the sixties has shown, this is certainly not the case of neoclassical theory;

b) second, the claim regarding the "remoteness" of the theory from the actual reality of contemporary capitalist systems appears difficult to accept: neoclassical economics cannot be thought simply to represent a refined intellectual game with no connection whatsoever with reality, but must be seen as the result of the ingenious and generous life-long efforts made in order to construct a representation, a "mirror" of that same reality, or at least of its relevant aspects;

c) last, but certainly not least, the idea of a "fully decentralized" system – or, to put it differently, the idea of a market economy "in its purest form" (Pasinetti [7], p. 5) – is falsified by the need that the theory has to make recourse to the role of the so-called "auctioneer" in order to determine prices. In the worlds of Nicola ([5], p. 109) «this [procedure] amounts to the centralization of this crucial aspect of the economy. But then it is no longer true ... that general equilibrium (with private property of the means of production) represents the prototype of an economic system capable of functioning in a totally decentralized way».

The point appears particularly relevant from the perspective of the present paper – the search for an appropriate combination of theoretical framework and institutional context. The neoclassical scheme refers to an institutional framework which in no way resembles that of present day economic systems. In fact the atomistic, freely competitive structure of property-owning and utility-maximizing agents, who are however centrally coordinated by a sort of "social planner" (the auctioneer)[2] who performs the crucial role of

[2] The institutional nature of this crucial "meta-agent" remains a mystery to be solved.

determining equilibrium prices, does not coincide either with a "pure" competitive market economy (that is with a totally decentralized economic system), or with the diametrically opposed scheme of a centrally planned economic system in which the economic plan identifies the objectives of the system and assigns productive tasks to all state-owned firms. The "neoclassical" institutional framework cannot therefore be employed in the construction of an institutionally-oriented theoretical scheme. Nowhere, except perhaps in the Paris stock exchange of the times of Walras, are transactions allowed only at "equilibrium" market clearing prices; nowhere are economic agents placed on an exactly identical footing with respect to the role played in the economic system, to their behaviour, to their objectives, to their "power"; nowhere does perfect information and perfect foresight characterize the choices made by individual agents; and the list can continue.

The problem cannot be solved with the introduction of modifications of the basic assumptions of the theory, for the simple fact that no other type of institutional framework is compatible with the model. We must then turn elsewhere for a solution of our problem.

Fortunately, the traditional neoclassical approach is not all there is in the history of economic thought. Early classical and Keynesian economic theory supply a promising alternative in which a number of crucial features of actual economic systems can be conveniently placed (such as the different role played by different social groups, or the presence of uncertainty and the crucial importance of the expectations held by agents); and in which a sufficient degree of flexibility regarding the institutional set-up can be found. But before proceeding along this "alternative" path, a preliminary question of method must be raised.

4. - Pasinetti's "Two Phases" Distinction

This question – extremely relevant from a methodological viewpoint – bears on the way in which institutions should be taken account of in the construction of the theory. Pasinetti's recent contribution to the analysis of the relation between institutions and economic theory (Pasinetti [7]) supplies the occasion for a reflection on this crucial theme.

Pasinetti ([7], pp. 11 ff.) writes that, in his view, «economic theory» – an expression by which he intends «*strict* or ... *pure* economic theory, not all economic analysis in its broad sense, has, so to speak invaded, and has thus constrained unduly, social science investigations in general, and institutional investigations in particular. It has done so by imposing, in a way which appears exclusive and sometimes even arrogant, its own set of assumptions concerning individuals' behaviour. Strict economic theory – Pasinetti continues – should be pushed a little bit back, or rather a little bit deeper, at a more fundamental, *pre-institutional* level, thereby opening up – without undue interference – the whole field of institutional analysis, and at the same time providing sturdy and rocky theoretical foundation for it».

«The objective of a fruitful integration of economic theory and institutions cannot be reached – according to Pasinetti – with the Walras-Arrow-Debreu theoretical framework... [which] is crucially based on the maximization principle and thus on a specific rule of individuals' behaviour, which lead straightaway to specific social institutions. But it can be done with a theoretical framework whose basic lines can be traced... back... to the Classics. In fact, in the development of economic theory, parallel to the pure exchange model... one can detect another basic model (... [the] model of pure production) which is at the basis of a whole series of economic theories reconducible to what may be called the Classical/Keynesian paradigm».

According to Pasinetti ([7], p. 13) «within this theoretical framework... it is possible to confine strict economic theory to a really fundamental framework of relations that can be dealt with at a level of investigation that is *pre-institutional*». The problems of economic theory that emerge at this stage relate to the conditions that must be satisfied if certain goals are to be reached (e.g. full employment, price stability), or to logically consistent relations, or... normative rules, or... those problems which are generated by the basic forces at work in a dynamic context. No one of these relations require that any specific stand is taken on the economic institutions that have to be set up to bring the economic magnitudes considered into existence».

Referring to his previous work (Pasinetti [6]), the author in question claims to have shown «that it is possible to construct a solid, strong skeleton of basic economic relations, which refer to a production economy expanding through time with structural change». The evolution of the "natural" economic magnitudes is, according to Pasinetti, ([7], pp. 14-5) «traced out, at a stage of analysis at which behavioural and organizational devices – and therefore institutions – are indeed not considered. The "natural" magnitudes possess a series of remarkable ... properties, but are singled out in a way that is independent of how they may be actually achieved. At the same time, they bring out a series of problems that have then to be solved at the institutional level, i.e. by setting up the appropriate institutions».

«Here then comes a *second stage* of investigation on which economic analysis can no longer claim exclusiveness... The whole field of enquiry is... open for the investigation of institutions. It is at this stage that hypotheses on individuals' and social behaviour become relevant. It is at this stage that the evolutionary approach to individual and social behaviour is given full possibility of displaying its enormous potential».

5. - Conclusion

Pasinetti's conception, though far reaching and extremely stimulating, seems to be open to two interconnected criticisms: the first relates to the compatibility between his two-phase distinction and his "preliminary" choice of a theoretical perspective (in his case, the Classical/Keynesian approach); the second refers to the possibility of identifying a *distinct* pre-institutional stage of the theoretical process if an essential part of this latter process is represented precisely by the systematic consideration of the insitutional features (social framework and individual agent's behaviour within this framework). Both points are complex and can only be discussed briefly in very general terms.

a) As it has been just recalled, Pasinetti ([7], pp. 14-6) "proposes" to identify two distinct phases in the process of economic theorizing: (*i*) the pre-institutional phase in which «a series of 'natural' relations are defined and investigated, concerning the determination of a complete set of 'natural' economic magnitudes (prices, wage rate, rate of profit, sectoral productions, sectoral employment, rate of interest) without making any reference to behavioural and organizational devices – and therefore [to] institutions»; and (*ii*) a second stage in which institutions are introduced in the theoretical framework, in order to assess their appropriateness, and «to bring [their] fundamental features (which have normative properties, such as 'efficiency') into existence». In Pasinetti's view, the analysis of this perspective cannot be carried out within the neoclassical Walras-Arrow-Debreu theoretical framework, but it can be done with a theoretical framework reconducible to what may be called the "Classica-Keynesian paradigm". In other words the choice of the theoretical framework in which the two-phase analysis is to be carried out apprears to be preliminary with respect to the identification of the first of the two phases of which the analysis should consist (the pre-institutional one). But this preliminary choice is made precisely on the basis of the evaluation of arguments relating to institutions: in fact the rejection of the neoclassical framework of analysis is explicitly linked to the circumstance that this framework «is crucially based on the maximization principle and thus on a specific rule of individuals' behaviour, which lead straightaway to specific social institutions».

b) As regards the second aspect, the problem is to clarify what conception of economic theorizing underlies Pasinetti's proposal of the above mentioned distinction in two phases. Apart from the fact that the ambition to identify a pre-institutional stage may be seen as dangerously close to the neoclassical pretence to identify the "eternal economic laws", what is the nature and what is the scope of economic theory implicit in the "proposal"? For if Economics, or Political Economy, is conceived as the social science whose principal aim is that of spelling out the regularities that characterize the phenomena of value, production and distribution in given social and institutional contexts, Pasinetti's "proposal" seems to based on a rather weak foundation. In other words, if the systematic consideration of the institutional framework, of the type of agents operating in it, of their behavioural patterns, represents an integral part of the process of economic theorizing, how is it possible to conceive of one phase of this same process of economic theorizing which should be explicitly pre-institutional in nature? How can the basic "natural" relations be identified and investigated abstracting from the framework in which economic agents make their decisions, carry out their activity? Clearly, in spite of apparent similarities, in different contexts the same activity (e.g. the entrepreneurial function) can be carried out in totally different ways, in totally different perspectives; moreover, the same type of decision would be bound to have radically different type of outcomes in different institutional contexts.

In order to ignore all this, and to maintain the idea of a process of economic theorizing based on the distinction in two phases proposed by Pasinetti, it would be necessary to reject the classical type notion of Political Economy indicated above. But in this case the only alternative would be the neoclassical idea of Economics as the study of rational choices in the face of scarse resources – the negation of which represents the starting point of Pasinetti's proposal.

Research must then be addressed to the direct integration of the basic features of the institutional context in an adequately "opened" theoretical framework - for the construction of a tool capable of helping us interpret the economic dimension of historical reality. This task, obviously, cannot be carried out here, but certainly represents an ambitious and exciting research programme.

BIBLIOGRAPHY

[1] ARROW K. - DEBREU G., «Existence of Equilibrium for a Competitive Economy», *Econometrica*, n. 22, 1954.

[2] CARAVALE G., «Alcune considerazioni sulla nozione di equilibrio nella teoria economica», *Studi Economici*, n. 47, 1992.

[3] COASE R.H., «The New Institutional Economics», *Journal of Institutional and Theoretical Economics*, n. 140, 1984.

[4] LANGLOIS R. (ed.), *Economics as a Process - Essays in the New Institutional Economics*, Cambridge, CUP, 1986.

[5] NICOLA P.C., *Equilibrio generale imperfetto*, Bologna, il Mulino, 1994.

[6] PASINETTI L., *Structural Change and Economic Growth*, Cambridge, CUP, 1981.

[7] PASINETTI L., «Economic Theory and Institutions», *Quaderni dell'Istituto di Teoria Economica e Metodi Quantitativi*, Milano, Università Cattolica del Sacro Cuore, 1992.

[8] ——, *Structural Economic Dynamics*, Cambridge, CUP, 1993.

Conclusions

Edmund S. Phelps *
Columbia University, New York

I conclude with a look back at what has been written. The papers and discussions of this volume would challenge anyone's ability, even one as experienced as I, to find the one or two unifying themes. The institutions examined vary enormously and the perspective on the institution often differs from one paper to another.

Luigi Paganetto and Pasquale Lucio Scandizzo have offered a highly original contribution on the long-standing problem of the underdevelopment of the South of Italy. It goes well beyond the generalities of Edwin Banfield, whose emphasis on the role of trust were suggestive but not concrete enough to have the shape of an economic model. It builds not only on Banfield but also on the recent work by Robert Putnam. His study of the centuries-old differences in the political institutions and traditions among the Italian communes and city-states has served to inspire the present paper. The hypothesis of the authors is that the peculiar success of the North of Italy, not shared by the South, rested on the ability of producers of consumer goods in the North to team up with producers of capital goods there in order to develop improved machinery. This ability to work together in a project of mutual interest, though one fraught with risks of free riding and opportunistic dishonoring of commitments, is laid to the civic background of the North, which was one of widespread cooperation in local government. By constrast, the South's history was that of a centralized monarchy.

Corruption in the public sector was the subject of more than one paper this year. The paper by Mancur Olson analyzed such corruption

---

* The author is McVickar Professor of Political Economics at Columbia University and visiting Professor at Università degli Studi di Roma «Tor Vergata» in summer 1995.

GRAPH 1

MODEL OF POLITICAL EQUILIBRIUM
IN THE CORRUPTION - ENTERPRISE PLANE

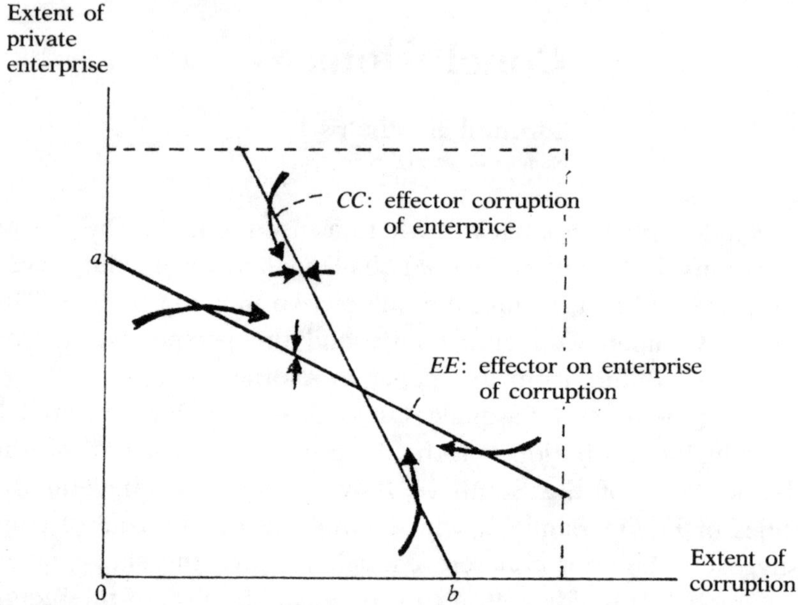

in relation to private enterprise. But Olson's was just one such one-way relationship. In economics, as someone once commented to Kenneth Arrow, everything depends upon everything else in two ways. There are two connections between Private Enterprise and Public-Sector Corruption. Olson's connection is the salutary effect of a strong private sector on the volume of corruption. In Graph 1 this is shown by the curve *CC*. There is also the tendency of corruption to choke off private investment and thus to leave the field to state enterprises. That channel carries an effect of corruption on the volume of private enterprise. This second connection is shown by the curve *EE*. Given the two curves, the level of private enterprise and the level of corruption are jointly determined.

The upshot of this joint determination is that an upward shift of the *EE* curve – an increased supply of private enterprise at any given level of corruption – leads both to increased private enterprise and to decreased corruption, since *EE* is flatter than *CC*. (If *EE* were the steeper curve, the equilibrium would be either at maximum enterprise or at maximum corruption; in the former case, the upward shift of *EE* would increase the corruption accompanying the maximum enterprise level, while in the latter case there would be no effect on either corruption or enterprise).

A somewhat similar diagram arises in another dimension. Here we replace private enterprise by the size of the public sector (which bears no obvious relationship to the public sector in the normal sense of the term) and we replace corruption by a broad indicator of economic performance – say, cumulative economic growth (of potential net national product) or, in other words, productivity. The diagram in Graph 2 illustrates. The curve *PP* shows the effect of the size of the public sector on "economic growth". Such a relationship has been investigated in the study by Robert Barro and Xavier Sala-i-Martin, for example. Yet there also exists a relationship showing the effect of economic performance on the size of the public sector. This is the curve *PUB*. Again, one can expect that there is a tendency for the economy to gravitate toward the intersection of the

GRAPH 2

ANOTHER DIMENSION OF POLITICAL EQUILIBIUM

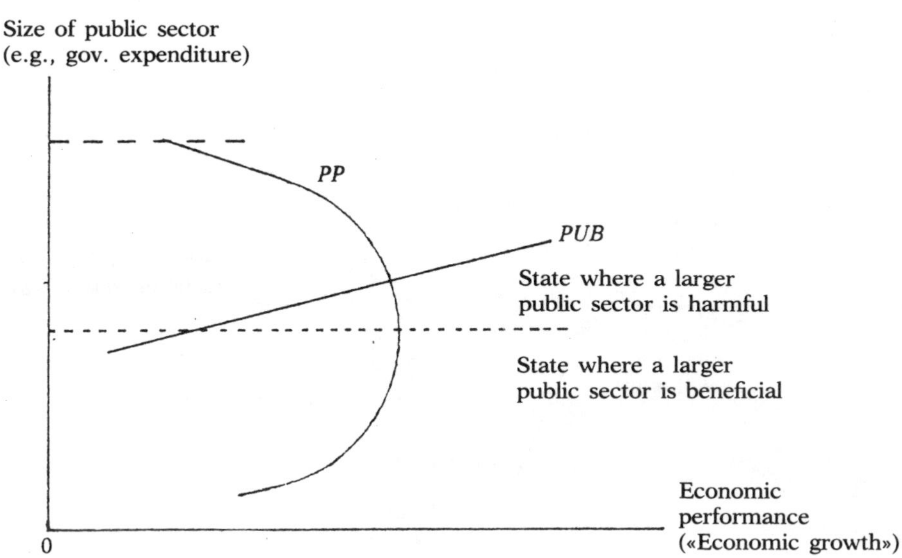

two curves. If each of these two curves is identical in some subset of economies, the timepaths of "growth" and the public sector in those economies will tend to "converge" toward the same path and end-point.

The message here, of course, is that there is a nonlinearity. At high levels of the public sector, a further small expansion would be harmful for economic performance; at low levels of the public sector,

GRAPH 3

CORPORATION POLITICAL EQUILIBRIUM
WITH SOME CHEATING

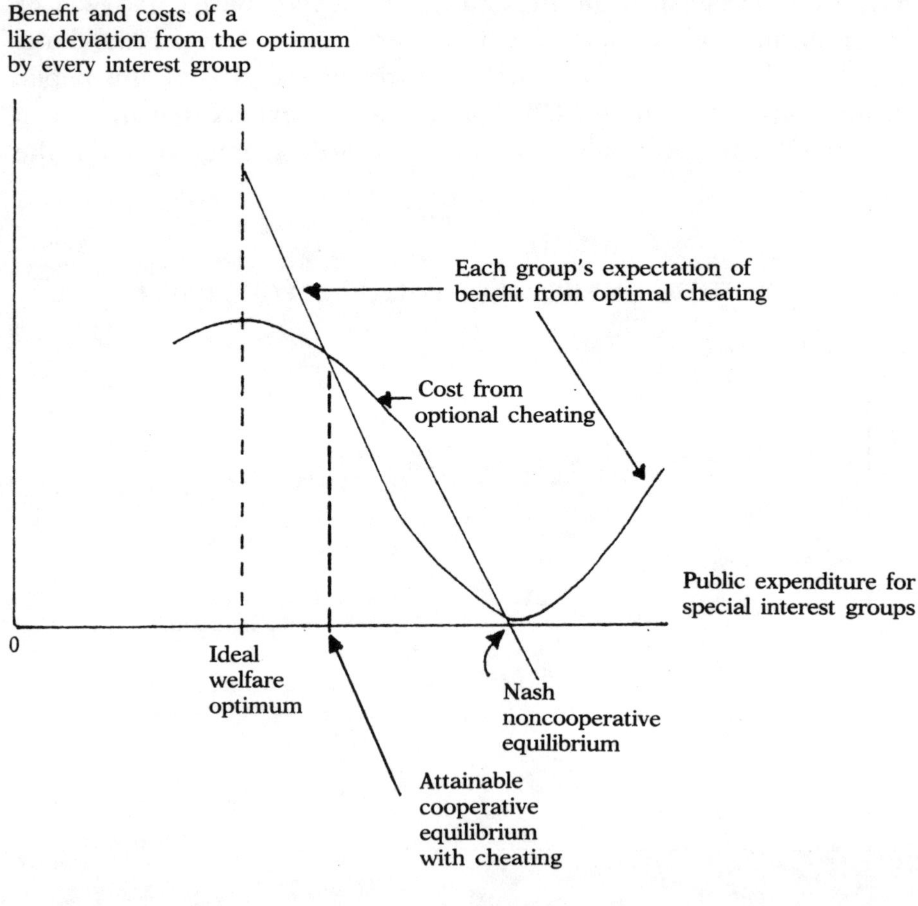

a small expansion would be beneficial. Such a nonlinearity, and a very similar diagram, may also lie behind the equations in a recent paper on inequality and economic growth by Nicola Rossi and Andrea Brandolini. Where inflation is high it is a threat to growth, but not when it is low.

The third diagram conveys other ideas in this volume. I have simply copied from the paper by Avinash Dixit. A construction he credits to Dilip Abreu. Only the application is different. Graph 3 illustrates the diagram using the size of the public sector – government expenditure on final goods and services. As the diagram illustrates, there is some Ideal Optimum size of the public sector. At the other extreme we find the noncooperative pork-barrel political equilibrium of all the special-interest groups, each with its desire for its uniquely preferred kind of public spending. This Nash equilibrium brings a bloated public sector, one well above the Lindahl non-equilibrium, or Ideal Optimum. Yet this Nash "equilibrium" is a bit pessimistic. There will generally be some cooperation among the interest groups, which may take the form of an agreement not to misrepresent their respective benefits and costs from obtaining more of what each wants. That possibility is illustrated by an intermediate point between Nash and Lindahl where the benefit of cheating (how much cheating is not capable of being shown in the diagram) is positive but counterbalanced by an equal cost arising from the risk of being caught and being punished by the other groups.

The themes expressed by these three diagrams are not by any means all the themes dealt with in this volume. But they are among the more important themes.

Index

UNIVERSITY OF BRISTOL
15 NOV 2013
WITHDRAWN
UNIVERSITY OF BRISTOL LIBRARY